The Jubilee Challenge

The Jubilee Challenge

Utopia or Possibility ?

Jewish and
Christian
Insights

Hans Ucko
Editor

WCC Publications, Geneva

Cover design: Rob Lucas

Cover illustration: Sounding the *shofar*, the ram's horn used for the Jewish new year and day of atonement festivals. In kabbalistic literature it is credited with the power of softening the divine judgment and dispelling the forces of evil — something that it appears to be doing in this 13th-14th century miniature of a German Yom Kippur rite. (Used by permission of the Bibliothèque de l'Alliance Israélite universelle, Paris, MS 24 H, fol. 79 v. Photo: Jean-Loup Charmet.)

ISBN 2-8254-1231-7

© 1997 WCC Publications, World Council of Churches, 150 route de Ferney, 1211 Geneva 2, Switzerland

Printed in Switzerland

Contents

The Jubilee as a Challenge

Hans Ucko

But I, being poor, have only my dreams;
I have spread my dreams under your feet;
Tread softly because you tread on my dreams.

William Butler Yeats,
"He Wishes for the Cloths of Heaven"

It is possible that it is only a dream about a jubilee, a time of justice and freedom from the absolute tyranny of economic interests. Every seventh year, production is to cease: "a sabbath of complete rest for the land, a sabbath for the LORD: you shall not sow your field or prune your vineyard" (Lev. 25:4). Debts, too, are annulled. Seven of these cycles pass, and then freedom comes to the land, in the jubilee year: "you shall have the shofar sounded loud... throughout all your land... and you shall proclaim liberty throughout the land to all its inhabitants" (vv.9-10).

Henry George, a 19th century American advocate of the poor and oppressed, cites the institution of the jubilee as a measure designed to maintain an even distribution of wealth. Moses, he considered, had discovered from his experience in Egypt how the oppression of the masses arose from the monopolization of land in the hands of the few. Wherever the land was subject to absolute private ownership instead of being at the disposal of the nation, two classes are inevitably created: the very rich and the very poor; work becomes slavery, and corruption and demoralization set in. George draws attention to the biblical insistence that the land is a gift of the Creator to all creatures. We always read of the "land which the Lord your God has given you", never of "the land which you have acquired for yourself". The jubilee year is maintained by the poor as a protest against the conditions of abject poverty and enslavement. The jubilee year is the possibility to finally ensure a redivision of the land in accordance with its original equal distribution among all the people, ruling out the dominance of monopoly and in the end leading to the downfall of unjust empires.

But the question remains whether the jubilee is only a religious version of utopia — the equivalent of the perfect city of the philosopher Plato's *Republic* or the parallel to Thomas More's satirical account of life on the fictitious island Utopia? Is the Jubilee only one of many of a series of utopias to be counted together with Voltaire's *Candide*, Samuel Butler's *Erewhon* and William Morris's *A Dream of John Ball*? According to the jubilee regulations of Leviticus 25, the summation and culmination of the Code of Holiness, the land returns to its hereditary smallholders, who themselves hold it only on trust from God, preventing the concentration of wealth in the hands of the few; slaves go free, debts are remitted, the land "rests". Jubilee — isn't it only the inevitable dream of the poor, and we had better tread softly because we are treading on dreams? In the words of Agamemnon: "I know how men in exile feed on dreams of hope."

Whether a dream of hope or a utopia that is nowhere, the jubilee is a resolve against a status quo of continued oppression and exploitation of people and creation. Life can't simply be allowed to go on like it does. There must be at least a temporary suspension or reprieve, a change of mind and conditions. This is the jubilee. The jubilee legislation was designed to counter the natural acquisitive instincts of humans, reminding them that the earth is the Lord's and the fullness thereof. What is the meaning of this reprieve and freedom? "The land shall not be sold in perpetuity, for the land is mine; with me you are but aliens and tenants" (Lev. 25:23). All sales of land, all bids to concentrate means of production in the hands of one individual or one class are to be erased in the time it takes to blow the shofar. The jubilee restores each person to a state of pristine economic independence: "you shall return, every one of you, to your property and every one of you to your family" (v.10). The jubilee legislation requires society to recognize a basic right of entitlement as part of being human. Everybody deserves to have a place to be from, a place to return to. The meaning of the jubilee is that each person has his or her place, each culture its place; the selling of the world is undone, and globalizing presumptions are toppled.

And it is "not in heaven" (Deut. 30:12); it will not come to pass only in the beyond. The jubilee legislation is not conceived for another dimension, but it is set in time and in a regulated time, for everyone to count the days and years, when things will be changing, debts will be cancelled, the slaves will be freed and the land will lie fallow and rest. The jubilee is set in the context of shalom, which is the positive enjoyment of physical, economic and social well-being and not only an ideal to attain in days to come or in a spiritualized realm. But shalom is not just a given. It must be pursued. The very meaning of its root (from *shalem*, "to pay") suggests that there is no shalom without effort. Peace is costly and requires sacrifices.

Living with the sabbath

"Shabbat shalom" is the word of greeting on a Friday evening, ushering in the sabbath. The words belong together, "sabbath" and "shalom", "rest" and "peace", because they both require a sacrifice. Shalom requires the sacrifice of any holding on to the status quo for the sake of dominance and control. Peace and security are often joined together in political parlance, as if security could guarantee peace. But shalom is rather built on trust, where the end result cannot be controlled.

The sabbath is a celebration of God's creative power and an expression of trust: God has established order, meaning, purpose in the world. In this world humankind is to be the crown of creation and assigned the role of bringing creation to its goal and destination, to perfect what God has created but not brought to completion. It is as if God has left a margin for humankind to accomplish creation. God, said Rabbi Akiva, has created the bundle of flax. It is beautiful. But it is even more beautiful to see a fine linen cloth. A sheaf of wheat is a beautiful creation. But it is even more beautiful to see and hold in one's hand a loaf of newly baked bread. The work and ingenuity and cooperation of men and women go into the making of the fine linen cloth or into the baking of the bread. God must surely be in love with the crown of creation, allowing that much space for humankind to complete creation, holding back from being God, taking it all in God's own hands, from beginning to end, from flax to cloth.

In his book *Who Is Man?* A.J. Heschel writes: "Who is man? *A being in travail with God's dreams and designs*, with God's dream of a world redeemed, of reconciliation of heaven and earth, of a mankind which is truly His image, reflecting His wisdom, justice, and compassion. God's dream is not to be alone, to have mankind as a partner in the drama of continuous creation."[1] God has chosen humankind to be co-creators with God. The world is not perfect as created, and God knows it. God has put human beings on earth to refine their environment. It is a very particular dominion over creation that is entrusted to humankind, shouldering the responsibility of bringing creation to its completion. God ceases to be the absolute ruler. God and humankind instead become partners, and God is transformed from an "absolute" into a "constitutional" monarch, bound, as humankind is bound, to the conditions of the constitution. God has lost God's freedom to be arbitrary, and man and woman have gained the freedom of being able to challenge God in the name of God's own words and deeds.

To be co-creator is demanding. It takes the major part of our time, six days a week. From early morning to late night we are supposed to be co-creating. Roles are assigned, tasks are given, functions are meted out. There is a risk in all this of identifying ourselves only with what we do, while forgetting who we are. We may become so concerned with what we do and what others see us doing that we forget who we are. The role of the sabbath is to remind us of who we are. Once a week we are to give back the keys to God, to leave behind what we do and become again who we are, not a function but a human being. Once a week we should give up believing that we are indispensable. Co-creators indeed, but not prisoners of our own creation, being ruled by our function in creation and by creation itself. Once a week I rest from being co-creator.

It is certainly valid to pronounce that the sabbath was made for humankind and not the other way around. But in a certain sense humankind is created for the sabbath. Man and woman are to relinquish labour and effort to the sabbath, letting go of their control over creation, regularly practising detachment in relation to their own power and glory, setting creation free and setting themselves free. The biblical story is that the world was not finished and complete after six days. Only after rest was created and called the sabbath did God take a step back and look upon the whole of creation with a sense of completion.

Rest is not a side issue to creation or a break or interlude between one week of work and another. The sabbath is part of creation and provides the occasion for humankind to exercise the letting go of our heavy, iron-gloved hand of domination over creation. The unrelenting human interference in creation is not absolutely crucial or indispensable for its continuation. God's creative skills are sufficient for life to go on, and humankind is asked to let go every now and then from the anxiety of not being in unchallenged control. In a sense the sabbath requires the weekly sacrifice of our need to be in constant control. Six days a week work is needed for the betterment of the world, not more. The betterment of the world will also be furthered through rest, through letting go, through detachment.

This perspective is not only a biblical experience. It is a deeply human experience and wisdom, present in various cultures and religious traditions. The Way of Lao-tzu, for example, teaches, "To yield is to be preserved whole. To be bent is to become straight. To be empty is to be full. To be worn out is to be renewed. To have little is to possess. To have plenty is to be perplexed. To produce things and to rear them; To produce, but not to take possession of them; To act, but not to rely on one's own ability; To lead them, but not to master them. This is called profound and secret virtue."

The oppressed go free

The jubilee is about freedom from the yoke of exploitation, a time of freedom for the enslaved and restoration of human dignity. A closer look at the text, however, makes the contemporary reader somewhat disappointed, for the release of slaves seems to apply only to slaves of their own nationality. This is unfortunately not a text about the release of slaves in general. It would be wrong to read the text as a text from our times. Slavery was an accepted feature, essential to the economy and society. The ancient Mesopotamian, Indian and Chinese civilizations employed slaves, either domestically or for large-scale construction or agriculture. The ancient Egyptians used slaves to build the royal palaces and monuments. The coastal exploration of Africa and the invasion of North and South America by Europeans in the 15th century, as well as the subsequent colonization of the Americas during the next three centuries, provided the impetus for the modern slave trade. It is a sad truth that the traffic did not meet with much resistance from the church. There is in the New Testament no prohibition on holding slaves, for it merely regulates the conduct of masters and slaves. The apostle Paul sent the fugitive slave Onesimus back to his master Philemon. Slavery among Christians was similar to the practices in the Roman empire. Support for slavery went largely unquestioned throughout church history until the Enlightenment. *Uncle*

Tom's Cabin by Harriet Beecher Stowe contributed to the abolition of slavery in the US. Words like "My soul ain't yours, Mas'r! You haven't bought it, — ye can't buy it! It's been bought and paid for, by one that is able to keep it" were affirmed rather than the words of Paul on slavery: "Slaves, obey your earthly masters with fear and trembling, in singleness of heart..." (Eph. 6:5). We have come a long way since the days of regarding slavery as a normal feature of society.

It may therefore seem today as if the world of slavery lies centuries back in history and the words of the jubilee may not seem particularly relevant. And yet we know that slavery continues, although in different forms. From Khartoum to Calcutta, from Brazil to Bangladesh, men, women and children live and work as slaves or in slave-like conditions. According to the London-based Anti-Slavery International, the world's oldest human-rights organization, there are over 200 million people in bondage. Modern-day slavery does not fit our familiar images of shackles, whips and auctions. Contemporary forms of human bondage include such practices as forced labour, child labour and forced prostitution. Modern slaves might be children weaving carpets.

Can the jubilee vision about slaves being set free become a vision for our times? There is a linkage between the release of the slaves and the history of those who had the vision. The Levitical programme of jubilee is the programme of former slaves. Jewish history and memory begin with the words: "We were slaves to Pharaoh in Egypt." The first memory engraved is that of slavery and exploitation, of the humiliation and degradation of being subject to the arbitrary will of another. There is in Jewish history and in the very rationale of Judaism a movement from the memory of slavery through the revolt of the slave people against their oppressors, the breaking of the chains of human servitude and the beginning of a long march towards freedom. But this freedom is not a limitless space. It is a defined and circumscribed space. The way to freedom is not just a way out of the oppression of Egypt. Theologies of liberation may not be sufficient if they can only lead out of Egypt, even if they can point to a long-awaited freedom. They need to make halt at Sinai, where freedom is defined in the task of becoming a holy people. It is in Sinai that a nation of slaves heard a call to aspire to holiness and justice. But this call is as well a warning not to become a prisoner of one's own memories, of allowing one's psyche to be defined by one's suffering. The moral aspiration and hope is without fail founded in the memory of suffering in Egypt, but only as long as it is remembered in the light of the event in Sinai. There is sometimes a risk in our theologizing that we become only a people of sheer indignation, crying out against the ills and evils of our world, sometimes almost revelling in the suffering, exhilarating in an inarticulate call for an indefinite freedom.

The weight of poverty

The Levitical programme suggests the cancellation of all debts, announcing freedom from the oppression of economic interests. It is a vision that could carry beyond the debts of the particular economy of individuals in a given society.

National public debts, taken on a world scale, have almost without exception increased. The estimated total public indebtedness of the world at the end of the 18th century was about $2.5 billion. During the 19th century, Great Britain was the only world power to reduce its national debt, which suggests that the many colonies of the British empire seemed to have been profitable to the motherland. In 1890 the world total of public indebtedness had risen to an estimated $27.5 billion, an increase in a little less than a century of more than 1,000 percent. Following the onset of the worldwide economic crisis in 1929 and the outbreak of the second world war, national indebtedness soared. Beginning in the 1970s, inflation, high interest rates and a tenfold rise in the price of oil contributed to an ever-increasing world debt. Developing nations borrowed from international capital markets to finance their import bills. The borrowing, primarily in the form of floating interest-rate loans from major banks, precipitated a debt crisis in 1982, when worldwide economic growth fell. The calculated figure today of the third-world debt of about $1 trillion is so astronomical that it doesn't actually communicate anything at all. Today there are many third-world countries so deeply indebted that all their new loans are devoted entirely to servicing old ones. And it seems as if this does not matter to those who provide the loans. As long as interest is paid, the banks seem willing to allow the loans to be eternal. The longer the money is outstanding, the higher the profit.

As the presence of the debt crisis dawned on the world, the reality of the world's interdependence also became obvious. The inequitable distribution of resources, as exemplified in the vast differences of national per capita gross products, in the social and economic injustices within nations and in the over-exploitation and destruction of natural resources cannot be confined to the backdrop of world economy. The increasing globalization of the international system has made world affairs important for all countries. They touch our daily lives, influence our mode of behaviour and even determine the fate of nations. No more is it possible for countries to remain autarchic, and no more is it feasible for them to build walls around themselves. An economic initiative somewhere or a political crisis elsewhere has unavoidable ramifications on other countries and other continents. And even when nations build walls, construct barriers in the belief that globalization has not overtaken them or in the hope that they will be spared the ramifications of global developments, there is no safe way out. The debt crisis has to be addressed. In the words of the Talmudic tractate Exodus Rabbah, "There is nothing in the world harder to bear than poverty, for one who is crushed by poverty is like one to whom all the troubles of the world cling... If all the sufferings and pain in the world were gathered, and poverty was on the other side, poverty would outweigh them all" (31:14).

It is a deep religious insight that we are all responsible for each other. The religious traditions, including Judaism, Christianity, Buddhism and Islam, have also always recognized and encouraged the duty of materially well-off persons to aid the less fortunate. Almshouses, hospitals and orphanages were supported by donations from the rich and by church collections. But the phrase "alms for the poor" is today not automatically seen as the most constructive way towards more than a continued dependence upon the one who bestowed the gift. The same thinking seems to have been part of the reflections of the mediaeval scholar and philosopher Maimonides. In his work on the poor, he seems to realize that while charity is a laudable practice, the poor need more than a gift or a sum of money. He suggests that one should anticipate charity by preventing poverty. Charity can certainly be to assist the poor, either by a gift or a sum of money. But it can also be teaching them a trade, entering into a partnership with them, or helping them find work. The highest charity is, according to Maimonides, to put the poor where they can dispense with other people's aid and not be forced to the alternative of holding out their hand for charity.

Freedom comes to the land

The Levitical programme proposes that the land lie fallow in the jubilee year and be allowed to rest. "The earth lies polluted under its inhabitants; for they have transgressed laws, violated the statutes, broken the everlasting covenant... The earth is utterly broken, the earth is torn asunder, the earth is violently shaken" (Isa. 24:5,19). More than ever we have come to realize that the land needs to be given rest from us. We have to hold ourselves back from the land, lest it die and we die with it. The crisis in the world's environment is beyond anything yet known in history and is at a point where the very survival of the human species and other living species is threatened. The experience expressed in the Talmudic tractate Ecclesiastes Rabbah is ominous: "When God created Adam, he led him around the Garden of Eden and said to him: 'Behold my works! See how beautiful they are, how excellent! All that I have created, for your sake did I create it. See to it that you do not spoil and destroy my world; for if you do, there will be no one to repair it after you'" (7:13).

What does it mean to let the land lie fallow in a world where humankind is to have dominion over creation? It is obvious that our dominion is a major problem. The wish is sometimes expressed in the thought, prompted by the ecological crisis, that we abdicate from being the crown of creation and fuse, as it were, with creation, becoming one with trees and animals. The Bible does indeed affirm that humanity is an integral part of creation, "The LORD God formed man from the dust of the ground" (Gen. 2:7). But there is more to it. Creation comes about through the word of God: "Let there be...", and there is earth and heaven, sun, moon and stars, living creatures of all kinds. There is a remarkable difference when the creation of man and woman is mentioned: "Let us make humankind in our image, according to our likeness; and let them have dominion over the fish of the sea, and over the birds of the air, and over the cattle, and over all the wild animals of the earth, and over every creeping thing that creeps upon the earth" (Gen. 1:26). Being human seems to be equivalent to "having dominion". What does this mean? Maybe above all to recognize that we cannot become one with creation and hide "among the trees of the garden", throwing away our assignment to have dominion. Our relation to our environment cannot be based on the assumption that there is no difference between us and the rest of creation. It must begin with the opposite idea: We have a special responsibility, precisely because we are different.

Ours is the responsibility of realizing the consequences of the interrelatedness in our environment and the need for an economic and ecological reconciliation, a social restoration and personal renewal. In chapter 15 of his *Guide of the Perplexed* Maimonides remarks: "In the realm of Nature there is nothing purposeless, trivial or unnecessary." This is our task to discover, remember and realize. Nowhere can the ecological chain be violated. The interrelatedness of our environment goes beyond its own immediate confines. There is an intrinsic connection between peace, justice and environment. Peace is dependent on justice, justice on equal distribution of resources, resources to be used only in so far as there is not an over-exploitation of resources. The debt crisis of the third world is intertwined with the ecological crisis. The depletion of the rain forest in the South for furniture in the North has effects on global warming throughout and is caused by the infinite debt of the South to the banks and nations of the North. To reduce environmental degradation and for humanity to save its habitat, societies must recognize that the environment is finite. As populations and their demands increase, it becomes more and more obvious that the idea of continuous growth must give way to a more rational use of the environment, but this can be accomplished only by a dramatic change in the attitude of the human species. The human attack on the environment has been compared with the dramatic upheavals of the earth in the geological past; whatever a society's attitude may be towards continuous growth, humanity should recognize that this attack threatens more than just human survival.

In discussing the viability of the jubilee vision for the land, we must not forget the Old Testament guidelines on the meaning of "having dominion" over the environment. Specific rules apply, where respect for creation is never abandoned. When people are building their houses from fruit-producing trees, they should remember that God instructed that only trees that did not bear fruit should be used for the Temple according to the tractate Exodus Rabbah (36:20). Instructions for wartime situations include ecological considerations: "If you besiege a town for a long time, making war against it in order to take it, you must not destroy its trees by wielding an axe against them. Although you may take food from them, you must not cut them down. Are trees in the field human beings that they should come under siege from you?" (Deut. 20:19) The overall consideration is that "the earth is the LORD's and all that is in it, the world, and those who live in it" (Ps. 24:1). The rest follows from this fundamental principle.

Jews, Christians and the jubilee

Jews and Christians believe that their respective religious traditions can speak to them, and to the world beyond them as well. The affinities between Jews and Christians have been the object of many statements and ecumenical documents in recent decades. In similar words these documents state that Jews and Christians, each from their unique perspective, have a common responsibility as witnesses in the world to God's righteousness and peace. Christians and Jews are as God's partners called to work in mutual respect and cooperation for justice, reconciliation and the integrity of creation. Following the last decades of Jewish-Christian dialogue, the Jewish-Christian relationship indeed has a chance of becoming more enriching than it has been before.

The Jewish-Christian dialogue in its beginning had to be a forum, where Jews and Christians could get to know each other, where Jews could discover that Christians were not a priori enemies of the Jewish people and anti-Semites. Christians learned in dialogue that Jews as well as Christians were a people of faith, that they were faithful to the God revealed to them in the Old Testament and that this faithfulness had carried them through centuries in the midst of persecution, often instigated by Christian triumphalism. The Jewish-Christian dialogue has been a movement of sharing, although it was maybe mostly Jews who shared with Christians about their faith and traditions instead of an occasion for reciprocity.

Through their dialogue Jews and Christians might realize the particular significance of sharing the major part of their holy scriptures with each other, the Old Testament, and of having, albeit from different perspectives, a common responsibility as witnesses to God's righteousness and peace. Jews and Christians are in a position to face issues of justice, peace and the integrity of creation because they have been nurtured by a particular sense of creation. We are not the works of our own hands — "It is he that made us and not we ourselves" (Ps. 100:3) — and "the earth he has given to human beings" (Ps. 115:16), not for its own disposal, but only "to till it and keep it" (Gen. 2:15). The exalted place of man and woman in the order of creation, precisely because it is not of their own making but a ministry to which they are appointed, is what makes the commandment to be responsible for the rest of creation intelligible.

The end of the cold war has given us no respite from the rising tide of violence and human suffering. Though we have crossed the point where large and powerful nations might risk the use of ultimate weapons to settle issues, the scene has now shifted to a myriad of small conflicts, the cumulative human and material costs of which outstrip the destruction caused by major wars. The growing complexity of the national and international environment is not catalyzing us to seek new ideas providing viable solutions to social maladies but is pushing many in the opposite direction. We need a vision sustaining our efforts away from the self-aggrandizing illusion of power and monetary gain.

The separation of power from responsibility and words from deeds is diminishing the credibility of national and international institutions, making them unable to contain the widening dimensions of poverty and to eradicate the structures of inequity. These paradigms have undergone many transformations but are still precariously perched on the pillars of shifting power equations, poverty aggregation, armament, technologies and cultural conflicts. Human ethical and cultural values are becoming victims of internal paralysis or external subversion. And behind all this is someone's greed, someone's power or national ego. We live today in a time when the last pretensions of the Enlightenment seem to have floundered: the notion of the human individual as a rational, self-legislating being. The fall of state socialism has led to a void with many uncertainties. The bipolar world of a communist bloc and a capitalist bloc provided, at least in its very polarity, possibilities to seek societal alternatives. Today we see that not only socialism has failed. "The liberal project" does not seem to provide a sustainable and responsible society in its emphasis on self-interest. The neo-liberalism of the political right puts the individual too much at the centre, glorifying selfishness and naked competition. It allows too small a role, if any, for altruism or the common good. Neo-liberal spokespersons seem to pretend that there is no such thing as society. New societal values are needed to give meaning to a responsible society.

Although new challenges in this area call for fresh thinking on the part of all members of our society, Jews and Christians ought to be prepared to deal with them inasmuch as they have not severed their links with tradition. Thus, Jews and Christians, both informed by what they have learned about the integrity of creation from the Old Testament or the Hebrew Bible, need not try to invent anew ecological ethics for example. These resources should be present in their common heritage.

Is the jubilee vision a resource and a possibility for a new discourse on sustainable societal values? In May 1996 the Ecumenical Institute, Bossey, hosted a meeting of Jews and Christians on the jubilee as the theme of the WCC's eighth assembly in 1998. The contributions, from economists, ecologists, sociologists, theologians and educators, provide material for our thinking. They elaborate on the jubilee vision from different perspectives. It is obvious that the rules of Leviticus cannot be naively applied to the contemporary world; a straightforward remission of debts, for instance, as the rabbis found, would make people reluctant to give credit, on which our economic system depends. With the abolition of slavery in most of the world, however, we have made progress towards social equality, which is one of the clear aims of biblical legislation. But we need to continue asking how we can realistically implement, in contemporary society, the great aims of the Levitical programme regarding the equitable distribution of wealth and the sustainable utilization of land, including minerals such as oil. We now have to address these issues on a global scale, where both the inequitable distribution of wealth between North and South and encroachment on the environment caused by growing populations and increasing material expectations have reached threatening proportions. Which spiritually founded values that derive from these traditions can effectively be brought to bear on our own situation? We need to avoid naive, well-meaning responses to problems which, though urgent, are complex, calling for constant evaluation rather than glib solutions. While we may not have the tools to solve the debt crisis, our concern should remain, leading beyond moral indignation, hopefully providing an instrument for the discussion and giving a human dimension to an economic issue.

As far as we know the jubilee vision has never been implemented. We may surmise the reasons why, and some of these reasons are also recorded in this publication. One reason could be that it was difficult to deviate from what was perceived as the normal course of history. For some, history remains as fixed and certain as nature. Copper does

not become iron. Sheep do not give birth to frogs. Yesterday's enemies
are tomorrow's. There have been masters and slaves, therefore there
will always be masters and slaves. The door seems closed to allowing
hope to take a hold of the course of history, leading it another way.

The key to hope is breaking boundaries. A hopeful person sees
three answers where others see one. To teach hope, one must imbue
children with "the logic of water", not "the logic of rock". One must
step out of Aristotelian logic to imagination, which flows around
barriers till it finds a way through. The exodus from Egypt is God's
course in how to hope. To teach people who believed their fate as
Pharaoh's slaves was a law of nature, God carried them to the far
extreme, showing them a natural world that had suddenly become
mutable. Already in Egypt, nature (frogs, locusts, eclipses, etc.)
turned impulsive. Nothing precisely that could not happen, but
nothing as one would expect. Then came the entrance exam to the
course itself: the people had to be to be willing to go, and not everyone
was. A midrash says that only one in five was capable of leaving
Egypt, and even those who left had second thoughts during their long
journey. Once on their way, things continued to be different. Nothing
would go normally in the desert: Bread fell from above, and water
rose from below. This is the course of hope. The vision of jubilee is a
vision against reason. It is a vision of hope. It can be discarded
immediately with the help of the abacus or the calculator. It can, if
allowed to live on, be deferred to become an inoffensive spiritual
exercise. The question now before us is whether the jubilee vision
could be the impetus and challenge to a necessary rethinking towards
addressing concretely the conditions that once prompted the Levitical
programme. It is likely that for a jubilee to be truly effective, more
time may be needed than the time it takes to blow the shofar. But we
could begin, all the time remembering that "nothing great is created
suddenly, any more than a bunch of grapes or a fig. If you tell me that
you desire a fig, I answer you that there must be time.."

NOTE

[1] Abraham Joshua Heschel, *Who Is Man?*, Stanford, CA, Stanford UP, 1965, p.119.

Utopia and Responsibility

Konrad Raiser

This consultation, which is sponsored jointly by the Ecumenical Institute and the Office for Interreligious Relations of the World Council of Churches, opens the cycle of events that will mark the 50th anniversary of the Ecumenical Institute of Bossey. The institute was established in 1946, two years before the inauguration of the World Council of Churches, thanks to a generous gift of David Rockefeller. The decision of the first general secretary of the WCC, Willem A. Visser 't Hooft, to use these funds for the creation of an institute for ecumenical education and learning is a manifestation of his far-sighted vision. He saw the ecumenical movement as a movement of people, young and old, clergy and lay, men and women, who together, through encounter and dialogue, were to learn what it means to live and to manifest the unity of the church for the sake of the wholeness of the human community. Now, 50 years later, this vision has lost nothing of its challenging character. Since then, many ecumenical institutes have been established, and many academies and lay training centres have strengthened the common efforts for ecumenical renewal and for leadership formation. In this expanding network, Bossey has retained a unique place and vocation: to bring together people from all Christian traditions and from diverse cultures and languages, and to provide the space for ecumenical exposure and continuing dialogue.

Both in individual and in corporate life, celebrating a jubilee is an occasion for remembering, self-assessment and anticipating the future. It is therefore a fitting tribute to the special vocation of the Ecumenical Institute to begin the series of events marking this anniversary with a dialogue consultation, bringing Christian and Jewish scholars together to examine the jubilee tradition of the Bible and its relevance for today. It serves as a reminder that the common study of the Bible has been an integral part of the programme of the Ecumenical Institute from the beginning, inspired particularly by Suzanne de Diétrich, who was part of the first leadership team of the institute. Her ability to penetrate the biblical text and to let it speak afresh to contemporary conditions profoundly shaped the early generations of ecumenical leaders.

The choice of the subject for this dialogue consultation points beyond the immediate context of the 50th anniversary of the Ecumenical Institute. When, more than two years ago, discussions began with a view to determining the theme for the eighth assembly of the World Council of Churches, to take place in 1998, the year of the 50th anniversary of the council, attention began to focus on the biblical jubilee tradition. In fact, it represents a secularized echo of the biblical tradition that a 50th anniversary in common English usage is called a jubilee. This originates from the Latin translation of the Bible which rendered the Hebrew word *yovel* in Leviticus 25:10ff. as *iubilaeus*. The *yovel* in Leviticus 25 is the 50th year that follows seven sabbath years. The prescriptions for this "holy" year (see Lev. 25:12) — liberation of all slaves, remission of debts and restitution of land — have remained one of the powerful sources of biblical inspiration in both the Jewish and Christian traditions, notwithstanding their seemingly utopian character. The Central Committee of the World Council of Churches therefore accepted the challenge to approach the 50th anniversary of the World Council of Churches as an "ecumenical jubilee", reappropriating the biblical jubilee tradition for the present context of the ecumenical movement.

This decision raises the obvious question whether the appropriation of an important part of the Torah by a Christian assembly, particularly outside its Jewish and specific historical context, is legitimate, and how such reinterpretation can be done without continuing the history of Christian expropriation of the traditions of the Jewish people. Reference can be made to the fact that here, as in so many other instances, the New Testament is itself part of the process of reception and interpretation of the Hebrew Bible, which is continuing in the Jewish community until this present day. In particular, the meaning of the kingdom of God as proclaimed by Jesus of Nazareth can be understood fully only against the background of the jubilee tradition of the Torah.

However, the Christian reading of the Hebrew Bible, which the church has acknowledged as an inseparable part of the holy scriptures, must expose itself to and be challenged by the continuing process of biblical interpretation in the Jewish tradition. The Council therefore recognized the opportunity for dialogue with Jewish scholars to penetrate more deeply into the meaning of the biblical jubilee tradition, to widen and correct the dominant Christian perception, and to explore the significance for today, in particular in the context of the ecumenical movement. This consultation is therefore important not only for the Ecumenical Institute of Bossey but for the World Council of Churches as a whole. It gives me particular joy to welcome you, as General Secretary of the WCC, at the beginning of this consultation and to thank you for your readiness to contribute to this process of mutual questioning and enlightenment.

I

In this opening address, I have been asked to reflect on the theme "Utopia and Responsibility". This is a suitable topic to begin our reflection together, since indeed many of our contemporaries would consider the jubilee prescriptions in Leviticus 25 as manifestations of utopian thinking. No society and no economy, they would tell us, could function and survive on the basis of these rules. While they would concede that it might be interesting to explore the origins and the meaning of these regulations in the context of the early Jewish history, they would deny that they have any continuing validity for the contemporary situation.

What is meant when an idea is called utopian? "Utopia" was the name given by Thomas More to the imaginary island that he used as the setting for the perfect society depicted in his treatise of that name, written in 1516. The term, derived from the Greek, means "no place" and suggests that a utopia is precisely an ideal not realized anywhere.

Since the time of Thomas More, the word "utopian" has been used to characterize an entire genre of literature, though idealized portrayals of how the world ought to be go back much further — to Plato's *Republic*, for example, or the eschatological vision of Isaiah 65, which is reflected in Revelation 21. Particularly perhaps in periods of uncertainty and despair, writers and thinkers have constructed utopias, often with the hope or even expectation that the gap between the ideal they project and the dismal reality of the status quo might generate the energy for change and transformation.

In our own century, writers such as Aldous Huxley in *Brave New World* and George Orwell in *1984* put this literary form to a much different use. In their terrifying projections of future society, they exposed the unacknowledged consequences of developments that could already be seen in society and thus unmasked the fundamentally utopian character of the spirit of modernity.

In our day, the term "utopian" has come to be used almost exclusively to disparage the visionary character of any models or proposals for changing "the way things are". To be utopian is to be an idealist and a dreamer, to indulge in fantasies, to lose contact with reality. In a world governed by scientific calculation and the technological approach of "problem solving", there seems no room for utopian thinking. And is this not the basic message of the thesis of "the end of history", namely, that with the collapse of communism after 1989, the last rival utopia projecting an alternative to the liberal system of the global market has disappeared? Whatever subversive influences utopias may have had are banished forever. There is no alternative, no utopian challenge, for we already live in the best of all worlds.

The idea that the global market economy creates "the best of all worlds" is itself thoroughly utopian. This is evident if we look at it from the perspective from below, the perspective of those who are excluded from enjoying its benefits. But it is a utopia that, far from being a subversive challenge, has become an ideology that serves the interests of defending power and domination.

This might be considered an added reason for being sceptical and critical of all utopias, but those who are excluded from the benefits of the process of globalization will not cease to hope for a better world and to entertain dreams, utopian as they might be. And if we have become captives of a utopia turned into an ideology that has blinded our eyes so that we can no longer see reality and its contradictions, should we then not try to regain the critical sense of utopia and of its inevitably partial realizations? Indeed, the common-sense understanding that sets utopian thinking over against a realistic view of the world must be questioned. Any perception of reality, in particular of social reality, is shaped and conditioned by a perspective that reflects the social position and the interests of those who speak or act. This was brought home to me very dramatically at an ecumenical hearing about the international debt crisis. A senior representative of the World Bank, fully convinced of the validity and realism of his analysis, was confronted with the testimony of people from countries that had experienced structural adjustment programmes. They spoke about a reality that he had never seen or experienced personally. Under the impact of these testimonies, he said somewhat helplessly: "Could it be that we have become blind and cannot see reality?" The question of utopia and ideology leads into the struggle about ultimate reality.

There is also a particular ecumenical angle to our topic. The ecumenical movement of our century has had a strong utopian element. To speak of the unity of the church for the sake of the renewal of human community is indeed a utopian project that aims at subverting the status quo of divided churches so that they might be transformed into signs of the new humanity in Christ. Twenty-five years ago Ernst Lange wrote: "Ecumenism can no longer be toyed with as a mere possibility. It has become the test case of faith. Today, there is... only one way for the church to be the one, holy, catholic and apostolic church, and that is the ecumenical way." His book *And Yet It Moves...* [1] was a powerful apologia for the ecumenical utopia, of "the utopian dream of a united and renewed Christendom which would be the 'leaven', the pattern, the stimulus of the coming world community, the custodian of a source of humanization which is not only inexhaustible but also always far in advance of every form of human achievement yet realized in history, namely, the humanity of Jesus of Nazareth".

Just as others have declared the utopia of world peace to be the critical condition that must be met if our world shaped by science and technology is to have a future, so Ernst Lange proclaimed the ecumenical utopia as the critical test for what it means to be the church today. However, this vision seems no longer to inspire a sense of allegiance among a new generation. It falls under the verdict that is being passed on all utopias today. The churches seem to have accommodated themselves to a situation of friendly coexistence in continuing separation. Can the ecumenical vision be brought to life again?

Through this preliminary exploration of our topic, we have come across different layers in the understanding of utopia. The most basic is the tension that exists between the utopian ideal and the commonly accepted reality. While utopian projections may be interesting and an exciting play of human imagination, they should not be taken seriously.

In a second level, utopian projections and explorations may assume the role of a critical test for the existing reality, unmasking the ideological element in what is considered a realistic view and opening the eyes to the dangerous and destructive consequences if the present course of events continues unchanged. It is in this sense that the biblical prophets and their later followers engaged in utopian thinking.

This leads finally to the examples of utopian reflection that anticipate and describe a different reality in the future in order to mobilize the potential for change, to liberate human community from captivity to the past, from fatalism and resignation that accept that things will and can never change. On all three levels, utopia challenges our understanding of a responsible assessment of reality. By transcending everyday reality in imaginary reflection, in critical contestation or in visionary mobilization, utopian thinking has an affinity to the mystical or prophetic dimensions of religions. It is ultimately in this context that the question of responsibility must be considered.

II

Against the background of these reflections about utopia, reality and responsibility, I turn now to the biblical jubilee tradition and thus to Leviticus 25. The detailed exegesis of this text will be a continuing thread throughout this consultation, and not being a biblical scholar myself, I look forward to receiving new insights from our dialogue here with and on this passage. What I will say is formulated from the perspective of a Christian theologian who receives and studies the Hebrew scriptures as the Bible of Jesus of Nazareth, through which God continues to speak today to Jews and Christians, even though they read and interpret the scriptures differently in the context of their traditions.

The jubilee year, as it is described in Leviticus 25, shall be opened on the Day of Atonement at the beginning of the 50th year following upon seven sabbath years. The opening of this year by the sound of the trumpet shall be a proclamation of "liberty throughout the land to all its inhabitants. It shall be a jubilee for you: you shall return, every one of you, to your property and every one of you to your family" (v. 10). The central regulation that in the jubilee year all shall return to their original share of the land is combined further with the intentions of the sabbath year, namely, there is to be no sowing or harvesting (v. 11) so that the land can enjoy a complete rest. No land, in fact, shall be sold in perpetuity, for "the land is mine" (v. 23) and all ownership is only that of a tenant or trustee.

The jubilee year and the sabbath year belong to the same line of tradition in the Torah. Leviticus 25 is part of what biblical scholars call the Holiness Code (Lev. 17-26), which is one of the three collections of ancient Jewish legislation. The other two are the Book of the Covenant (Ex. 20-23) and Deuteronomy. The Covenant Code is generally considered to be the oldest of these collections, reflecting the situation of an egalitarian community of free peasants. There is at present a lively debate among biblical scholars about the dating of Deuteronomy. Traditionally, it is linked with the reform movement under King Josiah, which would place it 200-300 years after the time of the Covenant Code, reflecting the social development under the monarchy, including the emergence of a monetary economy, of class differentiation and of taxation. The Holiness Code is generally linked with the exilic period after the destruction of the temple in Jerusalem.

The sabbath year occurs in all three collections (Ex. 23:10-13; Deut. 15:1-18; and Lev. 25:1-7) but is being reinterpreted in the light of changing conditions. The basic notion of the sabbath tradition is a regular period of rest for the land, the animals and the servants. In the context of Deuteronomy, this basic notion is extended and reinforced by the idea of remission with regard to debts and slaves (the Hebrew *shamat* and *shemittah* mean to withdraw one's hand, to let go or to liberate). This new interpretation is a response to the distortion of social relationships through an imbalance of power and an accumulation of wealth. The sabbath year is intended to restore just relationships in society.

Under again radically changed conditions, Leviticus 25 reappropriates the same tradition. Here the remission of debts and the release of slaves is demanded for the 50th year, which could appear as a weakening of the earlier sabbath year regulation. The main focus, however, is now placed on the restitution of the original distribution of land to all families. There is no direct evidence that the jubilee year as described in these regulations was ever actually observed, even though there is some indication that the programme of reconstruction under Nehemiah followed the jubilee principle (Neh. 5:1-13). This could suggest that the concept of the jubilee year emerged at the end of the exile in Babylon in the situation of an impending return of the exiled people. The time from the destruction of Jerusalem to the edict of Cyrus announcing the possibility of return was approximately 50 years. The jubilee year might therefore have been a genuine utopia in its origin, expressing the vision of a new beginning, a return to the order of community life instituted by the will of God. This is underlined by the fact that the jubilee year is to be proclaimed on the Day of Atonement. The intention of the biblical jubilee was to break periodically the inevitable historic dynamic of acquisitiveness and domination, leading to exclusion, and to restore the opportunities for life in community to all.

This jubilee principle is reflected in the Hebrew Bible also beyond the Torah, particularly in the prophets. One of the key passages is Isaiah 61:1-2, where the jubilee as "the year of the LORD's favour" is a symbol of salvation. As such, it was reappropriated by Jesus, who interpreted the sabbath and the jubilee tradition as a concrete representation of the coming kingdom of God, proclaiming it as a promise particularly to those who were considered as unacceptable before God. In the sermon at Nazareth as recorded in the gospel of Luke (4:18-19), Jesus proclaims liberty in quoting Isaiah 61, leading up to the affirmation: "Today this scripture has been fulfilled in your hearing" (v. 21). The specific sabbath rule of the cancellation of debts, which already in Leviticus 25 is integrated into the jubilee framework, is reflected in the Lord's prayer as taught by Jesus, which thus becomes a jubilee prayer: "Forgive us our debts, as we also have forgiven our debtors" (Matt 6:12); the Greek word for the act of forgiving, *aphesis*, is also used in the LXX to render the Hebrew word for the "release" of captives and prisoners found both in Lev. 25:10 and Isa. 61:1). The parable of the unforgiving servant (Matt 18:23-35) vividly recalls that the failure to repay debts could lead to the loss of liberty. A further, more distant echo of the jubilee message is found in 2 Corinthians 6:2: "See, now is the acceptable time; see, now is the day of salvation" — which immediately follows the proclamation of reconciliation.

Through these reinterpretations of the jubilee tradition, the utopian legislation of Leviticus 25 was transformed into a powerful prophetic vision of the new life in community in the horizon of the kingdom of God. The periodicity of the sabbath and the jubilee year is radicalized by Jesus and Paul by being focused on the eschatological now, or today. Any moment can become the year of God's favour, the time of salvation. Now is the time of liberation, remission, forgiveness, reconciliation. It is God who offers the jubilee of healing and restoring life, of forgiveness and liberation from bondage. These affirmations have become central for the Christian understanding of the gospel of Jesus Christ. In the further process of Christian reception and interpretation, however, the original and very concrete focus of the jubilee principle has largely been forgotten. It is only now that we begin to discover how deeply Jesus in his proclamation was rooted in the original jubilee tradition and that we cannot pray the Lord's prayer without being confronted with the jubilee role of cancelling all debts. It is my expectation that our dialogue here will help us recover and discern the critical and prophetic note of the jubilee tradition and thus counteract the tendency of spiritualizing, which has characterized much of the Christian reception of the Hebrew scriptures.

III

While we do not know much about the social and historical context in which the idea of the jubilee year was first formulated and while the rule that a jubilee should be observed every fifty years seems to have remained an expression of the priestly need for ordering communal life, the jubilee principle of the restitution of the land, the liberation of slaves and captives, and the cancellation of debts has remained one of the powerful utopias in Jewish and Christian history. Its potential of critically unmasking the status quo of domination and dependency and of sustaining the hopes and visions for a transformation of the existing reality seems to be inexhaustible.

This is expressed with particular poignancy by the fact that the Liberty Bell in Philadelphia, one of the great symbols of the American revolution, carries an inscription quoting Leviticus 25:10: "Proclaim liberty throughout all the land unto all the inhabitants thereof." It should be admitted that in the Christian tradition the spiritualizing tendency very often has turned the utopia of the jubilee into an ideology manifesting and defending the power of the church. This is true in particular for the origin of the practice of holy years in the mediaeval church in connection with the crusades. The granting of indulgences, which became the central feature of the holy year, must be considered as a distortion of the original jubilee principle. More recently, the emphasis of the holy year has moved to spiritual renewal in the love of God, faithfulness to the gospel, reconciliation and commitment to justice and compassion in human society. The jubilee or holy years have often been occasions to affirm Roman Catholic integrity, notably in the year 1950 with the promulgation of the most recent mariological dogma and the encyclical *Humani generis*. It is therefore a welcome change of orientation that Pope John Paul II in his letter to prepare the great jubilee of the year 2000 offers a full biblical explication of the jubilee concept, showing the rich and very concrete meaning of this idea in the biblical tradition.

A more direct reappropriation of the biblical jubilee motif is found in sermons and religious writings in the context of the 19th-century struggle for the emancipation of slaves in the United States. Several Afro-American spirituals from that period mention a "year of jubilee". The promulgation of the emancipation of slaves in 1863 was interpreted as the beginning of a year of jubilee. Following the same line, the original biblical tradition has been reappropriated more recently in reflections coming from the context of the historic peace churches. Here the radical imperative of the jubilee regulations (i.e., leaving the soil fallow, cancelling debts, freeing slaves and redistributing land and capital), have been applied to the structures of injustice that characterize relationships within and between societies today.

In particular, the jubilee imperative to cancel debts has been used as a biblical reference in discussions about the global debt crisis. This is true for many statements from Christians and churches in Latin America, but also for an Asian-African initiative to mark the year 1998 as a jubilee year to commemorate the 500 years since Vasco da Gama sailed round the cape in southern Africa to reach the Indian Ocean. This initiative calls for the cancellation of debts, for the restoration of land to the original owners and for the repatriation of what has been taken away by the colonial powers. Reference could also be made to the fact that the Korean churches have been celebrating the year 1995 (i.e. the 50th year since the end of the second world war and the division of Korea) as a jubilee year. Their hope was that this year would inaugurate the process of the reunification of Korea and of the reconstitution of national unity.

These examples of reappropriating the biblical jubilee tradition show its continuing critical and visionary potential, but also the dangers that are associated with all utopias. Appealing to the jubilee tradition today could indeed be understood as raising expectations that are unlikely to be fulfilled. The utopia of the jubilee obviously is in tension with reality as we know it. A cancellation of the international debts, in particular of the poor countries in Africa, contradicts the logic of the global financial system and is therefore not being considered. After the abolition of slavery and more than 70 years of efforts to establish international standards for labour regulations, the slave-like exploitation of labourers is on the increase under the pressure of competitiveness on the global market. The expropriation of land, in particular of indigenous peoples, for the purposes of mining and in the interests of the timber industry is continuing unabated, and the cries of landless farmers are being met with violent repression. To proclaim a jubilee year under these conditions would indeed seem hopelessly utopian.

However, if we consider the critical and prophetic potential of the jubilee principle, then it can help to uncover the self-destructive tendencies of the present global system of finance and economy and thus become a powerful call to responsibility. Unless the inherent dynamic of this system aiming at the accumulation of power and wealth and the limitless exploitation of the land can be interrupted, it will lead to increasing conflict, violence and potential self-destruction. The utopian belief in the self-regulating power of the market has turned into an irresponsible ideology of domination that is unable to correct itself in view of the long-term consequences.

The jubilee tradition, like all genuine utopias, focuses attention on very basic and elementary features of human life in community, power and domination, acquisitiveness and exploitation of nature. The basic principle is that of the self-limitation of power as exercised in domination over people, as accumulation of capital and wealth, and as exploitation of natural resources. The jubilee tradition is a powerful reminder of the fact that the Creator God is the source of all power and liberty and the provider of what is needed for human life. Where this dimension is being negated, reality becomes distorted, and the realism of the powerful reveals itself as an ideology of self-defence. In such situations the utopia of the jubilee must be understood as an expression of true realism, namely as the affirmation of creation and human community before God.

After having accepted the biblical jubilee tradition as the framework for preparing the eighth assembly of the WCC and its 50th anniversary, the Central Committee struggled with the formulation of an appropriate theme to capture the thrust of the biblical concept. Eventually a consensus was reached for the theme "Turn to God — Rejoice in Hope". This theme emphasizes that it is in turning to God that we will see the reality of our world. Turning to God means repentance, but also reorienting the basic perspective and transcending the realism of the closed system. Turning to God means accepting God's offer of reconciliation and liberation, that is, of entering into the relationship with God that, in the biblical tradition, is called holiness. This is the essential condition for the jubilee and thus for hope, joy and celebration. In God's perspective, we can see the world and human community as it is meant to be in its true reality. For this reason the jubilee tradition continues to be a source of inspiration.

I conclude these reflections on utopia and responsibility with a brief reference to a novel published in 1942 by the German writer Stefan Andres entitled *Wir sind Utopia* (We are utopia). The book takes us to Spain at the time of the civil war. A former monk returns as a prisoner of war to the Carmelite monastery he had left 20 years earlier when the world of the monastery had become too narrow for him. Back in his previous cell, he is captivated by the memory of how he used to project an ideal island of bliss on to the ceiling of his cell. His spiritual father, an old mystic, had tried to convince him that none of these utopias had ever become true, but he had clung to this projection, which he needed in order to maintain the zeal of his faith. Before he had left the monastery, his spiritual father had given him this final piece of advice: "God does not go to utopia! But he comes to this world, wet with tears — again and again! Because here, there is infinite poverty, infinite hunger, infinite suffering! God loves the wholly Other, God loves the abyss... God loves this world, because it is imperfect. — We are God's utopia, but in the process of becoming!" Andres's novel then follows this lead, and in a very moving way God's utopia becomes visible in the midst of war, betrayal and brutality, in the act of forgiveness of sins and absolution given against all canonical rules and human insight. The jubilee principle indeed contradicts the established rules and human insight, but it opens the horizon for God's utopia, which we are meant to become.

NOTE

[1] Geneva, WCC, 1979, p. 9. German original 1972.

Leviticus 25 and Some Postulates of the Jubilee

Jacob Milgrom

The basic postulate of the jubilee is Leviticus 25:23-24: "Further-more, the land must not be sold beyond reclaim, for the land is mine; you are but resident aliens under my authority. Therefore, throughout the land you hold, you must provide redemption for the land." "Land" here is Canaan, the promised land, and "you" refers to the people of Israel. They are to keep in mind that the owner of the land is God and they are only resident aliens; that is, God is the landlord, and the Israelites are tenants. And the deity-landlord-owner has decreed that "the land must not be sold beyond reclaim". Each Israelite clan has been assigned a plot of land (Num. 26) that must always remain in its possession.[1] Even when it is sold, it can always be reclaimed, a process called redemption, and every 50th year (jubilee), it must be restored to its original owner. Cancellation of debts and return of forfeited land was also known in the ancient Near East.[2] It usually occurred when a king acceded to the throne. Its purpose was to "prevent the collapse of the economy under too great a weight of private indebtedness".[3] However, it was generally limited to the king's retainers and subject to his whim.[4] The biblical jubilee, in contrast, was inexorably periodic and incumbent on every Israelite.

What are the circumstances that necessitate the sale of the land? The key verses are 25-28, 35-43. They represent three stages of destitution.

Stage 1: Sold land and its redemption (vv.25-28)

When your brother becomes impoverished and has to sell part of his holding, his closest redeemer shall come and redeem the sold property of his brother. If a man has no redeemer but prospers and acquires enough for his redemption, he shall compute the years since its sale, refund the difference to the man to whom he sold it, and return to his holding. If he does not acquire sufficient means to recover it, his sold property shall remain with its buyer until the jubilee year; it shall be released in the jubilee, and he shall return to his holding.

It is assumed that an impoverished farmer takes out a loan for the purchase of seed. In the event of crop failure, he is forced to sell part of his land to cover the previous loan and purchase new seed. Then his closest kinsman (the redeemer) is required to intervene. The buyer must allow the redeemer to repurchase the land. The buyer is paid the value of the crop years remaining until the next jubilee. In effect, the buyer has never even purchased the property; he has only leased it until the jubilee or earlier if it is redeemed.

It must be emphasized that the redeemer does not return the land to the original owner but keeps the land until the jubilee. In this way he gets back his redemption costs and will not incur a loss. One might ask: What purpose does redemption serve if, whether the land remains sold or is redeemed, the original owner does not get his property back until the jubilee? The answer lies in the basic principle: The land should not be alienated from the clan to whom it was assigned by God.

Stage 2: Lost land (vv.35-38)

If your brother, being (further) impoverished, falls under your authority, and you hold him (as though he were) a resident alien, let him subsist under your authority. Do not exact from him advance or accrued interest. Fear your God, and let your brother subsist under your authority. Do not lend him money at advance interest, or lend him food at accrued interest. I, the Lord, am your God, who freed you from the land of Egypt, to give you the land of Canaan, to be your God.

Here it is assumed that the sold land was not redeemed. The owner incurs a crop failure on his now reduced property and is forced to take out a new loan, and again he defaults. This time he is forced to sell all of his land, and he becomes a "tenant farmer" for the creditor. Technically, he has lost all his land, but its usufruct is still his. He may not be treated as a foreigner on whom interest may be charged. Since he pays no interest, the produce from the land can amortize his loan. It is assumed that if he cannot repay the loan, the land will return to him (or his heirs) at the jubilee. The redeemer is not obligated to intervene in this case (and the following one), since his redemptive duties fall only on sold land (and persons) but not on loans (see below).

Stage 3: "Slavery" (vv.39-43)

> If your brother, being (further) impoverished under your authority, is sold to you, do not make him work as a slave. He shall remain under you as a resident hireling; he shall work under you until the jubilee year. Then he and his children with him shall be released from your authority; he shall return to his kin group and return to his ancestral holding. For they are my slaves, whom I freed from the land of Egypt; they shall not be sold as slaves are sold. You shall not rule over him with harshness; you shall fear your God.

If as a tenant (stage 2) the debtor still cannot repay his loan and otherwise cannot support himself and his family, he and they enter the household of the creditor. He no longer enjoys the usufruct of his forfeited land. Nonetheless, his status is not that of a slave but that of a resident hireling; he receives wages, all of which pay off his debt. They may even provide him with a surplus with which to free himself of his debt and status. Thus, for Israel slavery is unequivocally abolished. As far as we know, this law remains utopian; there is no hard evidence it was ever enacted.

Stage 3, as well as stage 2, is startlingly conspicuous by the absence of the provision for redemption, a fact that the rabbis confirm when they declare that relatives are under no obligation to redeem their indentured kinsman (Babylonian Talmud, Qiddushin 15b). Furthermore, it would not be true redemption. The redeemer might give him a free loan, an act of charity, but he may not hold him and his land until the jubilee, which he could do if it were a case of redemption.

The superior status of the hireling over the slave is manifest not only in his economic advantages but also in his working conditions. This is implied by the repeated admonition "do not treat him harshly". After all, the terms of the hireling's labour are stipulated in advance; the slave, in contrast, is subject to the demands and whims of the master. Considering that the hireling is a free person, it may well be that if he finds the creditor's conditions too harsh or his wages too low, he can seek another employer.

Note that he returns "to his ancestral holding". The significance of this clause rests in the supposition that the jubilee cancels his entire debt. His restored land can now provide him with subsistence so that he need not fall immediately into debt and ultimately have to be sold once more into servitude.

Many more postulates undergird the jubilee. I would add only one more: the statement in the last verse (v. 42), which forms an inclusion with the first (vv. 23-24): "For they are my slaves whom I freed from the land of Egypt." God owns Israel because he is their redeemer. Freedom means simply a transfer of masters: henceforth the Israelites are servants of God, and of *no one else*. Thus, just as the nearest relative (the redeemer) is obligated to redeem the land of his kinsman sold (or forfeited) to another, so is he obligated to redeem the person of his kinsman sold to (i.e., enslaved by) another. The debtor falling into the hands of a non-Israelite creditor is considered a captive. The obligation to redeem captive Israelites is traceable back to Abraham and Lot (Gen. 14), and it persists in biblical and rabbinic tradition. Indeed, when King Herod wanted to sell Jewish criminals who had been punished with slavery to a foreign nation, he was warned that the people's hatred of him would only increase (Josephus, *Antiquities* 16.1-4), an indication that the repugnance of selling Jews to Gentiles — even criminals — was not a theoretical desideratum but a tradition practised by the people at large.

To recapitulate: God is Israel's landlord and redeemer. Thus, as God's tenants and servants, Israel is doubly obligated to follow the deity's laws. These include redemption and the jubilee. If inherited land is alienated, the nearest kinsman (the redeemer) is required to buy it back; if he fails, the land automatically returns to the owner at the jubilee; simultaneously his debt is cancelled, and he begins his life anew. Redemption is not charity. The redeemer keeps the land until the jubilee. His purchase price is thus covered by the land's usufruct, and he will be induced to redeem.

Descent into poverty can never terminate in slavery. Even at its nadir, a poor man's status is that of a wage-earning resident hireling. His loan is interest-free, which allows his wages to amortize it, possibly allowing him to be released from the creditor even before the advent of the jubilee. Redemption, however, is not prescribed, since it applies only to sold land and persons, not to loans.

Thus, the jubilee is a socio-economic mechanism to prevent latifundia and the ever-widening gap between the rich and the poor which Israel's prophets can only condemn, but which Israel's priests attempt to rectify in Leviticus 25.

NOTES

[1] J. Milgrom, *The Book of Numbers*, Philadelphia, Jewish Publications Society, 1990, pp.219,480-82.

[2] M. Weinfeld, "Sabbatical Year and Jubilee in the Pentateuchal Laws and their Ancient Near Eastern Background", in *The Law in the Bible and in Its Environment*, ed. T. Veijola, Göttingen, Vandenhoeck & Ruprecht, 1990, pp.39-62; *idem, Social Justice in Israel and in the Ancient Near East*, Jerusalem, Magnes Press; Minneapolis, Fortress Press, 1995.

[3] D.O. Edzard, *The Near East: The Early Civilizations*, ed. J. Bottero et al., trans. R.F. Tannenbaum, London, Weidenfeld and Nicolson, 1965, p.225.

[4] Y. Bar-Maoz, "The 'Misharum' Reform of King Ammisaduqa", in *Research in Hebrew and Semitic Languages* (in Hebrew), Tel Aviv, Bar Ilan, 1980, pp.40-74.

The Biblical Jubilee:
In Whose Interests?

Norman K. Gottwald

Among those who have studied the jubilee regulations of Leviticus 25 most intensively, there has emerged virtually no consensus on any of the major points at issue in their interpretation. Are the jubilee provisions clear and coherent in and of themselves? What specific economic conditions do they address? When did they originate? How do they relate to other biblical economic relief measures? Were they ever practised? If they were practised, what would have been their effects?

The terms of our symposium are shaped by widely divergent views about the precise nature of the jubilee. While our focus will be on the implications of jubilee for contemporary economic and social life, our appropriations of the text will be sharply conditioned by the answers we individually give, however provisionally, to the disputed textual issues.

From my perspective, there is one set of questions that has not been pursued with the same vigour as the literary, historical and religious questions. This can be described as the political-ideological locus and dynamic of the jubilee. This is the issue I wish to concentrate on because I believe that similar political-ideological factors operate powerfully in any attempt to draw on jubilee for our common life today.

In order to address the political-ideological issue, however, it is necessary to posit a working hypothesis concerning the biblical jubilee in its literary, social historical and religious dimensions. I do so with an admission of the tentative and provisional nature of my reconstruction.

The jubilee of Leviticus 25 fits within a broad family of texts (*torot*, or narratives, prophecies, wisdom sayings) concerned with economic relief among which the most pertinent are Exodus 21:2-11; 23:10-11; Deuteronomy 15; Ezekiel 45:7-12; 46:16-18; Jeremiah 34:8-22; and Nehemiah 5. These texts do not resolve into a single harmonized system but reflect relief measures proposed or practised in various Israelite circles over some hundreds of years. Taken together, they attest to a political economy that repeatedly generated tax and debt burden that led to landlessness and impoverishment for sizeable numbers of people and, in turn, undermined communal stability. They also attest to frequent efforts to ameliorate the baleful effects of this economic impoverishment, or even to actually halt the economic juggernaut that caused them. The Bible describes these abuses and their remedies largely in the moral and religious discourse of "sin" and "redemption".

The type of political economy that prevailed in the biblical world has been variously described as advanced agrarian society, aristocratic empire, bureaucratic empire, rent capitalism, Asiatic mode of production, or tributary mode of production. This tributary mode of production was dominated by a small elite and their bureaucratic servants who lived on the agricultural and pastoral surplus of a vast peasant majority. This surplus was extracted by causally connected and mutually reinforcing cycles of taxation and debt. For most of the biblical period, from independent monarchy to eventual colonial subjection by great empires, Israel's economic life lay within the sphere of this tributary mode of production.

Typically, in such a political economy the non-elite populace languishes in "a culture of silence", their voices muted and only obliquely heard in the official records and the high literature. Significantly, however, Israel's beginnings were shaped under a communitarian mode of production practised by farmers and herders resisting domination by elites. For this reason, the voices of these little people are heard more frequently in the Bible than elsewhere in the ancient Near East, although not unequivocally, since from David onward they had to reckon with the superior power of native and foreign elites. Thus the Bible contains an admixture of what have been contrasted as "the Great tradition" and "the little traditions" that coexist within elite-ruled peasant societies.

The economic relief laws of the Bible occupy the contested ground between the elites and the small producers, whose blood, sweat and tears made monarchies and colonial regimes possible. On the one hand, the pressure from below exerted by peasants seeking to improve their life conditions could not be satisfied in any fundamental way within the tributary mode of production. On the other hand, this pressure from below could not be entirely ignored, especially when it threatened economic productivity and the foundations of political regimes. From time to time, elites would issue measures of relief: reducing or cancelling debts, freeing debt slaves, and/or restoring land lost to indebtedness. Unscheduled relief of this type is known from Mesopotamia in royal manumission decrees.

Israel participated in this wider dynamic of fluctuating pressure from below and sporadic relief from above, but with some significant differences. The leverage for relief measures in Israel rests on a fulcrum that preceded the monarchy and the tributary mode of production: Moses, who is made the progenitor of these economic easements. But as these relief measures weave through biblical history, it is kings and priests who initiate them. Thus, it is probable that the Covenant Code of Exodus was promulgated under Jeroboam I or Jehu in the northern kingdom. Josiah is widely viewed as the southern monarch who gave his backing to the Deuteronomic Code. And one of the few points on which interpreters of Leviticus 25 tend to agree is the hypothesis that the jubilee laws in their present form come from the Priestly Code towards the end of the exile. In all these so-called codes, the relief is offered within a sabbatical system of seven years or multiples of seven in the case of the jubilee, in contrast to the royal decrees in Mesopotamia, which occurred randomly.

Leviticus 25 operates on the premise of a unified cultic community with responsibility to keep family units intact on cultivated land. It aims to accomplish this by providing a 49- or 50-year waiver of all debt and debt servitude and a return of lost land holdings. In the interim between the jubilees, debtors who have lost their freedom or their land or both have the opportunity to raise the means to buy their release and recover their land. Land "sold" to creditors is conceived as "on lease", the amount needed to buy back the land being adjustable according to the number of harvests that the buyer/creditor has enjoyed. Unlike the related provisions of Exodus and Deuteronomy, Leviticus 25 does not include remission of debts or release of debtor slaves every seven years. It does, however, incorporate the seventh-year fallow of Exodus.

The jubilee programme posits the benign cooperation of God in providing a bounteous sixth-year harvest to feed the community over the two or more years before crops are once again harvested after the seventh-year fallow. This optimism defies the irregularity of drought conditions which occur on the average of every two to four years. It also overlooks the inflation of food prices in conditions of scarcity. The jubilee programme further premises sufficient prosperity for debtors and debtor slaves to be able to work their way to solvency and freedom long before the next jubilee. Moreover, it assumes that creditors will honour the solidarity of the community and facilitate this mandated recovery of land and personal freedom. There is a large measure of naiveté in thinking that those destitute enough to lose land and freedom would be able to recover their losses. It would only be imaginable if creditors were generous towards "brother" Israelites. For most debtors and debt slaves, the jubilee would be their only salvation. Indeed, the plight of those in the majority who suffered loss more than seven years before the next jubilee could be far worse under the jubilee release than under the seven-year releases of debts and debtor slaves granted in Exodus and Deuteronomy.

Such considerations, coupled with the absence of any certain reference to the enactment of the jubilee in biblical or other records, have prompted a general suspicion that this is a utopian programme that was never implemented and perhaps never intended to be implemented — "a counsel of perfection", as it were, sharing in some respects with the vision of Ezekiel for restoration of a purified religious cult and a just civil order. I do not see any evidence that jubilee was ever enforced, but I do imagine circumstances in which it could have been seriously proposed.

The extension of the seven-year sabbatical principle to 49/50 years by a priestly party vying for leadership in restored Judah could have offered an attractive fresh start. It proposes a "clean slate" to sweep away past economic and political encumbrances on land. It would be attractive for returning exiles whose land had fallen into other hands in their absence. It would also promise to honour the just claims of those remaining in the land who had fallen prey to Samaritan, Babylonian or other non-Yedahite creditors or expropriators. The initial jubilee could have been proposed as the framework within which to restore former holdings, whereas the long wait between jubilees would ensure stability in the settlements agreed upon at the restoration. The 50 years between the fall of Jerusalem in 587 and the edict of Cyrus in 538 could have been the historical impetus to begin the jubilee programme with all possible speed following the restoration of Judah. The jubilee programme can thus be viewed as the political and economic ploy of the Aaronid priests to achieve leadership in restored Judah by dispensing benefits to a wide swath of the populace, presumably with civil and military support from the Persians.

If the jubilee was advanced as a workable programme of restoration, why was it not put into effect? Several obstacles come to mind. For one thing, the restoration from exile did not occur in one stroke but was strung out over decades as successive waves of exiles returned. For another, it is not evident that the Aaronid priests gained undisputed leadership in Judah at once. More likely they were locked in struggle with other groups for decades. Although their cultic programme may have won the day in the rebuilt temple, their economic proposals probably encountered fierce "secular" opposition. Moreover, the holdings of Israelites at the fall of Jerusalem in 587 were very unevenly distributed. If the unbalanced distribution of land under the monarchy was to be adhered to in instituting the jubilee, it would incorporate gross inequities and ensure the vulnerability of small landholders to indebtedness. Furthermore, the very slow economic recovery of Judah would not have provided optimal conditions for enforcing the jubilee, which depended so much on high productivity and general goodwill of those with power.

Perhaps, above all, the jubilee programme provides no way to settle jurisdictional disputes over land ownership. What should be done about land formerly owned by exiles, but occupied for the last 50 years by other Israelites? The grounds for settling such cases would likely be more political-ideological than legal. Returning exiles would press their case as a "purified" remnant entitled to recover their former status. Non-exiled Israelites would counter that the exiles had forfeited their rights because their disastrous policies led to the fall of the state in 587. Only newly developed lands could give all parties in this dispute a secure place in the restored Judah, but the jubilee has no provision for such historical disruptions.

Often overlooked in assessing the jubilee is the economic role of the priests. It is noteworthy that houses and land in walled cities are exempt from the jubilee. Within the fortified administrative and commercial centres, the priests functioned as temple officials, tribute gatherers and profitable entrepreneurs. If the jubilee denied them some advantages in land ownership, they were left free to pursue trading ventures under Persian protection or to court the advantages of alternative commercial enterprises in the developing commercial axis between Athens and Arabia. It should also be noted that jubilee does not probe the reasons for Israelites becoming impoverished, which would include not only Persian taxes but also tithes and offerings taken in by the priests. It is not surprising that a century after the edict of Cyrus, Nehemiah found debt and debt slavery rampant in Judah, threatening the foundations of "social peace". Nehemiah's release of debt and debtor slaves is described not in jubilee terms but rather as an urgent one-time emergency measure analogous to steps taken by Greek tyrants. Nehemiah thereby alleviated the worst hardships of the populace in order to consolidate the threatened colonial regime in Persian-sponsored Judah. Under Ptolemaic, Seleucid and Hasmonean regimes, however, the old inequities were once again ascendent.

My social historical scenario for the priestly jubilee programme is indeed speculative, yet plausible in terms of what we know about the operations of the tributary mode of production and what is implied or hinted at in the biblical record. In any case, this sort of exercise in historical imagination has pinpointed practical considerations that need to be kept in mind as we assess economic-reform proposals that are given religious endorsement. The following issues in appropriating such proposals from our religious past emerge as of critical importance:

1. Will the redistribution and use of the land proposed be able to produce in accord with the reform promises? Do the proposals take into account drought, soil conditions, climate and rainfall, farming practices, and existing technology? Land reform does not succeed simply because of religious motivation or general goodwill. If the physical and technological parameters for agrarian productivity are ignored, the reforms may be ineffectual and contribute to disillusionment and fatalism among those most in need of empowerment.

2. Will the cultural and religious traditions of the cultivators facilitate or obstruct the reform proposals? Peasants have particular attitudes and values with respect to the land that constitutes their livelihood. Their religious beliefs may tend towards insurgency or resignation, combining optimism and fatalism about social change in unpredictable ways. In particular, peasant notions of personal honour

and family integrity must be assessed carefully in land-reform proposals. To be effective, the changes proposed must be seen by peasants as embodying and advancing their way of being in the world. Do the reforms treat them with respect and dignity?

3. Will the land-reform proposals provide for an effective way of settling jurisdictional disputes over ownership? Are the land claims individual, familial, tribal, village or cooperative based? When claims conflict, as is the situation faced, for example, by the Land Commission in the Republic of South Africa, what is the equitable way to do justice to all parties? What role will civil and religious institutions play in adjudicating these claims?

4. Internationally, will the larger economic systems permit these reform proposals to work? Leviticus 25 does not take Persian imperial and commercial interests into account. In our day, international corporations in the world market have far-reaching impact on local agrarian conditions. For the most part, the larger economic systems that fix prices and favour one-crop exports are not favourable for meaningful land reform. To be blunt, can piecemeal reforms country by country be effective without major changes in the international economic networks?

5. Locally and nationally, who will gain and who will lose from the land-reform proposals envisioned? Indigenous comprador classes have long profited as middlemen in the exploitation of peasants and workers. In a number of ways the priestly group behind Leviticus 25, as well as figures like Ezra and Nehemiah, fit the role of a comprador class. Does our focus on biblical reform traditions take serious account of the frustrating reality of a privileged comprador class and its links to political power?

6. Will religion as believed and practised facilitate or obstruct meaningful land reform? Do we who specialize in religious traditions of social justice recognize how much institutional religion has obstructed land reform? Does the land-reform proposal tap into the progressive dimensions of the prevailing religious traditions and counter the reactionary dimensions of the same religious traditions? Are we fully aware that the jubilee, and other biblical traditions of economic relief, are Jewish and Christian in their canonical origin and cannot automatically awaken the allegiance of adherents of other religions? What are the extra-Jewish and extra-Christian religious traditions that bear on indebtedness and land ownership? Is there a secular equivalent of the claim to divine ownership of the land?

7. How is moral discourse about corporate "sin" and corporate "redemption" to interface effectively with entrenched systemic power? It is evident from the ambiguity and political-ideological entanglement of biblical land reform schemes that there is no innocent and obvious route from our traditions, motivations and aspirations for social justice to particular programmes of land reform. The routes to lifting the burden from peasants, as from workers at large, are circuitous and complexly mixed with politics and ideology. We have grounds for hope. Our hope, however, is not lodged in pushing the adoption of an ancient proposal from our revered heritage. Our hope lies rather in encouraging an interplay of social conscience and social analysis that will engage in the political and ideological battle necessary to make a significant difference in the lives of millions of marginal cultivators the world over.

Jewish Understandings
of Sabbatical Year and Jubilee

Leon Klenicki

The book of Nehemiah points out the post-exilic community's firm agreement to suspend all agricultural work during the seventh year and to forgo all debts as commanded in the law of God: "The peoples of the land who bring their wares and all sorts of foodstuff for sale on the sabbath day — we will not buy from them on the sabbath or a holy day. We will forgo [the produce of] the seventh year, and every outstanding debt" (10:31). This passage alludes to three passages in the Torah, each one of them devoting its attention to a different aspect of the seventh-year release. Exodus 23:10-11 calls on the Israelites to let the land lie fallow and the vineyards and all they grow untouched, that the poor people may eat of them, as well as the wild beasts. The text says: "Six years you shall sow your land and gather in its yield; but in the seventh you shall let it rest and lie fallow. Let the needy among your people eat of it, and what they leave let the wild beasts eat. You shall do the same with your vineyards and your olive groves."

The second reference is found in Leviticus 25:1-7 and 18-22:

> Then God spoke to Moses on Mount Sinai: Speak to the Israelite people and say to them: When you enter the land that I assigned to you, the land shall observe a Sabbath of the Lord, six years you may sow your field and six years you may prune your vineyard and gather in the yield. But in the seventh year the land shall have a Sabbath of complete rest, a Sabbath of the Lord: You shall not sow your field or prune your vineyard...
>
> You shall observe my laws and faithfully keep my rules, that you may live upon the land in security; the land shall yield its fruit and you shall

---

• Background information taken from classical sources and Jewish encyclopedias compiled by the author.

eat your fill, and you shall live upon it in security. And should you ask, "What are we to eat in the seventh year, if we may neither sow nor gather in our crops?" I will ordain my blessing for you in the sixth year, so that it shall yield a crop sufficient for three years. When you sow in the eighth year, you will still be eating old grain of that crop; you will be eating the old until the ninth year, until its crops come in.

The text of Deuteronomy 15:1-11 commands the Israelites to observe the seventh year "as a year of release":

Every seventh year you shall practise remission of debts. This shall be the nature of the remission: Every creditor shall remit the due that he claims from his fellow; he shall not dun his fellow or kinsman, for the remission proclaimed is of the Lord. You may dun the foreigner; but you must remit whatever is due you from your kinsmen. There shall be no needy among you — since the Lord your God will bless you in the land that the Lord your God is giving you as a hereditary portion, if only you heed the Lord your God, and take care to keep all the instruction that I enjoin upon you this day. For the Lord your God will bless you as He has promised you: You will extend loans to many nations, but require none yourself; you will dominate many nations, but they will not dominate you. If, however, there is a needy person among you, one of your kinsmen in any of your settlements in the land that the Lord your God is giving you, do not harden your heart and shut your hand against your needy kinsman. Rather, you must open your hand and lend him sufficient for whatever he needs. Beware lest you harbour the base thought, "The seventh year, the year of remission, is approaching," so that you are mean to your needy kinsmen and give him nothing. He will cry out to the Lord against you and you will incur guilt. Give to him readily and have no regrets when you do so, for in return the Lord your God will bless you in all your efforts and in all your undertakings. For there will never cease to be needy ones in your land, which is why I command you: Open your hand to the poor and needy kinsmen in your land.

Note that this Deuteronomy text cautions the people not to let the recurrence of the seventh-year release harden their hearts against the distressed who seek loans at the time of their need.

There is a clear relationship between the surrender of the produce of the seventh year to the poor (Ex. 23:11) and the liberation of Hebrew slaves following the sixth year of their purchase (Ex. 21:2-6; cf. Deut. 15:12-18). The text of Deuteronomy 15:12-18 is clear concerning the liberation of the slaves:

If a fellow Hebrew, man or woman, is sold to you, he shall serve you six years, and in the seventh year you shall set him free. When you set him free, do not let him go empty-handed: Furnish him out of the flock, threshing floor, and vat, with which the Lord your God has blessed you. Bear in mind that you were slaves in the land of Egypt and the Lord your God redeemed you; therefore I enjoin this commandment upon you today. But should he say to you, "I do not want to leave you" — for he loves you and your household and is happy with you — you shall take an awl and put it through his ear into the door, and he shall become your slave in perpetuity. Do the same with your female slave. When you do set him free, do not feel aggrieved; for in the six years he has given you double the service of a hired man. Moreover, the Lord your God will bless you in all you do.

The jubilee year is described in detail in Leviticus 25:8-17 and 23-55. Its provisions include the dating of the recurrent jubilee year, the proclamation of its start with the sounding of the shofar on the Day of Atonement, the return of all Israelites to their ancestral land and families, the observance of the fallow, the fixing of prices for the sale of land (except for houses in cities) in relation to the occurrence of the jubilee, the redemption of the land of next of kin, especially land regulation for Levites, and the freeing of defaulting debtors and all Israelite slaves. The text justifies these proscriptions in terms of two basic principles: God's ownership of the land (v. 23) and God's possession of all Israelites as his slaves (v. 55).

A reference to the seven-year cycle appears in the Joseph stories (Gen. 41:25-36) in the dream of Pharaoh of seven good years and seven bad years. Earlier Near Eastern texts also talk about the land being blighted for a seven-year period because of the death of Aqhat, just as it flourishes for seven years after Baal defeats Mot. Similarly, Anu warns Ishtar that a seven-year drought would follow the slaying of Gilgamesh (Gilgamesh Epic 6, lines 101-6).

It has been pointed out that the concept of both the sabbatical and the jubilee years originated under simple economic and social conditions, possible when agriculture was not yet the major source of the food supply of the Israelites. This relates to a time not long after the conquest, which also provides a proper setting for the idea of the jubilee. At this early date, tribal solidarity was still strong, the consciousness of the common possession of the ground and soil fresh in their minds, and the memory of the patriarchal relationships in the desert vivid.

The ideas of the desert period lived on among the people for many centuries, especially outside the large centres. At any rate, "Neither the sabbatical nor the jubilee year appears in the Bible as a nascent institution. While they drew on earlier Semitic practice for some of their ideas, in their present form they represent a unique Israelite attempt to combat the social evils that had infected Israelite society and to return to the idyllic period of the desert union when social equality and social concern had prevailed."[1]

Jubilee in the post-biblical period

It is known that the laws of the jubilee were not in practice at the time of the second temple, "but since the laws of the Jubilee and the calculation of the years of the *shemittah* (Sabbatical Year) are linked with the laws of the Sabbatical Year, which were in force, one can find in these laws something of the life and customs of that period".[2] Halakhah, Jewish religious law, stipulates that rules that relate to the sabbatical year — for example, the prohibition of land cultivation, the renunciation of ownership of produce and the obligation of the householder to remove all produce gathered for his needs — apply also to the jubilee: "What applies to the Sabbatical Year applies equally to the Jubilee" (Sifra, Be-Har 3:2).

The rabbinic teachers taught that the sanctity of the produce of the sabbatical year was such that if the householder sold it and bought meat with the proceeds, the stringencies of the sabbatical year applied both to the produce itself and to the meat, that is, they deduced the laws of the sabbatical year from verses dealing with the jubilee and vice versa. Thus, in the verse applying to the jubilee, "You shall eat the increase cleared out of the field" (Lev. 25:12), the rabbis taught, "As long as you eat from the field, you may eat from your house. When what is in the field has been consumed, then you must clear out what is in the house" (Sifra, Be-Har 3:4), applying it to the sabbatical year.

The *Jewish Encyclopedia* points out that "only the law on the remission of debts which comes into force at the end of the Sabbatical Year" (Sifra Deuteronomy 111) does not apply on the Jubilee; against this, however, there are, according to the *halakhah*, two precepts of the jubilee which do not apply to the sabbatical year — that land sold returns to their owners during the jubilee years (Lev. 25:23, 24) and that slaves go free (Sifra, Be-Har 3:6). The verse, "And in the seventh he shall go out free for nothing" (Ex. 21:2) was interpreted as referring not to the seventh year which was the sabbatical year but to the seventh year from the date on which he was sold (Jerusalem Talmud, Qiddushin 1:2, 59a); if the Jubilee came in the middle of his six-year term, however, the slave went free then (Qiddushin 1:2). This law was also applied to the Hebrew bondsmaid, although it is not explicitly mentioned in the Torah, and was apparently an innovation of the *tannaim*. A Hebrew slave sold to a gentile did not go free in the seventh year but only in the jubilee (Sifra, Be-Har 8:4). In addition, the Hebrew slave who refused to go free in his seventh year went free on the jubilee (Mekh., Nezikin 2; cf. Josephus, *Antiquities* 4.273).

The sabbatical year in post-biblical times

Rabbinic literature points out that the precept of the sabbatical year includes three positive commandments and six prohibitions. The three positive commands are (1) in "the seventh year thou shalt let it rest and lie fallow" (Ex. 23:11); (2) "the seventh year shall be a Sabbath of solemn rest for the land" (Lev. 25:4); and (3) "At the end of every seven years thou shalt make a release. And this is the manner of the release; every creditor shall release that which he hath lent unto his neighbour" (Deut. 15:1-2). The six negative precepts are (1) "Thou shalt neither sow the field (2) nor prune thy vineyard. (3) That which groweth of itself of the harvest thou shalt not reap, (4) and the grapes of the undressed vine thou shalt not gather" (Lev. 25:4-5). (5) "He shall not exact it [the loan] of his neighbour" (Deut. 15:2), and (6) "Beware that there be not a base thought in thine heart, saying: 'The seventh year, the year of release, is at hand'; and thine eye be evil against thy needy brother, and thou give him nought" (Deut. 15:9).

According to the rabbis, the laws of the sabbatical remittance of debts are applicable both in the land of Israel and in the diaspora. But the obligation to let the land lie fallow is limited to the land of Israel. The biblical background points out that these laws begin only "when ye come into the land which I give you" (Lev. 25:2). The Talmud, however, discusses and debates whether the sabbatical laws are still biblically relevant after the destruction of the first temple, when apparently the jubilee year is no longer operative. According to Judah II, it is observed today only because of rabbinic enactment to "perpetuate the memory of the Sabbatical Year".

In temple days, rabbinic law established that it was also biblically forbidden to work the land during the 30 days prior to the start of the sabbatical year. "The rabbis extended this pre-sabbatical prohibition until the preceding Shavuot for orchards, and Passover for grain fields. After the destruction of the Temple, these additional restrictions were no longer in force, and today it is permissible to work the land until Rosh Ha-Shanah of the Sabbatical Year."[3]

The community was concerned about produce that grows of itself during the sabbatical year. The rabbis considered it holy, and its usage was restricted. Farmers were forbidden to harvest the growth for commercial purposes (Mishnah, Sheviit 7:3) or to remove it from the land of Israel (Mishnah, Sheviim 6:5). It may only be eaten or utilized in its usual fashion, so that items such as wine and vinegar may be used only for nourishment and not for anointing purposes (Mishnah, Sheviim 8:2). The sabbatical produce may be eaten only as long as similar produce is still available in the field for the consumption of animals (Mishnah, Sheviim 9:4). Once such produce has been consumed, all remaining sabbatical products of the same species must also be destroyed (Mishnah, Sheviim 9:8).

The rabbis stated that the sabbatical money release was intended to free the poor from their debts and to enable them to attempt again to achieve financial stability. However, when Hillel later saw that people refrained from lending money before the sabbatical year, he instituted the *prosbul* (Gittin 36a). The following are excluded from cancellation by the sabbatical year: wages, merchandise on credit, loans on pledges, a note guaranteed by mortgage, a note turned over to the *bet din* for collection, and the debtor's waiving the cancellation of his debt (Gittin 36a-b, 37a-b).[4]

The meaning of *prosbul*

Prosbul is a legal rabbinic formula whereby a creditor could still claim his debts after the sabbatical year despite the biblical injunction against doing so (Deut. 15:2). The text of the *prosbul* reads, "I declare before you, so-and-so, the judges in such-a-such a place, that regarding any debt due to me, I may be able to recover any money owing to me from so-and-so at any time I shall desire." The *prosbul* was signed by witnesses or by the judges of the court before whom the declaration was made (Mishnah, Sheviit 10:4, Gittin 36a). The principle underlying the *prosbul* was based on the passage "and this is the manner of the release: every creditor shall release that which he hath lent unto his neighbour; he shall not exact it of his neighbour and his brother... Of a foreigner thou mayest exact it; but whatsoever of thine is with thy brother thy hand shall release" (Deut. 15:2-3). The rabbis and rabbinic teachers deduced that the operation of the year of release did not affect debts of which the bonds had been delivered to the court (*bet din*) before the intervention of the sabbatical year (Sheviit 10:2), since the court was regarded as a corporate body to which the words "thy brother", suggesting an individual, did not apply. The court would therefore collect its debts after the sabbatical year (Maimonides, Yad, Shemittah ve-Yovel 9:15). "Through a slight extension of this precedent, the *prosbul* was instituted, which in effect amounted to entrusting the court with the collection of the debt. Without actually handing over the bond to the court as previously required, the creditor could secure his debt against forfeiture by making the prescribed declaration.

> The *prosbul* was instituted by Hillel. The Mishnah states that when he saw that the people refrained from giving loans one to another before the Sabbatical Year, thereby transgressing "Beware that there be not a base thought in thy heart," etc. (Deuteronomy 15:9), he instituted the *prosbul* (Sheviit 9:3). The Talmud therefore explained *prosbul* as *pruz buli u-buti*, meaning an advantage for both the rich and poor. It benefitted the rich since it secured their loans, and the poor since it enabled them to borrow (Gittin 37a). The word, seems, however to be an abbreviation of the Greek expression πρὸς βουλῇ βουλευτῶν, meaning "before the assembly of counsellors." The rabbis later explained that Hillel only abrogated the Mosaic institution of the release of all debts every seventh year since the law of release itself was only of rabbinic authority during the Second Temple period when the Jubilee was not operative because the land was not fully occupied by Israel (Gittin 36a-b). It was only permitted to write a *prosbul* when the debtor possessed some real property from which the debt could be collected. The rabbis were very lenient with this rule, however, and permitted the writing of a *prosbul* even when the debtor possessed a minute amount of land such as a flowerpot or the trunk of a tree. The creditor was also permitted temporarily to transfer to the debtor a small parcel of land so that the *prosbul* could be written (Sheviit 10:6, 7; Gittin 37a). An antedated *prosbul* was considered valid, but a postdated one was void (Sheviit 10:5).[5]

The *Encyclopedia Judaica* has the following on the post-biblical period understanding of the sabbatical year:

Following the destruction of the Temple (69 C.E.), the observance of the sabbatical prohibitions imposed ever increasing economic hardships upon the agrarian society of ancient Israel. It became a constant source of challenge to the religious tenacity of the farmers. The rabbis constantly exhorted the masses to continue to observe properly the sabbatical restrictions, declaring that exile (Shabbath 33a), poverty (Suka 40b), and pestilence (Avot 5:9) result from the transgression of these laws. Immediately following the destruction, most of the land was left in Jewish hands and the sabbatical year was observed. Permissible organized distribution of sabbatical produce was arranged by the rabbis in order to ease the burden of the farmers although there was some opposition to this procedure (Sheviit 4:2). However, after the unsuccessful Bar Kohkba Revolt (132-135 C.E.), the Roman government abrogated its previous tax exemption (Safrai, 320f.). Many Jews now compromised their observances due to the new economic pressures engendered by the demand for taxes during this year (Mekhilta, Shabbata 1). Some gathered sabbatical crops in order to pay these taxes while others even traded in the produce (Sanhedrin 3:3, 26a). An entire city was described in which all the residents transgressed the sabbatical laws (Tosefta Demai 3:17). An instance was even recorded where a proselyte retorted to the reproaches of a native Jew by exclaiming, "I will merit divine reward since I have not eaten the fruits of the Sabbatical Year like you" (Berakhot 30a; Gittin 54a). Nevertheless, even during this period, there were individuals who resolutely observed the sabbatical restrictions. R. Eleazar b. Zadok remarked about such a person, "I have never seen a man walking in the paths of righteousness as this man" (Sukkah 44b).

As a consequence of the hardships now encountered in sabbatical observances, the rabbis relaxed many of the prohibitions. Their actions were probably also prompted by the viewpoint of Judah II that the institution of the sabbatical year was rabbinic only during the second temple period, when the jubilee was not operative because the land was not fully occupied by Israel (Gittin 36a-b). Areas such as Ashkelon (Tosefta, Oho. 18:4), Beth-Shean, Caesarea, Bet Guvrin, and Kefar Zemah (Jerusalem Talmud, Demai 2:1, 22c) were exempted from the restrictions of the sabbatical year. Judah ha-Nasi also permitted the buying of the vegetables immediately after the close of the sabbatical year (Sheviim 6:4) and the importing of produce from the diaspora during the sabbatical year (Jerusalem Talmud, Sheviim 6:4, 37a; 7:2, 37b), both transactions having been previously forbidden. Many Jews still transgressed the sabbatical prohibitions that remained in force, since they knew that their institution was only rabbinic (Jerusalem Talmud, Demai 2:1, 22d). It was related that an individual disobeyed the sabbatical laws but carefully observed the *hallah* rules since the latter was still a biblical commandment (Jerusalem Talmud, Sheviim 9:8, 39a).

Rabban Gamaliel, the son of Judah ha-Nasi, continued his father's policies and also relaxed sabbatical restrictions. He permitted the previously forbidden actions of tilling the fields until the actual start — Rosh Ha-Shanah — of the sabbatical year (Moed Katan 3b; Tosefta, Sheviit 1:1), and the preparation of olives with an olive-crusher during this year (Mishnah Sheviim 8:6; Tosefta, Sheviim 6:27). During the third century, conditions worsened for the Jewish farmers. Taxes were increased so that the constantly changing Roman rulers could support their armies and military expeditions. The rabbis therefore permitted the actual sowing of the seeds that produced the necessary food for the foreign armies (Sanhedrin 26a; Jerusalem Talmud, Sanhedrin 3:6, 21b; Maimonides, Yad, Shemittah 1:11). They also extended the time that fruits could be harvested and eaten during the sabbatical year (Mishnah, Sheviim 9:3; Pesahim 53a). Even during this difficult period, individuals continued to be meticulous in their observances. It was related that R. Safra investigated the rules governing his removing a barrel of Erez Israel sabbatical wine to the diaspora before he did so (Pesahim 52b). The rabbis declared that the verse "Ye mighty in strength, that fulfill his word" (Ps. 103:20) refers to those who leave their fields and vineyards untilled for a full year and still do not complain when they pay their taxes under the Roman government (Leviticus Rabbah 1:1). The observance of these laws remained sufficiently widespread so that the Gentile nations were able to mock the Jews by stating, "The Jews observe the law of the Sabbatical Year and therefore have no vegetables. Consequently, the Jews sadden camels by eating the thorns which otherwise would have been consumed by the camels" (Lamentations Rabbah, Proem 17).[6]

The contemporary experience

The agricultural settlements in the land of Israel and Zionist redemption of the land brought about practical problems for the settlers in respect of the sabbatical year. Before the *shemittah* of 1889, the leading rabbis of the generation debated whether it was permissible to enact a formal sale of all the Jewish-owned fields and vineyards to non-Jews in order to permit the working of the land during the sabbatical year. R. Isaac Elhanan Spektor of Kovno issued the following statement permitting this transaction:

> I was asked several months ago to express my opinion concerning Jewish colonists, who live on the produce of the fields and vineyards of our Holy Land, as the *shemittah* year is approaching in 1889. If we do not find a

hetter it is possible that the land will become desolate and the colonies will turn into wasteland, God forbid. Hundreds of souls will be affected by it. Although I am very much preoccupied and very weak, yet I find it necessary to deal with this important problem; and permit the work in the fields, by selling them to the Muslims for a period of two years only. After that period, the vineyard and the fields go back to the owners; and the sale must be to Muslims only and may take place during the coming summer. I prepared, with the help of God, a special brochure dealing with this subject, but in practice I never came out with a *hetter* because I did not want to be the only one in this new matter, as is always my practice in such things.

But now that I received a letter informing me that my good friends, the rabbis: R. Israel Joshua of Kutna, R. Samuel Mohilewer of Bialystok, and R. Samuel Zanwil of Warsaw gave due consideration to this problem and came out with a *hetter*, and wait for my approval, I am greatly pleased to find that I am not alone in this great issue. My opinion is, therefore, to follow my above mentioned suggestion [sell the land to non-Jews]. Furthermore, the work in the fields and vineyards is to be done by non-Jews, but in the case of poor people who cannot afford to engage non-Jewish labour, let them consult the aforementioned honoured rabbis; and may the Lord grant us the privilege to come joyously to our land, and observe the *mitzvah* of *shemittah* as it was originally ordained for us and in accordance with all its rules and regulations.

It must be explicitly stated that this *hetter* is only for the year 5649 (1889) but not for future *shemittot*. Then further meditation will be necessary, and a new *hetter* will be required; and may the Lord help His people so that they should not need any *hetter* and should observe *shemittah* in accordance with the Law as I have fully explained it, in the special brochure, with the help of God.[7]

Spektor's lenient decision was opposed by some rabbinic leaders. Many of the colonists originally refrained from work during the sabbatical year in accordance with the stringent ruling, but the rise in farms compelled Jewish farmers to abide by the lenient decision during the next *shemittah* of 1896.

The *Encyclopedia Judaica* points out that

before the sabbatical year of 1910, the controversy regarding the sale of the land to Muslims revived. Rabbi Abraham Isaac Kook, then the chief rabbi of Jaffa, was the leading proponent of the sale, while Rabbi Jacob David Willowsky of Safed opposed it. During the ensuing *shemittah* years, the chief rabbinate of Erez Israel continued to abide by the lenient ruling, although there was always opposition to its decisions. Most prominent among the opponents has been Rabbi Abraham Isaiah Karelitz of Bene-Berak. In Kibbutz Hafez Hayyim attempts to grow vegetables in water (hydroponics) have met with some success as a method of observing the restrictions of the Sabbatical Year. Sabbatical Years during the second half of the 20th century fall during 5712 (1951/52); 5719 (1958/59); 5726 (1965/66); 5733 (1972/73); 5740 (1979/80); 5747 (1986/87); and 5754 (1993/94). [8]

A final reflection

The concepts of sabbatical year and jubilee belong to a moment of Jewish history. Their meanings developed from early biblical understandings to mediaeval and contemporary interpretations because of specific events. Contemporary understanding relates to the situation of the State of Israel, religious or secular farms, and even ecological reasons.

To interpret the meaning of the sabbatical year in our own days may tempt ideologists to use the text as a pretext. This is a reality when critics of the contemporary economic situation recommend using the year 2000 as a sabbatical for the international debt. The biblical concept of sabbatical year, however, refers to the Jewish calendar, not the Christian (specifically the Gregorian) yearly account. The international debt, especially of third-world countries, is the consequence of banking as well as national irresponsibility. Military juntas or leaders with little political wisdom accepted loans beyond any realistic possibility of return. These loans generally did not help the masses but rather benefited only individuals, military leadership or the new post-colonial civil administrations, who have learned quickly the lure of corruption, both economic and political.

I am concerned about the use and abuse of biblical laws, a dimension of theological contempt that might seduce religious leadership in their fight for social justice. I am recommending prudence, a theological virtue that seems to have disappeared from religious organizations. The gift of prudence should be used to guide wisely at times of crisis. It should help denounce economic injustice, but also educate people to be responsible in economic dealings. This was done by the Pharisees and the rabbinic scholars for centuries in their understanding and interpretations of the sabbatical year and the jubilee.

NOTES

[1] *Encyclopedia Judaica*, Jerusalem, 1974, vol. 14, col. 577.
[2] *Idem*, p.578.
[3] *Idem*, p.582.
[4] *Idem*, p.582.
[5] *Encyclopedia Judaica*, Jerusalem, 1974, vol. 13, 1182.
[6] *Ibid.*, vol. 14, pp.583-584.
[7] E. Shimoff, *Rabbi Isaac Elchanan Spektor*, 1959, pp.134f.
[8] *Encyclopedia Judaica*, vol. 14, p.585.

BASIC BIBLIOGRAPHY

Encylopedia Judaica, Jerusalem, 1974.
The Jewish Encyclopedia, New York and London, Funk and Wagnalls Company, 1901.
Edward Neufuld, *Socio-Economic Background of Yobel and Smitta*, Roma, Rivista Degli Studi Orientali, Volume 33, 1958.
Robert North, S.J., *Sociology of the Biblical Jubilee*, Roma, Pontificio Instituto Biblico, 1954.

The Jubilee: Some Christian Understandings throughout History

Jacques Nicole

The imminence of the third millennium CE, as well as the perspective of its 50th anniversary (1948-98), has led the World Council of Churches to suggest to its member churches a reflection on the jubilee. Such a theme includes dimensions of penitence, repentance and reparation, but also of joyful celebration and adoration of the Creator of the universe, all necessary components for the pilgrimage leading to the eighth assembly at Harare (Zimbabwe) and to the year 2001.

In this article I provide a sampling of the various interpretations the notion of jubilee has received in the Christian churches over the course of the centuries.

The New Testament

There is no direct reference to Leviticus 25 in the New Testament, but the traditional Christian interpretation of Isaiah 61:1-2, incorporating part of Isaiah 58:6 ("let the oppressed go free"), in Luke's gospel 4:18-19 has often seen the "year of the Lord's favour" as a clear allusion to Leviticus 25. It is part of an account (Luke 4:16-30) of the first public exposition of the scriptures by Jesus in the synagogue of Nazareth. He interprets it eschatologically in reference to his own ministry: "Today this scripture has been fulfilled in your hearing" (v. 21). The same messianic interpretation of the jubilee by Jesus is implicit in his reply to the disciples of John the Baptist in Matthew 11:2-6 (Luke 7:18-23).

Two important modifications however have occurred. First, perhaps because the early church never was in a position to organize socially, politically and economically a nation within the boundaries of a particular country, there is no mention of the land. Second, the advantages of the jubilee are explicitly extended to foreigners, with a reference to Elijah and the widow of Zarephath (Luke 4:25-26), as well as to Elisha and Naaman the Syrian leper (v. 27).

Jesus' self-understanding certainly explains why jubilee themes such as the remission of debts and the redistribution of wealth play such an important role in the whole of the New Testament. One good example can be taken from Matthew's version of the Lord's prayer (6:9-13). In verse 12 ("And forgive us our debts, as we also have forgiven our debtors") the Greek word translated "forgive" — *aphiēmi* - strongly echoes the LXX translation of the jubilee words *deror* (liberty) and *yovel* (jubilee).

This is forcefully illustrated in the same gospel of Matthew by the parable of the unforgiving servant (18:23-35). After he himself is forgiven a debt of astronomical proportions, a slave turns around and has one of his own debtors, who owes a sum that is trifling by comparison, thrown into prison. The parable concludes with what might be called the jubilee moral: "if you do not forgive your brother or sister from your heart", you cannot expect God to forgive you your own debts (v. 35).

Another example can be found in the two descriptions of the community of the apostles in Jerusalem in Acts 2:42-47 and 4:32-35, showing how the first Christians sought to ensure there were no needy among them by voluntarily practising a radical form of redistribution of wealth (cf. also Deut. 15:4). On a larger scale, Paul develops a similar idea when he invites the Corinthian Christian community to participate in his vast project of collection for the needy fellow Christians of Jerusalem, as a response to "the grace of God that has been granted to [them]" (2 Cor. 8:1).

Echoes in the patristic tradition

While reacting against an allegorical interpretation often based, as in Philo of Alexandria, on the mystical meaning of the numbers 7 and 50, the rabbinic schools had already emphasized the spiritual — and more interiorized — sense of the jubilee. The Book of Jubilees insists on inner conversion, and the Fourth Book of Maccabees introduces the expiatory character of the suffering of the just in a way that calls to mind the epistle to the Hebrews.

In his translation of the Hebrew Bible, Jerome renders *yovel* by *iubilaeus* and explains it as a *remissionis annus* (year of remission).

It was therefore soon understood as a time of penitence inciting the human soul to turn back to its Creator.

The Hebrew meaning is further altered by the assimilation in Latin of *iubilaeus* and *iubilare* (to shout), which usually renders the Hebrew word *teru'a* and was used, particularly in monastic circles, to describe the *iubilatio*, the inner joy that comes from the contemplation of the divine mysteries.

Thus in a comment on Leviticus 25:8, Richard of St. Victor, (d. 1173) writes:

> The one who deserves to possess spiritual gifts in the full quietness of soul, after the cycle of seven times seven years, seems in some ways to enter in the forty-ninth year. Then comes the fiftieth, called the jubilee... Then the flesh "sabbatizes" when earthly desires no longer prevail, and it delights in spiritual exercises... Therefore the spirit of the human, overjoyed in jubilation, is carried away into praise of God perfectly and fully. [1]

The Holy Year

The association of the jubilee with the doctrine of expiation and indulgences is not a Christian invention. It is present in the Talmud, which states that on the year of jubilee a large indulgence was granted. The penitent is urged to go on a pilgrimage of expiatory value.

In this sense the Christian concept of jubilee was developed in relation to the crusades. Bernard de Clairvaux (1090-1153) associates the indulgence given on the occasion of the second crusade to a jubilee: "annus placabilis Domino, annus remissionis, annus utique iubilaeus" (a year of appeasing the Lord, a year of remission, and especially a year of jubilee). The crusade is the Christian jubilee because of the abundance of the indulgence offered to those participating in it. However after the fall of Ptolemaïs in 1291 and the end of the eighth and last crusade, the plenary indulgence was granted to pilgrims travelling to places more accessible than Jerusalem, such as Santiago de Compostela and, above all, Rome.

Jubilee was also applied by Cardinal Stephen Langton, around 1200, to the indulgence granted on the occasion of the translation of Thomas Becket's remains, 50 years after his martyrdom.

The penitential doctrine of the Christian church finds its classical expression in the writings of Thomas Aquinas (1225-74). The magisterium disposes of the treasure of merits common to the whole church.

The pope can therefore pronounce a remission of the penalty because of sins committed in the present life, shortening the time to be spent in purgatory. From then on, the practice of indulgences underwent a tremendous expansion.

The first historically attested Christian jubilee, or holy year, was proclaimed in 1300 by Pope Boniface VIII. It coincides with the great revival preached by the mendicant orders, particularly the Franciscans, as well as the vibrant millenarian expectation that traversed the 13th and 14th centuries.

The emphasis in such Roman Catholic jubilee years has in recent times moved from the traditional notion of indulgence to spiritual renewal in the love of God, faithfulness to the gospel and commitment to justice and compassion in human society (e.g., see *Iubilaeum maximum*, by Pope Pius XII, 1949). In proclaiming the most recent such year (1975), Pope Paul VI emphasized the theme of reconciliation.

The Protestant churches

The Protestant churches appear to have been reluctant, particularly during the 16th and 17th centuries, to use the concept of jubilee. No doubt it was because of its link with the doctrine and practice of indulgences, which played an important role in the controversies of the Reformation. The fact that the holy years have been also occasions to promulgate dogmas and encyclicals, such as the mariological dogma and *Humanae generis* in 1950, which could not be fully accepted by Protestants, might also be a possible explanation.

However, Calvin writes on the jubilee that "this was the most illustrious Sabbath, since the state of the people, both as to their persons and their houses and property, was renewed; and although in this way God had regard to the public good, gave relief to the poor, so that their liberty should not be destroyed, and preserved also the order laid down by Himself". Quoting 2 Chronicles 36:21, he notes that the land "enjoyed her Sabbaths, when it had vomited forth its inhabitants, for since they had polluted it by violating the Sabbath, so that it groaned as if under a heavy burden, He says that it shall rest for a long continuous period."[2] While acknowledging that the jubilee has a direct relevance to the social, economic and ecological organization of Israel, Calvin clearly states that its deeper meaning is spiritual, pointing to the theology of the sabbath.

Another noteworthy exception is the appearance of the term "jubilee" in sermons and religious writings in the context of the 18th- and 19th-century struggle for the emancipation of slaves in the United States. Fugitive slaves from the Southern states often found refuge with the Federal troops, and some were even enrolled to fight against their former masters. This produced a number of African-American spirituals mentioning specifically the jubilee:

O brethren, rise and shine,
And give God the glory, glory
Rise and shine and give the glory, glory
For the Year of Jubilee.

Don't you want to be a soldier, soldier, soldier,
Don't you want to be a soldier, soldier, soldier,
Don't you want to be a soldier, soldier, soldier,
For the Year of Jubilee.

Lincoln's proclamation emancipating the slaves as of 1 January 1863 was clearly acclaimed as the beginning of a year of jubilee, extending to the African-American people the freedom from which most of them had previously been excluded. Ironically, one of the famous icons of the American Revolution, the Liberty Bell in Philadelphia, has inscribed on it a quotation of Leviticus 25:10: "Proclaim liberty throughout all the land unto all the inhabitants thereof."

Conclusion

In the past 30 years widespread interest has been stimulated in the implications of the jubilee theme for Christian social ethics. John H. Yoder's book *The Politics of Jesus* (1972) includes a chapter entitled "The Implications of the Jubilee", which traces allusions in the gospels to the four jubilee prescriptions: leaving the soil fallow, remitting debts, freeing slaves and redistributing capital. No doubt the present symposium will be the occasion of a much wider inventory of jubilee-inspired literature. May it be also a powerful source of inspiration for us all.

58   *The Jubilee Challenge*

NOTES

[1] Quoted by Raymonde Foreville, "Jubilé", in *Dictionnaire de Spiritualité*, vol. 8, Paris, Beauchesne, 1974, p.1480.
[2] John Calvin, *Commentaries on the Four Last Books of Moses*, Grand Rapids, MI, Eerdmans, 1950, 2.450-51.

BIBLIOGRAPHY

A. Biéler, *La Pensée économique et sociale de Calvin*, Geneva, Librairie de l'Université, 1959.
E. Delaruelle, "L'idée de Croisade chez St. Bernard", in *Mélanges St. Bernard*, Dijon, 1954.
E.M. Dörfuss, "Das Jobeljahr in Verkündigung und Theologie der Kirche: Systematisch-Theologische Implikationen", *Ökumenische Rundschau*, 44, July 1995, 311-27.
R. Foreville, "L'idée de Jubilé chez les théologiens et les canonistes", *Revue d'histoire ecclésiastique*, 56, 1961, 401-23.
R. Forewill, "Jubilé", in *Dictionnaire de Spiritualité*, 8.1478-87, Paris, Beauchesne, 1974.
M.B. Friedland, *To Proclaim the Acceptable Year of the Lord: Social Activism and Ecumenical Cooperation Among White Clergy in the Civil Rights and Antiwar Movements of the 1950s and 1960s*, Ann Arbor, MI, University Microfilms, 1993.
M. Harris, *Proclaim Jubilee: A Sprituality for the Twenty-First Century*, Louisville, KY, Westminster/John Knox Press, 1996.
E. Jombart, "Jubilé", in *Dictionnaire de droit canonique*, 6.191-203, Paris, 1957.
R. North, *Sociology of the Biblical Jubilee*, Rome, Pontifical Biblical Institute, 1954.
J.H. Yoder, *The Politics of Jesus*, Grand Rapids, MI, Eerdmans, 1972.
World Council of Churches, "Biblical and Theological Dimensions of Jubilee", unpublished staff paper, Geneva, 1993.

Sabbath and Jubilee

Geraldine Smyth

Sabbath and jubilee as life symbols have travelled long distances since their conception within the Jewish tradition. Finding a home in many contexts, they have sometimes kept faith with their original religious significance, sometimes developed another religious meaning, and sometimes taken on a more generalized spiritual or ethical significance. The celebrating of a golden jubilee of marriage or of religious vows comes to mind. Another example is the inauguration by the UN Environmental Programme of an "Environmental Sabbath" kept on June 1 each year: resources drawn from different world faiths are circulated, suitable for use in education or worship, and encouraging more caring and respectful practices that will give the earth rest.

In this article, we consider how the symbol of sabbath and, in some measure, of jubilee influenced the WCC conciliar process (covenant) for justice, peace and the integrity of creation (JPIC). While acknowledging that these symbols did help to shape a more integrated ethical vision, the limiting of their scope and influence will be related to the failure within Christian theology in recent centuries to develop a vital and coherent theology of creation. Sabbath and jubilee will then be explored in terms of their symbolic potential to act as pathways that bridge areas within Christian theology that need to be reconnected: God and creation, creation and liberation, creation and covenant, creation and eschatology. In the final section, I offer some reflections on my own context of Northern Ireland, centring on the particular contribution of women in the struggle to move from violence to peace, by correlating some dimensions of the Jewish understanding of sabbath with the insights of feminist writer Julia Kristeva on "women's time". This I do with deep respect for the essentially Jewish roots and context of this symbol of sabbath, and with a sense of gratitude that my Jewish teachers and friends have encouraged me to draw life from such symbols for my own spiritual and ethical living as a Christian woman and theologian.

A backward glance

At the JPIC convocation at Seoul in 1990, the symbols of sabbath and jubilee took on a special focus in several ways. For example, the notion of jubilee was lifted up in relation to the division of the land where the convocation was hosted. For Koreans at the convocation such a division was viewed as the original sin. Participants affirmed the dynamic towards reunification in terms of the call for a jubilee in 1995, when the land might be one again, divided families might be reunited, and severed political links might be restored. The year 1995 has come and gone with no jubilee horn bringing down walls of division; instead there are threats of war and stronger walls.

Also within the JPIC process, some of the affirmations made at Seoul were phrased in language that echoed the jubilee texts of Leviticus and Exodus. The theme of justice for the earth was a strong focus in Affirmation 8, for "the earth belongs to God". Affirmation 7 that "creation is beloved by God", carried a similar resonance, but it satisfied neither participants from the East nor those who called for an ecological approach, who were uneasy about the anthropocentric perspective. These affirmations were not well grounded in a sturdy theology of creation, but they nevertheless offered a new framework for engaging the interrelated issues of justice, peace and the integrity of creation.

Furthermore, the symbols of both sabbath and jubilee were implicit in the prevailing language and ritual of covenant and covenanting — both in regard to the four official covenants made by participants to resist debt, militarism, abuse of the land and racism, but also in the many unofficial covenant-type commitments of solidarity entered into by participants from across the world.

Looking back over the conciliar process for justice, peace and the integrity of creation, one finds that the symbol of sabbath was not often adduced as a resource in the JPIC struggle for life. Rather than simply estimating the frequency or infrequency of references to jubilee and sabbath within the past tradition of JPIC, it may be more constructive to suggest that the reason these symbols did not play a fuller role was connected to the fact that despite several calls from various WCC consultations¹ creation did not attain a foundational place in the JPIC process. Thus, for example at the Kuala Lumpur meeting, which was focused on creation (one of the subthemes for the Canberra assembly, under the heading "Developing an Ethic for Justice and Sustainability"), the vision of *shabbat* was advanced as uniting the social and ecological aspects of justice. This vision was substantiated by analysis of interrelated aspects of injustice, poverty and the degradation of creation, and an ethics and economics of sustainability.²

There are historical reasons why creation has been relegated to the margins of Christian theological discourse, or why, even then, it was confined by a hermeneutical focus on Genesis 1-3, with a stress on individual sin and guilt. The reasons need not detain us, but the baleful consequences of such a theological narrowing of focus should be noted: the unity of Genesis was ruptured, and Genesis 4-11, with its attention to human community, was discounted. Thus too the dimensions of social responsibility and of blessing handed on in the "generations" were diluted. The sense of cosmic interrelatedness, dramatized in the flood story and in the universal covenant with all nations and with all creation, was all but lost. Thus the plurality of the creation theologies present also in the Psalms, Deutero-Isaiah and the Wisdom books or in Job 38-41 was flattened into a static view of the origins of the world and of humankind. The possibility of the liberation of creation tended to be held in a tight Christocentric way, cut off from its mythological and broader biblical roots.³

At the York and Kuala Lumpur consultations, the need to renew the correlation between creation and redemption, creation and covenant, creation and history, and creation and eschatology was specifically noted. But adequate theological attention has not yet been given to this task. It is my hope that the preparatory work for the eighth WCC assembly at Harare will not neglect this theological challenge.⁴

The focus on sabbath and jubilee offers the opportunity to substantiate the case for creation as foundational in JPIC and in the current "Theology of Life" process within the WCC.⁵ Furthermore, these offer "symbolic pathways" that can reconnect creation and salvation, creation and history, creation and covenant, creation and eschatology. I should like to explore these symbolic pathways further, and then share some ways in which these have opened a way within my own JPIC context: Ireland, a country riven by violence and sectarianism, yet inspired by a longing for a renewed sabbath of peace and for a jubilee time when prisoners can be released, when *all* the dead can be remembered, when parity of esteem for *every* cultural, political and religious tradition will be celebrated, and where the excluded will find economic justice and social inclusion.

Sabbath and jubilee: symbolic pathways of connection

God and creation

The sabbath recalls us to our identity and purpose and shows these to be closely connected to the purpose of the whole creation.[6] Within the Christian tradition, there are different accounts of the purpose of creation — God's glory or human well-being and salvation, or the well-being of all creation. South African biblical theologian Adrio König rightly insists that these should not be played off against one another but must be seen as complementary. Taking "sabbath" as a hermeneutical key to creation, we are confronted with the ultimate questioning of all our obsession with achievement. Through sabbath, our technocratic modes of knowing and relationship are challenged (Gen. 2:1-3). Both Claus Westermann and Jürgen Moltmann, commenting on the Priestly tradition, see the crown of creation in the sabbath rest of God on the seventh day. Neither work nor achievement is the goal of creation, but the gift and blessing of sabbath rest: "The crown of creation is not the human being; it is the sabbath. It is true that as the image of God, the human being has his special position in creation. But he stands together with all other earthly and heavenly beings in the same hymn of praise of God's glory, and in the enjoyment of God's Sabbath pleasure over creation."[7]

The tendency to de-contextualize and to interpret the divine command to care for the earth as to "subdue" the earth (Gen. 1:28) has led to a dominative epistemology bolstering an exploitative technology, and a theology that has viewed nature as something to be used for end gain or "transcended". In both cases, humanity and the whole future of creation are closed off from their innate telos.

Creation and liberation

The sabbath thus manifests something of the divine nature and of human nature made in God's image. The sabbath is constitutive of the whole of creation. It relates back to creation (Ex. 20:11), but it has links too with the Exodus tradition (Deut. 5:15). So too Leviticus 25 from the Holiness Code extrapolates from sabbath to the notion of the sabbath year and the year of jubilee for all the people and for the land itself. While there is abundant evidence for the literal practice of giving "rest" to the land, this is not so in respect of the returning of land to its original owners in the jubilee year.[8] Nevertheless, the persistence of this symbol and tradition over 2,500 years suggests that it has a deeply rooted significance in both the Jewish and Christian psyches, with overtones of renewal and justice and the radical restructuring of society in the direction of equality and solidarity with the poor.

Sabbath is a day of remembrance and blessing that makes it clear "that the God of the Exodus is the creator of the world, and that God the Creator is also the God of the Exodus".[9] It both anticipates the messianic era, the day of the new creation, and presupposes "the ecological 'day of rest' of the original creation".[10] Sabbath, then, as well as being the day of God's rest and humanity's, is also a day for nature to rest and see its blessings renewed.[11]

Relating creation and covenant

Although Exodus 16:22-30 suggests that the sabbath existed *before* the covenant at Sinai, and we have stressed the ancient association between creation and sabbath in the context of Genesis 2:2-3 (it is to be found, in fact, in all the traditions that constitute the Pentateuch), the sabbath symbol was primarily linked with the covenant between God and the people of Israel and was a day specially consecrated to God. Two theological perspectives emerged in regard to the sabbath. First, in Deuteronomy 5:14b-15, there is an insistence on the human need for rest, together with the remembering of God's liberation of Israel from slavery and bringing deliverance into a "resting place". Second, the Priestly emphasis of Exodus (20:11) draws explicitly on the notion of *God's* rest and *God's* hallowing of the day as in Genesis 2:2-3. This tradition too is thus an expression of covenant theology, though from God's perspective.

The great Christian theologian of the covenant, Karl Barth, asserted that creation was the larger context of covenant (*Church Dogmatics* III/I, 41).

Did we see this claim validated in the JPIC process, where covenant was, from the start, such a controlling symbol? Did the emphasis on covenant within JPIC open up the wider horizon of creation? It must be acknowledged that the covenant symbol, in relation to which JPIC commitments were from the start envisaged, did not fully realize its ecumenical possibilities. I would suggest that a significant reason why the covenant symbol was never fully "received" within the JPIC process was that it had become identified in a one-sided way with the human commitment rather than with the divine purpose. So, too, it was too firmly tied into a historical and confessionalized hermeneutic of election and disconnected from its creation and indeed "sabbath" context. The covenant symbol thus lost much of its universal and inclusivist potential. Thus sabbath emerges as a powerful integrative symbol, a symbolic pathway between God and creation, humanity and the nonhuman creation, creation and redemption. Through sabbath, creation in its origins opens to its eschatological fulfilment.

Creation and eschatology

The interrelationship between the life of creation, history and heavenly life is seen in a dynamic nexus when we explore "sabbath" in terms of its literal meaning in Genesis 1 — "ceasing from work; rest". This "rest" motif is clear also in Psalm 95 and in the version of Genesis that is given in the pseudepigraphic Book of Jubilees (most probably written by a Pharisee), for the author is intent on stressing the importance of the law at the earliest stages of history (Jub. 2:1-33). In serving this purpose, the sabbath motif is dominant: "Write the complete history of the creation, how in six days the Lord God finished all his works and all that he created, and kept Sabbath on the seventh day and hallowed it for all ages and appointed it as a sign for all his works" (Jub. 2:1). Sabbath is highlighted in 17 verses. [12] Besides the rules governing the keeping of the sabbath, it is claimed that the sabbath is kept in heaven, which can be extended to eternal "sabbath rest" for God's people.

The author of Hebrews (4:9-11) reads an eschatological meaning into the sabbath rest of Psalm 95. (The word for "rest" here is *menuha*, not *shabbat*, but the Septuagint in each case uses a word derived from the same Greek stem: *katapausis* in Psalm 94:11 [=NSRV 95:11) and *katapauō*, Gen. 2:2.) In reflecting on Psalm 95, where the historic promised land is seen in terms of "God's rest" ("They shall not enter my rest"), the New Testament author expands the context to include the promise to Christ's followers of entering heaven. While the echo back to Genesis is clear (creation), the author points forward to the sabbath rest still to come (the eschaton). Here the sabbath, or God's rest, relates creation to its innate dynamic of hope. The author stretches the meaning of the psalm to argue that it was not simply the land that was promised, "but a share in God's post-creation rest". This flows from the Jewish concept of the sabbath in its construing of that rest, as "'the image of the world to come' (Gen. Rab. 17 [12a])".[13] The declaration in the psalm connects land and rest: "They shall not enter my *rest*." Jesus is presented by the author in terms of a new Joshua ushering his followers into the heavenly rest of God. The promise is still open to be fulfilled.

Christians must guard here against any tendency to supersession-ism, and no doubt aspects of this text lean in that direction. Hence the importance here of recognizing the emphasis on the dynamic relation-ship between creation and eschatology, the origins of creation and the fullness of redemption, which structurally and thematically mirror each other. Thus, "a sabbath rest still remains for the people of God, for those who enter God's rest also cease from their labours as God did from his" (Heb. 4:9-10).

This same dynamic connection can be seen if we look at the central role of the sabbath in Jesus' ministry, as the time of compassion and healing, as the hallowed space into which outsiders are drawn. Jesus reveals the potential of sabbath, or God's rest, for reuniting creation and the reign of God, creation and new creation. For Westermann, salvation here is both liberative event and God's continuing blessing and blessedness. One can recall Jesus's acts of healing on the sabbath as acts both of healing and of liberation. So too Luke 4, where the explicit context of sabbath and the reference to the "Spirit of the Lord" (as in Gen. 1:2) frames the programmatic account of Jesus' ministry of liberation and healing. Here we note Jesus' appropriation of the jubilee imagery of Third Isaiah (61:1-2 and 58:6) and of Leviticus 25:8-12 — "to let the oppressed go free, to proclaim the year of the Lord's favour" (Luke 4:18-19). In the unfolding ministry of Jesus, the sabbath is associated with Jesus' prayer and praise of the Father, and also with compassionate acts of healing and liberation that herald the coming of the *basileia*, the new covenant and the new creation.

Within this messianic horizon, Jewish Christians first came to relate the sabbath both to the idea of the seventh day (the day of rest after the six days of work) and to the idea of the first day (celebrating the day of Jesus' resurrection into the new creation). As Moltmann expresses it: "The light of Christ's resurrection is the light of the Christian Sabbath. But it is more than that. It shines as messianic light on the whole sighing creation, giving it, in its transience, an eternal hope that it will be created anew as the 'world without end'." [14]

Later, Moltmann (adducing Riesenfeld and Rordorf), while careful to maintain the Jewish/Christian distinction in this regard, concludes that however opinions may have varied about the historical reconstruction, "there was a close connection between the celebration of the Jewish Sabbath and the Christian feastday, without the one feast's supplanting the other". [15] Under historical pressures and conflicts, this connection gave way to the separation of the two celebrations. But Moltmann urges Christians to recover the Sabbath connection of Sunday in a way that "the 'new creation' presupposes the ecological 'day of rest' of the original creation", completing rather than destroying the first. [16]

Here too Christians must be wary of conflating (and thereby expropriating *tout court*) the Jewish *shabbat* into the Christian Sunday. And yet, we can recognize that just as creation has been open at different times and places for new interpretations, so too sabbath, particularly in its eschatological horizon, within a world dominated by addiction to achievement, presents itself anew as a resource for healing and hope.

Time for sabbath: a different way for our world

Other ways of knowing

In recent centuries, Western culture and Western theology have been vitiated by an anthropocentric, progressivist worldview of "man the measure of all things". Within the ecumenical process for justice, peace and the integrity of creation, there were recurring conflicts of "interests" — between human rights and the needs of the earth, between the right to justice and the right to peace. If we deem dominative thinking the root cause, then dominative anthropocentrism, particularly in its patriarchal guise, must cease to be given legitimacy via a doctrine of creation devoid of sabbath. The creation of humanity "in the image of God", far from being a sanction for domination, is a call to *relatedness* with God and with the earth that is created good. Thus, creation is primarily experienced in encounter,[17] and sabbath is the fullness of that encounter.

The sabbath symbol invites us to recover a knowing that arises in relationship to the world, rather than the dominative knowledge deriving from the empirical-analytic worldview.[18] Such dialogic knowing is closer to the knowing-in-love suggested by the biblical word *hesed*[19] or to Augustine's "We know to the extent to which we love."[20] Again, Moltmann puts it well:

> Through this form of astonished, wondering and loving knowledge, we do not appropriate things, we recognize their independence and partici-pate in their life. We do not wish to know so that we can dominate. We desire to know in order to participate. This kind of knowledge confers community and can be termed communicative knowledge as compared with dominating knowledge. It lets life be and "cherishes its livingness". Christian theology must remember this, its own wisdom, if it wants to make its contribution to the conquest of the ecological crisis of scientific and technological civilization.[21]

This way of knowing that can let life be and cherish its livingness is alive with the creativity of sabbath. By entering into such wonder-ing, loving sabbath, we and the whole life-world to which we belong are gathered up into a new level of being-in-relationship.

Such participative knowing through contemplative presence to the life-world within and around us is grounded in a recovery of imagina-tion and the deepening of our capacity for symbol making. Feminist writer Julia Kristeva refers to this kind of knowing as radically different from the knowing derived from historic, or "linear", time — the mode of time that determines the world of work, politics and commerce. Through ritual and symbol we enter the realms of cyclic or "maternal" time, that draws us into "eternal" time. This symbolic or sacramental knowing is disclosed, not achieved, revealed through encounter with that which transcends us, and it opens us to the experience of the "eternal" within and beyond time.[22] We are very close here to the thought of Abraham Heschel, who spoke of the sabbath as relating us to eternity rather than utility, as the experience of the ineffable in the midst of life.[23] As Heschel observed: "The Sabbath is the counterpoint of living... our awareness of God's presence in the world... It teaches us... the grandeur of living in the face of eternity... The Sabbath is more than a day, more than a name for the seventh part of the week. It is eternity within time, *the spiritual underground of history*."[24]

I acknowledge Heschel's more explicit emphasis on sabbath (and I wonder if Kristeva is directly influenced by Heschel here), but it should become clearer why it is Kristeva's hermeneutic that I wish to follow when I turn presently to relate what has been said above about sabbath to the contemporary situation of conflict and peace in Ireland. It will be necessary first to look briefly at Kristeva's theory of "women's time" to see how relevant it might prove, not only to Ireland, but also to other contexts that are caught between violence and the sabbath time of peace.

Kristeva examines succeeding generations of the feminist movement — the first generation with its insistence on women's equality of access to linear, historical time and political power; the second generation, by contrast, on women's difference and separation from the world of linear time and political power. Kristeva insists, however, that it is not a matter of replacing one mode of time and experience with another, as a case of ideology and counterideology, but rather of the need to reconcile subjective, maternal time (motherhood) with the political, linear (male) time. While challenging any regression to the omnipotent "global mother", who resists separation, Kristeva challenges as unrealistic the rejection (by an earlier generation of feminists) of maternity. She reclaims the experience and discourse of motherhood as a way of healing and transformation for women and men. Kristeva affirms that because of undergoing in their own self the experience of birth with its "splitting apart" to allow separateness, women are disposed to defuse the violences outside. The birth into the world of a child in all its otherness poses the fundamental challenge to any identity — sexual, political or religious — as "sum total". This reality of birth is an invitation to love an other in attentiveness and self-forgetfulness.[25] Thus, for a new generation of women, any totalizing of one identity over another must be rejected. Kristeva insists that what is necessary is

> an apparent de-dramatization of the fight to the death between rival groups... And this not in the name of some reconciliation — feminism has at least had the merit of showing what is irreducible and even deadly in the social contract — but in order that... the implacable difference, the violence be conceived in the very place where it operates with the

maximum intransigence... so as to make it disintegrate in its very nucleus. [26]

We know that the dominant paradigm of political knowing and political ethic with its linear view of time and history, its language and meaning systems of power and control, winners and losers, largely excludes "maternal" understanding of time and space. What we need is an interplay of paradigms to assure an inclusiveness and transformation of the world we share with every living creature. Such a creative transformation will not simply return us to the repetitious histories of "nations, armies and destiny", where a different "other" will in time become victim or scapegoat. So how does this theory relate to the "place" of women in the conflict and struggle for peace in Ireland, or for that matter in the different places in which we live?

Women who cried "Stop!" — peacemakers, sabbath keepers
For two years, Ireland has found itself caught between violence, cease-fires and peace. After 25 years of bloody conflict, there has been a slow recognition in Ireland and Britain of the failure of the politics of linear time, with its principle of separating by excluding. The situation of sectarian violence has been — in theological terms — "anti-creational", with 3,500 killed and tens of thousands maimed; families threatened and broken by intimidation, burn-outs, forced exile or imprisonment with or without trial; neighbourhoods trapped in a culture of violence and racketeering; endemic social and economic deprivation, including the worst unemployment records in the EU; and a virtual male-only membership of parliament locked in adversarial clashes within a structural political vacuum. All this has bred deep frustration and suspicion. Social and political divisions are further institutionalized by the separatist patterns of church life and practice. For the most part we neither know nor are known by one another.
And yet in Northern Ireland, beginning in the 1970s, a new and different pattern has struggled to emerge in terms of maternal time. Attentive observers of the situation in Northern Ireland have discerned the vital but usually unacknowledged creativity of women who, in the face of the prevailing system, are willing to cooperate within a fragile life-world. I refer here to the networks and undercurrents of community activity to which the 1992 Opsahl Commission offered a forum and a space. [27] Suddenly, in that space appeared women's groups,

peace groups, community development projects that had moved sideways of the political-historical process, not by opting out (since from the start they were excluded). Rather than attempting to break into a closed system with its politics of linear historical time, these groups conceived politics in terms of solidarity that opened spaces within and between local contexts. These groups on a day-in-day-out basis, rather than through grand epoch-making ventures, have struggled and celebrated diversities from below, affirming life and "cherishing its livingness" in a culture of death.

These are the mothers who are in the streets at night, mediating with "joyriders" (young people who race stolen cars at high speeds and with danger to passers-by); they have set up neighbourhood cooperatives and opened centres where former prisoners can talk and be consulted as they try to find a place again within the community. These are the members of support groups, seeking to empower those who have been wounded or bereaved through violence, the formers of peace and justice networks who have documented abuses, lobbied for reform of the justice system or simply enabled people from different sides to meet and find possibilities of mutual understanding. So many seeds sown within the cracks of history, so many seekers after shalom.

It is no accident that many of these groups have been founded and have flourished largely within a maternal influence, though they are not gender exclusive. These groups represent a move in the transformation of the old political system of winners and losers by reclaiming the symbolic, retrieving a place for bodily and emotional experience, and the values rooted in home, community and neighbourliness — realms usually excluded by normative politics.

These women cried "Stop!" because they knew that life had some larger horizon of interrelationship and love. Such women have acknowledged from within themselves that the potential to be both victim and victimizer lies within each of us. Thus they have interrupted the cycle of violence, "the habitual and increasingly explicit attempt to fabricate a scapegoat victim as foundress of a society". [28] Such women have argued against totalizing one's own identity claims and have found a language to express respect for otherness and diversity.

Such movements, in detaching themselves from "the prevailing economy" and by seeking "other ways of regulating difference", have created diagonal human connections *across* political and denominational boundaries. This community solidarity against all the logic of history is rooted in the kind of subjectivity that puts a value on "maternal time". Those sacramental repetitions of birth and death, funerals and weddings, families claiming space to grieve over a murdered relative, or persevering in the week-in, week-out visits to a loved one in prison — all these are keeping faith with life in a culture of death and are true seekers after shalom. Just recently, the Women's Coalition, in an effort to bring together the reality of maternal time and linear time, have united across tribal boundaries and gained two elected representatives at the peace talks. They have formed a platform on a non-adversarial politics of shared space, determined that the time has now come to bring the experience of building community across differences inside the political system. It may well prove to be a kairos moment.

From cease-fire to sabbath?

The nationalist cease-fire broke down with the bomb in London's Canary Wharf. The Loyalist cease-fire has held, though not without fatal incidents. Attempts to broker a new cease-fire continue the struggle towards lasting peace. In this, one can perhaps reflect on the cease-fire and the pause that it has offered as a movement to sabbath. It has been a sabbath time in terms of a time to rest and breathe again. It has been a time of standing back to survey the anti-creation of violence, but also to reflect with a different mode of knowing on the small circles and quiet processes of compassion that have been at work within and between communities.

In so far as "sabbath", taken literally, means "to cease", in so far as sabbath is about re-symbolizing a sacred space where life can flourish, where we can commune with God and with one another, and we can experience God's creation renewed, sabbath is a model that can help move communities from cease-fire to shalom. Here, Kristeva's third category of "eternal time", as unveiling the eternal and spiritual in the midst of historical time, springs to mind. It is in the creative interplay of these time-spaces that new potential has been released. In the space of cease-fire, people have come to a sense of call to participate in the divine creating of sabbath peacefulness. There is here a resonance with the Christian tradition of *creatio continua* counterposing with the tradition of *creatio originalis*, and of the Spirit drawing the human contribution into the divine work of creation. The doctrine of *creatio continua* and the understanding of humankind as co-creators (the Orthodox church prefers "co-workers") with God find points of connection here with the Jewish tradition. In this respect, we might recall one Jewish reading of Genesis 2:3 — "God rested from all his work that God had created to make." The verb here (*la-asot*, "to make") is somewhat anomalous, and this interpretation suggests that God had created it to be made yet further by humanity. Everything but rest is created, as it were. This tradition intimated that creation would be finished by the rabbis. One notes the connection here with that other Jewish tradition — the *tikkun olam* where we are invited to work with God for the "mending of the world". Both the Talmudic and the Christian traditions, then, underline that we are *shutafim* (partners) with God in creation.

For all people of goodwill in Northern Ireland the period of cease-fire and broken cease-fire has involved a call to "continue to make", to cooperate with God's Spirit in the creating of sabbath peace and the healing of the world. Remembering has been a key part of this process, remembering all the suffering and death, the stories of pain, and the stories that give glimpses of the new creation. In such a spirit of remembering and from a new place of power-in-vulnerability, it is necessary for stories to be heard into speech. In this, there is something to be learned from the Jewish *Shabbat Zachor* or "Sabbath of Remembrance". It is on this sabbath before the feast of Purim that Israelites, looking back on their bitter experience at the hands of Amalek, hear the paradoxical instruction from Deuteronomy 25:19: "Therefore when the LORD your God has given you rest from all your enemies on every hand, in the land that the LORD your God is giving you as an inheritance to possess, *you shall blot out the remembrance* of Amalek from under heaven; do not forget*."

Now as then, in Ireland as in ancient Israel, one must both blot out the memory and keep the memory alive for the sake of the future. It is in the living of such a paradox that memory can revitalize hope. Memory severed from hope and imagination will imprison people in bitterness. We must remember, but realize that memory severed from hope and imagination will imprison us in a bitter past. We need, in the words of Emmanuel Levinas, an "anticipatory memory". Remembering is also an act of re-membering, of atonement (at-one-ment) — becoming one again in the solidarity of God's love. Cease-fire as a way towards sabbath creates a boundary between past and future and reveals God's love in the face of old enemies and of strangers.

In this perspective of sabbath as "eternal time", we can think afresh about the reconciling role of the churches in the peace process in Ireland. Unless the churches witness to the truth that reconciliation is God's will for us as churches, we cannot with much conviction call for healing in the body politic. The churches have contributed to the building of sectarianism; they need to collaborate in dismantling it, *letting go of* the role of "chaplains to their tribes" and *letting go to* the vision of "pastors to the peace". Maybe they will be able to draw on the resource of the newly founded Northern Ireland Council for Christians and Jews in their continuing search for hopeful remembering. In Heschel's phrase — "Living *sub specie Sabbatis*" — they may be open to the dawning of sabbath peace and joy.

One simple way of embodying this would be in joining together in shared rituals of healing and forgiveness. Another embodied symbol would be the declaration of an "ecumenical jubilee", where groups from one church would be welcomed for a period to join in the other church's worship, Bible study or pastoral activity, and so get to know the other tradition from within the other's view. In this way our attitudes would be shaped by the self-understanding of the other and their way of worship and of "sabbath keeping".

The logic of sabbath, the logic of jubilee, is the logic of God's superabundant grace. In the prodigal dispensation of God, there is no scarcity but generosity to the point of folly. Genesis 2, Leviticus 25, Matthew 5 or Luke 13 and 14 invite us to move beyond the human logic of strict exchange, merit and entitlement. [29] Wherever churches are struggling together to live in justice, peace and the integrity of creation; wherever God's people wrestle with such dilemmas as the forgiving of enemies, the release of prisoners, keeping faith with the memory of the dead, and the sharing of our space with the stranger in our midst, the symbol and logic of sabbath (as of jubilee) reminds us that the last word is God's. It is a word of letting go and letting be.

NOTES

[1] For example, at the York Consultation on Creation, 1986 (Church and Society and Faith and Order); at the Granvollen Conference "The Integrity of Creation", 1988; at the pre-Canberra consultation at Kuala Lumpur, 1990, and in contributions from indigenous theologians like George Tinker.

[2] "Implications of Sub-Theme I", *The Ecumenical Review*, 42, July-Oct. 1990, pp.319-22. The reference to *shabbat* most probably reflects Jewish presence and contribution within the consultation.

[3] The work of Claus Westermann, Jürgen Moltmann, Paul Ricoeur, Phyllis Trible, Elisabeth Schüssler Fiorenza and Adrio König has been influential in different ways in correcting this bias, whereby the only acknowledged link between creation and soteriology was of an anthropocentric and penal kind, and whereby creation was understood as disconnected from eschatology and from history. See also Geraldine Smyth, *A Way of Transformation: A Theological Evaluation of the Conciliar Process of Mutual Commitment to Justice, Peace and the Integrity of Creation*, Bern, Peter Lang, 1995, pp.141ff.

[4] *Ibid.*, pp.62-64,105.

[5] Although there is a close relationship between the symbols of sabbath and jubilee, we shall focus more explicitly on the symbol of sabbath.

[6] Adrio König reminds us of the need for complementary approaches to the purpose of creation — including God's glory, human or cosmic well-being, joy, the covenant or the kingdom. And he comments on the artificial tension introduced between Calvin (with his emphasis on God's glory) and Luther (with his focus on human salvation). These, he argues, must be made supplementary to one another. See his *New and Greater Things: Re-evaluating the Biblical Message on Creation*, Pretoria, UNISA, 1988, pp.148-56.

[7] Jürgen Moltmann, *God in Creation: An Ecological Doctrine of Creation*, London, SCM, 1985, pp.31,296.

[8] See Marc C. Tannenbaum, "Holy Year and the Jewish Jubilee Year", *Sidic*, 8, no. 3, 1974, pp.4-11, and Robert North, "The Holy Year and the Jubilee", *ibid.*, pp.12-16; also Ulrich Duchrow, *Alternatives to Global Capitalism: Drawn from Biblical History, Designed for Political Action*, Utrecht, International Books with Kairos Europa, Heidelberg, 1995, pp.142ff.

[9] Moltmann, *God in Creation*, p.285. It is helpful to see these sabbath texts alongside other complementary ones as part of a powerful central tradition in Judaism. See particularly Lev. 25:1-22, with its strong sense of corporate justice and respect for the cosmos. The New Testament sabbath stories emerge in this context as Jesus' retrieval and renewal of an ancient tradition that married the understanding of God's transcendence with God's continuing care for all creation but particularly the poor, the sick and the downtrodden; see Matt. 12:1-8; Luke 6:1-11; Mark 16:1-20.

[10] One agrees with Moltmann's suggestion about the ceasing of polluting actions so that nature too can be given sabbath rest. He urges that although Christianity celebrates only the messianic feasts of salvation history, "before all else it

celebrates the sabbath of creation. In the ecological crisis of the modern world it is necessary and timely for Christianity, too, to call to mind the sabbath of creation" (*God in Creation*, p.296).

[11] Moltmann, *God in Creation*. We encounter in the sabbath symbol God's feeling-awareness for creation, God's communicative rather than dominative knowing and relationship. Just as humanity experiences God's power and wisdom in the works of creation, so, according to Moltmann, "on the Sabbath the resting God begins to 'experience' the beings [God] has created. The God who rests in face of... creation does not dominate the world on this day: [but] 'feels' the world;... allows himself to be affected, to be touched by each of his creatures... In his rest... is close to the movement of them all" (p.279). The idea of humanity wielding "dominion" (Gen. 1:26), according to Moltmann, "is linked with the correspondence between human beings and God, the creator and preserver of the world" (p.29).

[12] I follow Adrio König here. See *New and Greater Things*, pp.67-70.

[13] Here I draw upon Myles M. Bourke's commentary on Hebrews, in *The New Jerome Biblical Commentary*, ed. Raymond E. Brown, Joseph A. Fitzmyer and Roland E. Murphy, London, Geoffrey Chapman, 1991, pp.920-941, quotations on p.928.

[14] Moltmann, *God in Creation*, pp.6-7. See also pp.292ff. for an exposition of the second-century Christian emergence of the idea of "the eighth day", still strong in the Orthodox church.

[15] *Ibid*, p.293. See also pp.6-7 and 292ff.

[16] *Ibid*, p.296. Thus the "ecological day of rest should be a day without pollution of the environment — a day when we leave our cars at home, so that nature too can celebrate its sabbath." Again we note the influence on Moltmann of Jewish practices, whereby the daily reliance on mechanization is set aside on the sabbath, in favour of simpler, natural means of living.

[17] Claus Westermann, *Creation*, London, SPCK, 1974, pp.64ff.

[18] Jürgen Habermas, *Knowledge and Human Interests*, Boston, Beacon Press, 1971, pp.308ff.; Ken Wilber, *A Sociable God*, New York, New Press, 1983, pp.111-35; Paul Ricoeur, "Hermeneutics and Critique of Ideology", in *Hermeneutics and the Human Sciences*, Cambridge, Cambridge UP, 1981, pp.80-82

[19] Thus *hesed* is frequently associated with covenant, with the movement of will that initiates the covenant and with the mutuality between covenant participants. See *The Theological Dictionary of the Old Testament*, ed. G.J. Botterweck and H. Ringgren, trans. David E. Green, Grand Rapids, MI, Eerdmans, 1986, s.v. *hesed*, pp.46ff.

[20] Cited in Moltmann, *God in Creation*, p.32.

[21] *Ibid*.

[22] Julia Kristeva, "Women's Time", in *A Kristeva Reader*, ed. Toril Moi, New York, Columbia UP, 1986, pp.187-213.

[23] Abraham Heschel, *God in Search of Man: A Philosophy of Judaism*, New York, Harper TorchBooks, 1955, pp.350-51.

[24] Abraham Heschel, *A Kristeva Reader*, pp.418-19.

[25] Kristeva, "Women's Time", p.206.

[26] *Ibid.*, p.209.

[27] Andy Pollak, ed., *A Citizens' Inquiry: The Opsahl Report on Northern Ireland*, Dublin, Lilliput Press, 1993.

[28] Kristeva, "Women's Time", p.210.

[29] Cf. Paul Ricoeur, *Figuring the Sacred: Religion, Narrative and Imagination*, Minneapolis, Augsburg Fortress Press, 1995, pp.279-83.

Sabbath, Sabbatical and Jubilee: Jewish Ethical Perspectives

Raphael Jospe

Methodology

Leviticus 25, which contains the core of the Torah's laws regarding the 7th year of sabbatical release (*shemittah*) and the 50th year of jubilee (*yovel*), begins with the words: "The Lord spoke to Moses on Mount Sinai, saying". Rashi (Rabbi Solomon ben Isaac, 1040-1105), the pre-eminent mediaeval Jewish Bible and Talmud commentator, quoting the ancient rabbis in the Sifra, asks: "What does the subject of the year of release have to do with Mount Sinai? Were not all the commandments given at Sinai? But just as the general rules, specific principles and minutiae of the year of release derive from Sinai, so were the general rules, specific principles and minutiae of all [the commandments] given at Sinai." [1]

Rashi and the ancient rabbis are asking here a profound question regarding the authority of the biblical text. They note that the Torah informs us, apparently superfluously, that the commandment of the year of release was given at Sinai. Why does the Torah inform us that this specific commandment was given at Sinai? Many of the commandments in the Torah were repeated and explained in the book of Deuteronomy. However, in Deuteronomy (15:1-11) the Torah specifically refers only to the release of debts, and not to the sabbatical rest of the land, which was to lie fallow. Rashi and the rabbis deduce from this anomaly that all the commandments, whether or not reiterated or explicated in Deuteronomy, and whether given only in general principles or in detailed minutiae, are equally authoritative, deriving from the revelation at Sinai.

I cite this technical, seemingly inconsequential exegesis because of its fundamental significance in developing a biblical hermeneutic. The laws of sabbatical release and jubilee appear in three major clusters in the Pentateuch: Exodus 23:10-11, Leviticus 25 and 27, and Deuteronomy 15:1-11. Much of modern Bible scholarship, following the "higher criticism" of the "documentary hypothesis", assigns the cluster in Exodus to the "Covenant Code", the cluster in Leviticus to "P", and that of Deuteronomy to "D".

While the questions raised by critical scholarship and the documentary hypothesis pose no ideological problems for me on religious grounds (indeed, many of the modern questions were anticipated centuries earlier by the outstanding mediaeval Jewish philosopher, grammarian and exegete Rabbi Abraham ibn Ezra),[2] the dissection of the biblical text into its supposed historical documents raises no fewer questions than it answers. At most, it can give us limited, albeit important, insight into the historic origins of fragmentary material. But it does not answer the question of redaction: how these disparate fragments came to be edited into the final text as it entered history. Following the example of Franz Rosenzweig and Martin Buber earlier in this century, I prefer to deal with what is to me a far more interesting and significant question than how the biblical text was written, and even how it was edited: namely, how it is read. The Bible, not as *ketuvim* (static scripture), but as *miqra* (the text as dynamically read): How has the text as it entered history been read and lived by the religious community over the centuries, and what enduring lessons and applications can we learn from it today? From this perspective, the classical rabbinic view that all of the commandments are equally authoritative, regardless of their specific textual source, and that even the often unwritten details transmitted over the centuries as oral Torah are ultimately, if indefinitely, derived from Sinai, forms a hermeneutic basis for Jewish reading, implementing and living the Torah today.

A second methodological point underlying my reading of the sources is that the dichotomy we tend to draw between the ethical and ritual dimensions of life is alien to the biblical mentality.[3] Differences of emphasis in various passages — whatever their historic or literary documentary sources — need not necessarily point to diverse ideological points of view but may be understood contextually. For example, the laws of the seventh year of release and the jubilee are commonly assumed to reflect the ritualistic priestly document P, and yet they are inseparable from basic ethical concern for the poor and dispossessed, and from the Levitical Holiness Code (Lev. 19). Furthermore, the notion that ritual per se cannot provide a mechanism for atonement for ethical offences (i.e., where the offence has involved harming another person) but that such ritual atonement is conditional upon prior ethical atonement, involving restoration and compensation, is not a later rabbinic or prophetic projection onto an earlier ritual structure. It is built into the Levitical system of sacrificial worship itself. Leviticus opens with describing various types of sacrifices to be offered on different occasions and for various offences. All of these are purely ritual, what the rabbis of the Talmud termed offences *bein adam la-maqom*, between a person and God (i.e., offences that involved no harm to another person). Then, in Leviticus 5:20-26 in the Hebrew Bible (in Christian Bibles, Lev. 6:1-7), the Torah for the first time cites the case of an ethical offence involving harming another person, what the rabbis of the Talmud termed offences *bein adam le-havero*, between one person and another. The Torah explicitly specifies that the man who had harmed another could not bring his ritual guilt offering (*asham*) until he first righted the ethical wrong by restoring the stolen, defrauded or lost object or principal and paid an additional penalty; only then could he begin the process of ritual, sacrificial atonement. Conversely, the statements by various prophets that are all too often understood as condemnation of ritual are opposed, in fact, not to ritual per se but to the perversion of ritual and the defiling of the sanctuary by ignoring the inherent correlation between the ritual and the ethical dimensions of life, by attempting to win God's favour by ritual behaviour while violating God's commandments concerning our obligations to our fellow humans. Both dimensions — the ritual and the ethical — are equally commanded by God, without differentiation.

A third methodological point concerns the differences of interpretation of the laws of the sabbatical and jubilee years that we find both in modern scholarly literature and in the traditional Jewish exegesis of these passages and halakhic sources (e.g., the Talmud, the Midrashim, and various mediaeval codes). We find, for example, disagreements regarding the implementation of these laws in actual practice in second temple times; whether the jubilee involved a release of debts (most scholarly and traditional opinion, including that of Maimonides, rejects this view, but there are arguments to the contrary);[4] whether the jubilee coincides with the seventh sabbatical year of release (i.e., year 49) or follows it (i.e., year 50) and accordingly, how to count the jubilee cycle. Our theme — ethical perspectives of the laws of the sabbath, the sabbatical year and the jubilee — deals with general underlying principles as they have evolved historically in Judaism and as they present continuing challenges to Jews today, especially in Israel. We need not deal, therefore, with the important disagreements in the scholarly and traditional literature regarding specific interpretations of these laws.

The sabbath: underlying principles

The priority of the sabbath

The sabbath was the very first commandment the Israelites received as a free nation after the exodus from Egypt, even before its inclusion in the decalogue at Mount Sinai.[5] A double portion of the manna *(man)*, which ordinarily rotted after a day, was to be collected on the sixth day, for on the sabbath they were forbidden to collect it in the fields (Ex. 16:5, 22-30). Because of its signal importance — the sabbath is a sign *(ot)* of Israel's covenant with God (Ex. 31:13) and of the creation (v. 17) — the rabbis understood the sabbath as taking priority even over reverence for parents and the construction of the sanctuary.

In the first case, the priority of the sabbath over reverence for parents is deduced by the juxtaposition of the two principles in Leviticus 19:3, "Each of you should revere his mother and his father, and observe my sabbaths; I am the Lord your God." Rashi, reflecting the exegesis of the Talmud and Midrash,[6] comments that the Torah "conjoins the sabbath to reverence for the parent, to teach you that even though I have warned you to revere your parent, if he should tell you to desecrate the sabbath, do not obey him; and the same regarding all the other commandments." As understood by the rabbis, the law of the sabbath thus teaches a fundamental lesson, that blind obedience to human authority, even the primary authority of parents, must ultimately yield to higher moral principle, and one must not obey orders that violate divine law.[7]

In the second case, the priority of the sabbath over the construction of the sanctuary (the portable tent-temple in the wilderness) is deduced from the juxtaposition of the two principles in Leviticus 19:30 and 26:2, "Observe my sabbaths and revere my sanctuary; I am the Lord."

Rashi, again citing the Talmud,[8] comments that the construction of the sanctuary does not supersede the sabbath. The rabbis had already deduced this principle from the verse, "Nevertheless (*akh*), observe my sabbaths" (Ex. 31:13), which seems to be a non sequitur after the appointment of Bezalel to construct the sanctuary. From the restriction "nevertheless", the rabbis deduce that the commandment to construct the sanctuary does not supersede the sabbath. We shall return later to the juxtaposition of the sabbath and the sanctuary.

Saving life supersedes the sabbath

Having established the principle that the sabbath takes priority over reverence for parents and the construction of the temple, we now reverse the inquiry: what, if anything, supersedes the sabbath? It is not clear whether in the period of the first temple any such principles were developed. As for the second-temple period, we should note that those types of Jews — Samaritans, Karaites and the Ethiopian Beita Yisrael[9] — whose traditions reflect a state of development of the second-temple period, or (in the case of the Karaites) a deliberate return to such developments, have certain similarities in their observance of the sabbath (as well as other practices, such as the laws regarding the *niddah*, the menstruant woman). Their approach to sabbath observance is stricter and more literalistic than that of Pharisaic Judaism and its heirs in rabbinic Judaism, which permitted certain leniencies (such as pre-lighting lamps for light and pre-cooking food, which was then kept warm on the sabbath day) and encouraged marital sexual relations on the sabbath, so that "you will call the sabbath a delight" (Isa. 58:13). So it is not clear whether the initial, disastrous refusal of associates of the Maccabees to fight on the sabbath (1 Macc. 2:32-38) was normative. Moreover, Mattathias and his followers, including the "Hasidim", thereafter resolved to fight on the sabbath, although it is not clear whether their resolution reflects initial Maccabean agreement (and a subsequent pragmatic change of mind) or disagreement in principle with their friends' behaviour: "And each said to his neighbour: 'If we all do as our brethren have done and refuse to fight with the Gentiles for our lives and our ordinances, they will quickly destroy us from the earth.' So they made this decision that day: 'Let us fight against every man who comes to attack us on the sabbath day; let us not all die as our brethren died in their hiding places'" (1 Macc. 2:40-41 RSV).

In the version of the story related by Josephus (*Antiquities* 12.274-78) the implication is that Mattathias disagreed and persuaded the survivors to change their minds:

> Many escaped and joined Mattathias, whom they appointed their leader. And he instructed them to fight even on the sabbath, saying that if for the sake of observing the law they failed to do so, they would be their own enemies, for their foes would attack them on that day, and unless they resisted, nothing would prevent them from all perishing without striking a blow. These words persuaded them, and to this day we continue the practice of fighting even on the sabbath whenever it becomes necessary. [10]

Josephus's comment that "we continue the practice of fighting even on the Sabbath whenever it becomes necessary" is clear testimony that, whatever the Jewish norm may have been in Maccabean times or earlier, by the time of the great Jewish revolt and the destruction of the temple in 70 CE, the halakhic norm clearly and consistently mandated that saving life supersedes the sabbath (*piquah nefesh doheh shabbat*). [11] This cardinal principle of rabbinic Judaism is deduced from two biblical verses: Exodus 31:13 and Leviticus 18:5.

The Jerusalem Talmud (Yoma 8:5) plays on the plural "sabbaths" in Exodus 31:13: "From where [do we learn] that even a doubtful [case of saving] life supersedes the sabbath? Rabbi Abbahu said in the name of Rabbi Yohanan: 'Nevertheless, observe my sabbaths'... The Torah says: For his sake, desecrate the sabbath, so that he may sit and observe many sabbaths... They taught: He who hastens [to save life by desecrating the sabbath] is praiseworthy; one who is asked is condemned; one who asks, sheds blood."

The Mishnah (Yoma 5:2) derives the same principle from Leviticus 18:5 ("Observe my statutes and my ordinances, which a person should do and by which he should live"), playing on the last two words *va-hay ba-hem*, "by which he should live": "From where [do we learn] that saving life supersedes the sabbath? Rabbi Judah said that Samuel said: As it is written, 'Observe my statutes and my ordinances which a person should do and by which he should live', and not by which he should die."

The great codes of Jewish law, such as the *Mishneh Torah* of Maimonides (1135-1204) [12] and the *Shulhan Arukh* of Joseph Karo (1488-1575) [13] elaborate further on these principles. According to Maimonides:

The sabbath and all the other commandments are superseded by danger to life... When there is doubt as to whether or not it is necessary to desecrate the sabbath... one desecrates the sabbath, for a dubious [case of saving] life supersedes the sabbath. The general rule is: In the case of a sick person who is in danger, the sabbath is like a weekday for anything [the patient] may need. These things [in healing on the sabbath] should not be done by non-Jews or by minors or by slaves or by women, so that the sabbath should not become unimportant [lit. "light"] in their view. [They should be done] by the leaders and the sages of Israel. It is forbidden to hesitate to desecrate the sabbath for a sick person who is in danger, as it says, "Which a person should do and by which he should live", and not by which he should die. Thus you learn that the ordinances of the Torah are not vengeful, but [bring] compassion and kindness and peace to the world.

Similarly, according to Karo: "When someone has a dangerous illness, it is a commandment to desecrate the sabbath for him. Whoever hastens is praiseworthy, and whoever asks [whether he should desecrate the sabbath], sheds blood." Rabbi Judah Ashkenazi, an 18th-century German commentator on the *Shulhan Arukh*, adds: "Even if the sick person does not want [the sabbath to be desecrated on his behalf], one coerces him, because this is the piety of fools."

It is clear, then, who "the one who asks" in such a case is. But who is "the one who is asked", whom the Jerusalem Talmud condemns? According to Rabbi Israel Meir Ha-Kohen Kagan (known as the Hafetz Hayyim, 1838-1933), in his commentary *Mishnah Berurah* on the *Shulhan Arukh*, the guilty party is the local rabbi (lit. "the wise student in his locale"):

That person who pretends to be pious and fears desecrating the sabbath for such a sick person... sheds blood, for while he goes to ask, the sick person may become even weaker and may be endangered... The local rabbi should have publicly taught this lesson, so that all the people might know, and would not need to ask him. If the sick person himself fears that others will violate the sabbath because of him, one coerces and consoles him, that this is the piety of fools.

The principle of *piquah nefesh* is thus invoked not only when active intervention is required in the face of actual danger but also when preventive measures are required in cases of dubious danger. The sabbath is thus routinely superseded for the preservation of human life and alleviating human suffering. In addition, we should note that the sabbath is also routinely superseded for the alleviation of animal suffering (*tzaar baalei hayyim*). For instance, animals must be fed and cows must be milked (although there can be no financial benefit from milk taken on the sabbath) to alleviate their suffering. [14]

Sabbath and sanctuary: sacred time and sacred space

The fact that the sabbath is superseded for the sake of the enhancement of animal as well as human life is fully consistent with the twin rationales listed in the Torah for its observance: the sabbath commemorates both the creation of the world (i.e., nature) and the exodus from Egypt (i.e., freedom). The theme of creation is frequently mentioned, not only in the version of the decalogue in Exodus 20:8-11 but also in the references to the sabbath elsewhere in the Torah (e.g., Gen. 2:3; Ex. 31:17), whereas the theme of the exodus from Egypt is found in the second version of the decalogue, in Deuteronomy 5:15-16. In these and other sources, the Torah explicitly indicates that the blessings of sabbath rest are intended to benefit one's animals and one's servants; thus nature and society, ecology and ethics, creation and freedom, are not only the sabbath's raison d'etre but also its beneficiaries. However, as Leo Baeck noted, these rights and benefits are extended not by the master but by God. [15]

These interrelated concepts of the sabbath as commemorating both nature and freedom in turn are based on the traditional Jewish view that the human being is God's partner (*shutaf*) in the ever-renewed work of creation (*ha-mehadesh be-khol yom tamid maaseh bereishit*), that people must implement and bring about the divine redemption of the world (*le-takken olam be-malkhut shaddai*). But if human beings are God's partners in the work of creation, they should also be God's partners in sabbath rest.

How, then, does Jewish tradition define the rest mandated for the sabbath? Rest is defined negatively, in contrast to work. Work, however, should not be confused with physical exertion. Rabbinic Judaism posits prohibited categories of work that involve little or no physical exertion, and there are types of physical exertion permitted, or permitted within limits (such as walking within one's town but not more than two thousand cubits beyond the municipal boundaries), or actually encouraged on the sabbath (such as marital sexual relations). What, then, is the definition of work?

The term for work is *melakhah*, which indicates an artificial activity or productive creativity, a way in which the human being creates (or destroys) something in the natural status quo. During the six weekdays of productive work, people impose their will upon nature. The sabbath is to be a time when people refrain from creating changes in nature and instead participate in the harmony of nature.

The juxtaposition of the sabbath (sacred time) and the sanctuary (sacred space) in Leviticus 19:30 and 26:2 ("Observe my sabbaths and revere my sanctuary; I am the Lord"), provided the basis for the rabbis to deduce from the types of work needed to construct the temple and maintain its sacrificial services 39 categories (many originally agricultural) of *melakhah* prohibited on the sabbath. Each of these categories has *avot* (lit. "fathers"), namely primary principles, and *toladot* (lit. "progeny"), namely derivative or corollary principles; these are considered to be of biblical authority (*mide-oraitah*). Additional extensions of these biblical principles form a protective "fence around the Torah" (*seyag la-torah*), a margin of safety around the biblical categories; these extensions are considered to be of rabbinic authority (*mide-rabbanan*).

The parallel between the creation of the world (the macrocosm) and the construction of the sanctuary (the microcosm) is reinforced by the Torah's identical terminology in describing both: "On the seventh day God completed [*va-yekhal*] his work [*melakhah*] which he had done" (Gen. 2:2), and "Moses completed [*va-yekhal*] the work [*melakhah*]" (Ex. 40:33). [16]

A different connection between the sabbath and the sanctuary is drawn by Abraham Joshua Heschel (1907-72). According to Heschel's view, the sanctification of time rather than of space enabled the Jewish people to survive the loss of sacred space (i.e., the temple and Zion). The Jewish emphasis was on an "architecture" of time rather than of space. The sabbath was the Jews' indestructible cathedral, a temple that could not be destroyed but that could serve as a spiritual sanctuary and central unifying religious symbol wherever they were exiled. In Heschel's words:

> The Bible is more concerned with time than with space... It pays more attention to generations, to events, than to countries, to things... Jewish ritual may be characterized as the art of significant forms in time, as architecture of time... The mythical mind would expect that, after heaven and earth had been established, God would create a holy place...

whereupon a sanctuary is to be established. Yet... it is holiness in time, the Sabbath, which comes first... The Sabbath... is not determined by any event in nature, such as the new moon, but by the act of creation. Thus the essence of the Sabbath is completely detached from the world of space. The meaning of the Sabbath is to celebrate time rather than space. Six days a week we live under the tyranny of things of space; on the Sabbath we try to become attuned to holiness in time. It is a day on which we are called upon to share in what is eternal in time, to turn from the results of creation to the mystery of creation; from the world of creation to the creation of the world. [17]

Thus far we have seen how the connection of sacred space (the sanctuary) and sacred time (the sabbath) has shaped both Jewish law (the definition of the 39 categories of *melakhah*) and Jewish theology (Heschel's view of the sabbath as sanctification of time rather than space). The space-time nexus has also been the subject of more purely philosophic discussion in Jewish literature. For example, Maimonides rejected both the Aristotelian arguments for the eternity of the world and the arguments for creation in time put forth by the Kalam (Islamic theology). In his *Guide of the Perplexed* Maimonides argues that there cannot have been creation of the world (i.e., space) in time, but that there must have been creation of time together with the world,

time itself being one of the created things. For time is consequent upon motion, and motion is an accident in what is moved... Time is a created and generated thing as are the other accidents and the substances serving as substrata to these accidents. Hence God's bringing the world into existence does not have a temporal beginning, for time is one of the created things... If you affirm as true the existence of time prior to the world, you are necessarily bound to believe in the eternity [of the world]. For time is an accident which necessarily must have a substratum. [18]

The space-time correlation (legal, theological and philosophical) is thus the key to understanding how, in rabbinic Judaism, the creation of the world, as the macrocosm, came to be understood as the prototype or blueprint for the construction of the sanctuary, as the microcosm; and conversely, how the 39 categories of *melakhah* (the term used to describe God's productive work in creating the world) necessary for the construction of the sanctuary and the maintenance of its system of sacrificial worship came to provide the basis for Jewish observance of the sabbath. As one scholar has described it: "The phenomenon is one of reversal: by doing all these labours in the particular prescribed configuration, one creates sacred space. By refraining from these same acts, in the context of the sabbath, one creates sacred time."[19]

On a historical level, for some 19 centuries, the sabbath served as a major force in the survival of the Jewish people and in the continuity of their religious life. The destruction of the temple, the loss of Jerusalem and the exile of the Jews from Zion, weakened (although they did not eliminate) the dimension of sacred space as a central factor in Jewish national and religious identity. Under such circumstances of dispossession and dispersion, the dimension of sacred time, as symbolized by the sabbath, became an even more important factor in Jewish cohesiveness.

That is why Ahad Ha-Am (Asher Tzvi Ginzberg, 1856-1927), Hebrew essayist and Zionist ideologue, could say: "More than Israel has observed the sabbath, the sabbath has preserved them."[20]

Sabbath, sabbatical and jubilee: to whom do they apply?

Israelites, resident aliens and foreigners

Who was eligible in ancient Israel for the rights and responsibilities of participating in the benefits of the sabbath, the seventh year of release and the jubilee? The situation is complicated by the fact that these three basic institutions are interrelated but by no means identical in their intent and purview. Each of the major sources in the Torah for these laws (described above) deals with aspects, and not with the total range, of these institutions; and there were different categories or classes of people referred to in the Torah's laws.

In addition, some of the terms mentioned in the Torah are ambivalent. The class of slaves or servants included both Israelite slaves or indentured servants (*eved ivri*, "Hebrew slave") and non-Jewish slaves (*eved kenaani*). Since the Torah frequently refers to slaves/servants in general, without further specification, when later rabbinic law attempted to understand the intention in each case, it did so contextually, with the result that some of the reasoning is circular: category *A* is entitled to rights *X*; category *B* to rights *Y*; in this particular passage we find a reference to rights *Y*; therefore in this case the intention of the Torah must be to category *B*.

The Torah also refers frequently to the *ger* ("alien" or "stranger"), without further elaboration.[21] Later rabbinic law distinguishes between the *ger tzedek*, "the righteous proselyte", who converts to Judaism and subsequently enjoys equally all the rights and responsibilities of full membership in the Jewish people, and the *ger toshav*, "the resident alien", a non-Jew who permanently resides among the Jewish people in the land of Israel, who (minimally) renounces at least idolatry or (maximally) adopts many Jewish practices, including the sabbath, without full conversion to Judaism. Maimonides defines the resident alien as a non-Jew, living among the Jewish people, who renounces idolatry and follows the "seven Noachide commandments", but does not fully convert to Judaism by circumcision and immersion. [22] He also notes that this category is only operative when the jubilee is operative.

Later attempts to clarify and codify rabbinic law, however, cannot be projected back onto the formative period of rabbinic law or late second-temple times, when the situation seems to have been rather more fluid, nor can the rabbinic understanding of the law necessarily be projected back to the first-temple period, at which time the laws and institutions were presumably even more fluid and undefined. Continued disagreements among rabbis and scholars regarding the meaning of these laws and institutions in ancient times, let alone regarding their implementation today (e.g., in contemporary arguments concerning proper conversion and "who is a Jew?"), attest to the complexity of the situation and the ambiguity of the relevant passages in the Torah.

We are left, then, with three basic categories of people for the purposes of eligibility in the rights and responsibilities of the sabbath, the seventh year of release, and the jubilee:

1. Jews, both native-born and the convert (*ger tzedek*), who have full rights and responsibilities.

2. Resident aliens (*ger toshav*), who permanently reside among the Jewish people in the land of Israel. Since, following the conquest of Canaan, the land was distributed among the tribes of Israel, and in fact many of the laws of the jubilee relate to the reversion of the land to its original owners, these resident aliens presumably were generally labourers, who worked for Jews. Although there obviously were cases of poor Israelites indebted or indentured to wealthy resident aliens (the Torah refers to such cases, e.g., in Lev. 25:47), presumably as a class the resident aliens, being landless, required legal protection and social support, which is why the Torah frequently classifies the *ger* with

other vulnerable and disenfranchised groups, such as the poor, the widows and orphans, for such benefits as the gleaning and the corners of fields during the harvest, support from tithes and fields left fallow during the seventh year of release. Their status is comparable, throughout the Torah, to that of the Israelites who had been "*gerim* in the land of Egypt", and therefore they deserved Jewish empathy and sympathy: "Do not oppress the alien; you have known the life [*nefesh*] of the alien, for you were aliens in the land of Egypt" (Ex. 23:9).

3. Foreigners (*zar*, "stranger", and *nokhri*, "foreigner"), who came to the land of Israel on a temporary basis (such as traders) and who are not part of the Jewish community or people. Unlike "your brother", they may be charged usury, and their debts are not released in the sabbatical year (see Deut. 15:3, 23:20). Both foreigners and resident aliens may be purchased into slavery (Lev. 25:44-45), whereas Israelites enslaved to them must be redeemed by their fellow Jews (vv. 25:47-49).

We thus have a hierarchy of rights and responsibilities, benefits and obligations, although there is some fluidity among the three categories. Resident aliens thus resemble Israelites in certain respects (e.g., social benefits for the poor and disenfranchised) and foreigners in other respects (enslavement to Jews). But the general lines of the hierarchy are clear in terms of sabbath, sabbatical and jubilee rights and responsibilities: the higher the degree of kinship (fellow Jews), the greater the extent of benefits and obligations. Conversely, the lower the degree of kinship (foreigners), the less the extent of benefits and obligations, with resident aliens forming an intermediate degree between Jews and foreigners.

The Torah's hierarchical concern for disenfranchised and dispossessed classes is reflected in its terminology, which has consistency, despite some fluidity of the boundaries. The primary interest, of course, remains with fellow Jews, "your brothers, the children of Israel" (Lev. 25:46), for whom there is the greatest degree of kinship and accordingly the highest extent of responsibility. Throughout the passages legislating the sabbatical and jubilee (Lev. 25 and Deut. 15), the Torah repeatedly emphasizes the term "your brother".

The rights and responsibilities of the sabbatical and jubilee years concern people (slaves or indentured servants), debts and land alike. Given an early agricultural society and economy, the need for such a correlation between enslavement, debt and land is clear. Crop failure would lead to indebtedness (to purchase food for the present and seed for the next year); indebtedness would lead to a forfeiture of ancestral land, resulting in further poverty to the point of being sold into enslavement for one's debts. Periodic release of debts, emancipation from enslavement or indentured servitude, and restoration of the land to the original owners (or their heirs) were therefore necessary, although different, features of the seventh year of release and of the jubilee, for the sake of economic stability and social justice. In this context, we should also note that the Torah's concern is not only for the rights of the individual but also for the rights of the nation, tribe and clan (or family), who should not be disenfranchised and dispossessed permanently from ancestral land. This is why the land itself had to be compensated for the "sabbaths" (i.e., the sabbatical years of release and jubilees) of which it had been deprived by Jewish failure to observe the commandments (see Lev. 26:24-25, 43). As in the case of the sabbath, these rights (individual and collective) are extended not by the authority of the human masters or creditors but by the authority of God, as repeatedly expressed in the Torah by the notion that all the earth (the land) is the Lord's and that Israel was liberated from Egyptian bondage to serve God, not people (Lev. 25:23,42,55).

The sabbath and women

In both versions of the commandment to observe the sabbath in the decalogue (Ex. 20:10 and Deut. 5:14), the commandment is addressed to "you [masc. sing.], your son and your daughter, your male slave and your female slave, your cattle and your alien who is within your gates". At first glance, it would appear that the omission of any explicit reference to women implies exclusion from the benefits of the sabbath. However, as I have argued elsewhere,[23] in this particular instance (and I am not generalizing from it), it is precisely the omission of any reference to the woman here that manifests her equality before the law. In the subsequent classes mentioned by the Torah (i.e., children and slaves), male and female are referred to equally. Why, then, is the woman not mentioned from the outset, together with the masculine "you"?

All the classical Jewish Bible exegetes (Rashi, Abraham ibn Ezra, Nachmanides and Sforno) follow the Mekhilta[24] in understanding the reference to the children as meaning minors, whose observance of the law is the responsibility of the parents to educate and enforce. One is similarly responsible for the actions of one's slaves and animals.

Who, then, is included in the masculine singular pronoun "you" (*ata*)? According to Ibn Ezra: "There is no doubt that the term *ata* applies to anyone who is *ben mitzvah* [a major, legally liable to observe the precepts]." Thus, if the woman were explicitly singled out here, as children and slaves are, and if the woman were thus not included in *ata* (since there is no neuter in Hebrew), we would have to conclude that the law in general does not apply to women, since the normal mode of expression is masculine (even for mixed company). In which case, imperatives such as the Shema ("Listen, Israel", Deut. 6:4), "do not murder", "do not steal", and so forth would also not apply to women, since they (like the commandment to observe the sabbath) are expressed in the masculine singular. Such an absurd conclusion can be avoided only if we follow Ibn Ezra in understanding *ata* here (and other masculine singular pronouns or imperatives elsewhere) as applying to any Jew of the age of majority, male or female. By contrast, the Torah had to mention female children and slaves because, in those cases, it would otherwise not be clear that the parents have the responsibility to ensure the education and observance of their minor daughters as well as that of their minor sons, and masters of their female as well as male slaves.

The sabbath thus applies to adult Jews, male and female; to their minor children, male and female; to their non-Jewish slaves, male and female (the sabbath applies in any event to Jewish slaves as Jews); and even to their animals.

When are the sabbatical and jubilee years operative?

The Torah introduces the laws of the sabbatical and jubilee years with the words "when you come to the land" (Lev. 25:2). The rabbis deduce from this wording two major principles. First, that the sabbatical and jubilee years are operative only in the land of Israel and when all the Jewish people actually live in the land of Israel; second, that the sabbatical and the jubilee are correlated; each is only operative when the other is operative. [25]

However, within a few centuries those conditions no longer applied, and therefore the sabbatical and jubilee years were no longer operative. In the words of Maimonides: "Since the tribes of Reuven and Gad and half the tribe of Menasheh were exiled, the jubilees were cancelled. As it says, 'Proclaim liberty in the land to all of its inhabitants' [Leviticus 25:10], i.e., at a time when all of [the land's] inhabitants are in it."[26]

Nevertheless, these halakhic principles do not mean that the sabbatical year of release and the jubilee were not observed at all during later first-temple and second-temple times. As we saw above, there is widespread disagreement of traditional and scholarly opinion regarding the extent of observance of the sabbatical and jubilee years in ancient Israel. The halakhic discussions in the Talmudic literature and the later codes refer not to practical historical fact (i. e., the extent of observance) but to theoretical legal principle. The question is theoretical; it relates to the level of authority of the law. But the theoretical question has, as we shall see, practical implications.

What the halakhah thus establishes is that, already in late first-Temple times (after the exile of the tribes that lived in eastern trans-Jordan), the sabbatical and jubilee years no longer had the authority of biblical law (*mide-oraitah*), which could be operative only in the maximal conditions of all of the Jewish people actually living in the land of Israel. Any subsequent observance of the sabbatical and jubilee years could be only on the basis of rabbinic authority (*mide-rabbanan*).

This distinction has immediate practical implications. First, it sunders the correlation between the seventh year of release (which remains practically relevant in its agricultural features and in its release of debts) and the jubilee (which no longer has any practical relevance in terms of the release of slaves and the restoration of original, ancestral property). Second, it permits the retention of at least some features of the sabbatical for moral and educational purposes. In the words of Maimonides: "In accordance with the words of the Scribes, the release [*shemittah*] of debts [in the sabbatical year] is operative [*noheget*] at this time in every place, although the Jubilee is not operative, so that the Torah of release of debts might not be forgotten in Israel."[27]

Third, the fact that the sabbatical year operates on rabbinic rather than biblical authority permits far greater leniency in making adjustments to its features. The sabbatical release of debts, which the Torah explicitly intends for the welfare of the poor (Deut. 15:1-11), had boomeranged to the detriment of the poor in second-temple times, with the evolution of an urban society and commercial economy:

"This is one of the things that Hillel the Elder instituted when he saw that the people were refraining from making loans to each other and were thus violating what is written in the Torah, 'Beware that you not have a worthless thought in your heart, saying, the seventh year, the year of release, is approaching, etc.'" [Deut. 15:9]. So Hillel instituted the *prosbul*. [28]

The *prosbul* was a legal formula enabling the creditor to claim his debts after the seventh year of release. The Torah had prohibited individual Jews from collecting debts from "his fellow and his brother" Jews (Deut. 15:2). The *prosbul* turned debts over to the courts before the sabbatical year for collection, since the Torah's restrictions apply only to individuals, not to the court. However, as Maimonides (following the Talmudic rabbis) notes, Hillel could not have instituted the *prosbul* had the authority for the seventh year of release still been biblical. It was only because the authority for the sabbatical was rabbinic, not biblical, that Hillel's innovation became possible: "The *prosbul* could benefit the release of debts at this time only because [the release derives] from the words of the scribes. However, the *prosbul* could not benefit the release of debts according to [the authority of] the Torah." [29]

In summary, because the residual observance of the sabbatical year of release is based on rabbinic rather than biblical authority, Hillel the Elder could effectively circumvent its restrictions in order to preserve its intended benefits — namely, economic relief and social justice for the poor. But where the lesser authority of the rabbis permitted, in Hillel's day, a circumvention of the sabbatical year, it may, in our day, permit at least a limited return to renewed observance of the sabbatical year.

Most of the features of the sabbatical and jubilee years (release of slaves, remission of debts, restoration of ancestral property) no longer have any practical effect, and their contemporary significance is largely symbolic in the struggle for economic security, social justice and freedom.

Since the late 19th century, with the Zionist return to the land (in both senses of renewed Jewish settlement and of renewed Jewish agriculture in the land of Israel), the question of reviving the agricultural features of the sabbatical year of release has been regularly debated. During 19 centuries of exile, the Jewish people had not only been removed from the land of Israel but also, to a large extent, been removed from agricultural pursuits in the countries of their dispersion. Should not, then, the restoration of the Jewish people to the land of Israel, their return to agriculture and the renewal of Jewish sovereignty in the state of Israel be accompanied by a revival of the sabbatical year of release?

Paradoxically, it is among non-Zionist ultra-Orthodox circles (who generally have little interest in agriculture or other Zionist endeavours in the rebuilding of the land) that we find the greatest degree of observance of the sabbatical year, during which time they purchase Arab produce. Conversely, among religious Zionists, although they have great interest in principle in the revival of the sabbatical, there is also recognition of the serious problems, both moral and practical, that such observance would entail.

On a practical level, after more than a century of Jewish settlement in the land of Israel and after nearly half a century of Jewish sovereignty in the state of Israel, the security and economy of the state are still precarious, due at least in part to the draining and detrimental effects of decades of continued hostility, and all too many active wars, between the Jews and the Arabs. Many Jews therefore argue for employing the legal fiction of "selling" the land in toto by the state-sponsored chief rabbinate, since one is allowed to use the produce of Israeli land owned by non-Jews. [30] Once again, it is because the legal authority for the sabbatical is rabbinic and not biblical that such leniency and flexibility become possible.

On a moral level, religious Zionists, who believe in rebuilding "the land of Israel for the people of Israel, according to the Torah of Israel", also hesitate to reinstate an ancient law that today effectively undercuts their Zionist goals and forces reliance on Arab produce.

In effect, therefore, the ultra-Orthodox non-Zionist Jews, who do not believe in "hastening" the messianic era by human initiative, are often the ones who take the initiative to revive one of the laws of the ancient Jewish state, whereas the religious Zionists, who see in Zionism and the Jewish state "the beginning of the flourishing of our redemption", are often reluctant to revive this symbol of Jewish sovereignty in the land of Israel.

The Sifra deduces from the verse "If there will be a jubilee" (Num. 36:4) that "in the future the jubilee will cease and will return". [31] Maimonides accordingly writes: "In the future, when for the third time [the Jews] come and enter the land, they will [again] begin to count the sabbaticals and the jubilees... Whatever place they conquer will be obligated [to observe] the tithes."[32]

The restoration of the sabbatical and jubilee years is, in Maimonides' view, one of the characteristics of the messianic era. Near the end of his code, he wrote: "In the future, the messiah-king [lit. the anointed king] will arise and restore the kingdom of David to its original sovereignty; he will rebuild the temple and gather the dispersed of Israel. They will return to the way they were originally, offering sacrifices and observing the sabbatical and jubilee years in accordance with the commandments of the Torah."[33]

From a religious Zionist perspective, the ingathering of the exiles, the rebuilding of the land of Israel, and the restoration of Jewish sovereignty in the state of Israel do not represent the messianic fulfillment of Jewish history but (at most or at least, depending on the point of view) "the beginning of the flourishing of our redemption". The renewal of the sabbatical year is a feature of the messianic era, according to Maimonides. The question is whether its revival should be initiated now, by us, or whether, like other features of the redemption, it should be postponed indefinitely, until the messianic era.

That is precisely what Jews today debate every seven years in the state of Israel. Has the time of the sabbatical come?

NOTES

[1] All translations into English are the author's, unless otherwise indicated. The Sifra is the Midrash Halakhah on Leviticus, dating from the period of the *tannaim* (rabbis of the Mishnah). It is often referred to in classical Jewish sources as Torat Kohanim. This passage is found in Sifra, Be-Har 1:1 on Leviticus 25:1.

[2] See my article "Bible Exegesis as a Philosophic Literary Genre: Abraham ibn Ezra and Moses Mendelssohn", in *Jewish Philosophy and the Academy*, eds Emil Fackenheim and Raphael Jospe (Cranbury, N.J.: Associated University Presses, Fairleigh Dickinson Press, 1996). A possible non-Israelite reference to the status of resident aliens, who are less than full citizens but more than foreigners, may be found in the Moabite Stele of Mesha (king of Moab, 9th century BCE). In lines 16-17, referring to his wars with Israel, Mesha says, "I completely killed seven thousand men, *gerin*, women, *gerot*, and maid-servants". The words *gerin* and *gerot* (aliens, masc. and fem.) , which may be

cognate to the biblical *gerim* and *gerot*, have also been interpreted as referring to boys and girls (cognate to the Hebrew *gur*, "cub" or "whelp").

[3] I discuss the correlation of the ethical and ritual dimensions in my articles "Ritual Exclusivity vs. Spiritual Inclusivity" (Foundation for International Studies, University of Malta, forthcoming) and "The Concept of the Chosen People: An Interpretation", *Judaism* 43, no. 2 (Spring 1994): 127-48.

[4] Maimonides (*Mishneh Torah*, Hilkhot Shemittah ve-Yovel 10:16), following midrashic sources, ruled that unlike the seventh year of release, the jubilee does not release debts. Josephus (*Antiquities* 3.282) wrote that the jubilee released both slaves and debts. For a recent discussion of the question, see Yitzhak Gilat, "Ha-Im Yovel Meshamet Kesafim" (in Hebrew), *Tarbiz* 64, no. 2 (Winter 1995): 229-36. For English summaries of current scholarly as well as traditional views, see "Sabbatical Year and Jubilee", *Encyclopedia Judaica* (1971) 14:574-86, and Baruch A. Levine's commentary to the Jewish Publication Society *Torah Commentary: Leviticus* (Philadelphia, 1989) on Leviticus 25 and excursus 10, "The Inalienable Right to the Land of Israel" (pp. 270-74). Nehemiah 5:1-13 seems to reflect a period of indebtedness and disenfranchisement when the laws of release and redemption of the land and of indentured kinsmen were not operative. Therefore, Nehemiah rebuked the landed gentry (*horim*) and creditors and remedied the situation by executive fiat. Jacob Neusner ("Scripture and Mishnah: Authority and Selectivity", in *Scripture in the Jewish and Christian Traditions*, ed. F. Greenspahn, Nashville, Abingdon, 1982, p. 79) cites the view of Morton Smith that Nehemiah was, in effect, "the archetype of a Greek tyrannos" in his "public works programmes, cancellation of debts, release of persons enslaved for debt, confiscation of the property of their wealthy opponents, and redistribution of land".

[5] On the sabbath, see "Sabbath" in *Encyclopedia Judaica* (1971) 14:557-72; Alfred Jospe, ed., *The Sabbath as Idea and Experience: An Introduction to the Meaning of Jewish Life in Our Time* (Washington, D.C.: B'nai B'rith Hillel Foundations, 1962); David Zisenwine and Karen Abramovitz, *The Sabbath: Time and Existence* (Tel Aviv: Open University of Israel, 1982); Arthur Green, "Sabbath as Temple: Some Thoughts on Space and Time in Judaism", in *Go and Study: Essays and Studies in Honor of Alfred Jospe*, eds Raphael Jospe and Samuel Fishman, (Washington, D.C.: B'nai B'rith Hillel Foundations, 1980), pp. 287-305.

[6] Cf. Sifra (Venice ed., 1545), Kedoshim, Parashah 1:10 (col. 174); Talmud, Yevamot 5:2, Bava Mezia 32a.

[7] Similarly, and presumably in reaction against the Nazi claims at the Nuremberg Trials that they were just following orders, the Second General Order of the Israel Defence Forces states that an order that is "manifestly illegal" is not to be obeyed.

[8] Talmud, Yevamot 6:1.

[9] The Ethiopian Jews call themselves Beita Yisrael and regard the term "Falasha" as pejorative. We should also note that the apocryphal Book of

Jubilees also requires extremely strict and literalist sabbath observance, including the prohibition of sexual relations.

[10] English translation by Ralph Marcus in the Loeb Classical Library edition of Josephus (vol. 7, p.143).

[11] The gospels clearly portray Jesus as getting involved in arguments with different groups of Jews on various occasions for healing on the sabbath (as well as for sabbath violations by others, such as his disciples). It is by no means always clear what the actual dispute concerned; which Jewish group was involved in the incident; whether in fact saving of life or alleviating suffering was at stake; whether Jesus healed by taking some action that per se involved a desecration of the sabbath, or by merely speaking to the patient. In at least one case, when Jesus healed a crippled man on the sabbath by talking to him at the pool of Bethesda (John 5), the argument had nothing to do with the healing itself but with the fact that after he was cured, the man followed Jesus' instructions and carried his bed on the sabbath. The story ends with John's conclusion that "therefore the Jews sought the more to kill him, because he not only had broken the sabbath, but said also that God was his Father, making himself equal with God" (v. 18 KJV).

[12] *Mishneh Torah*, Hilkhot Shabbat 2:1-3.

[13] *Shulhan Arukh*, Orah Hayyim 328:2.

[14] Interestingly enough, although Jesus is described in several places in the gospels as arguing with various groups of Jews about healing people on the sabbath, in Luke 13:15 and 14:5 Jesus cites the Jews' practice of alleviating animal suffering on the Sabbath.

[15] Cf. Leo Baeck, *The Essence of Judaism* (New York: Schocken, 1948), chap. 2, "Faith in Man: In One's Fellow Man — The Social Sabbath", p. 202.

[16] The connection between the 39 categories of prohibited *melakhah* on the sabbath and the work of constructing the sanctuary is explicitly mentioned in the Talmud, Shabbat 49b. For further parallels between the creation of the world and the construction of the sanctuary, see Green, "Sabbath as Temple" pp. 295-97.

[17] Abraham Joshua Heschel, *The Sabbath* (New York: Harper & Row, 1950), pp. 6-10.

[18] Moses Maimonides, *The Guide of the Perplexed*, trans. with an introduction by Shlomo Pines (Chicago: University of Chicago Press, 1963), 2:13, pp. 281-82.

[19] Arthur Green, "Sabbath as Temple", op. cit., p. 294.

[20] Ahad Ha-Am, "Shabbat Ve-Tziyonut" (1898), in *Al Parashat Derakhim* (in Hebrew) (Berlin, 1904), 3.79, and in *Kol Kitvei Ahad Ha-Am* (in Hebrew) (Tel Aviv, 1965), p. 286.

[21] For a brief English survey, see "Strangers and Gentiles", in *Encyclopedia Judaica* 15:419-21.

[22] *Mishneh Torah*, Hilkhot Issurei Biah 14:7-8. Cf. *Shulhan Arukh*, Yoreh Deah 124:2.

98   *The Jubilee Challenge*

23 "The Status of Women in Judaism: From Exemption to Exclusion", *Iliff Review* 35, 2 (Spring 1978), 29-39; see the discussion of this point on p. 31.

24 The Mekhilta is a tannaitic midrash on Exodus, primarily halakhic in nature.

25 See Maimonides, *Mishneh Torah*, Hilkhot Shemittah ve-Yovel 4:25, 9:2-3, 10:15.

26 *Ibid.*, 10:8.

27 *Ibid.*, 9:3.

28 Cf. Mishnah, Sheviit 10:3, and Talmud Gittin 36a.

29 Maimonides, *Mishneh Torah*, Hilkhot Shemittah ve-Yovel 9:16. Cf. "Prosbul" in *Encyclopedia Judaica* 13:1181-82.

30 Cf. Maimonides, *Mishneh Torah*, Hilkhot Shemittah ve-Yovel 4:29: "The produce of a non-Jew who purchased land in the land of Israel and seeded it during the seventh year is permitted."

31 Cf. Sifra (Venice ed.), Parashat va-Yiqra, Parashata 14:1 (col. 28).

32 *Mishneh Torah*, Hilkhot Shemittah ve-Yovel 12:16.

33 *Mishneh Torah*, Hilkhot Melakhim 11:1.

Sunday, Pentecost and the Jubilee Tradition: A Patristic Perspective

K.M. George

The Christian patristic reflection on jubilee involves a heavy dependence on number symbolism and the typological interpretations of the Hebrew Bible. Generally speaking, the fathers of the church do not resort to the idea of jubilee as described in Leviticus 25 as a model for socio-economic relations. In fact, they seem not to be impressed by the idea at all. I wish to point out briefly the interconnection between the biblical-liturgical elements and patristic hermeneutics in relation to the jubilee theme.

There are two sets of number relations in the Jewish tradition that the fathers use for a Christian understanding of history and eschatology: (1) the relation between sabbath and jubilee or the symbolism of 7 times 7; and (2) the sequential relation between 40 and 50. It should be clearly understood that there is no "number mysticism" in the thought of the outstanding representatives of the patristic tradition. They simply take for granted in their interpretation the special place attributed to the number 7 in the Jewish tradition.

Sunday and Pentecost are understood as the Christian parallels for the Jewish sabbath and jubilee. According to early Christian theology, the literal significance of sabbath and Pentecost ceases to exist. Gregory of Nazianzus (4th century) contrasts the literal with the spiritual by exhorting the Christians that while the Hebrews kept theirs in a literal way, Christians should observe theirs as "sacramentally reinstated", in a spiritual way ("On Pentecost", *Oration*, 41.1.4).

For the fathers, Sunday is the key. It is a purely Christian feast. Its sole theological basis is the belief in the resurrection of Christ. Sunday is the *weekly* Easter, the "icon" of the age to come. The weekly and the annual liturgical cycles of the church are centred on Sunday.

The notion of Sunday as the first day of the week as well as the eighth day was a favourite theme in the patristic interpretation.

In the Alexandrian theological tradition, the cycle of the seven-day week was the symbol of history, both human and cosmic. The problem of this cycle is that it returns to itself endlessly. The recurring cycle of the week provides no exit, no hope. Human life is caught in the vicious circle of this dismal return.

So Sunday is proposed both as the first day of the week and as the "eighth day", which breaks the cycle. Sunday as the first day stands for the beginning of all creation. As the day of the resurrection of Christ, it represents the renewal of all creation. All life that is subject to death and corruption is renewed in Christ. As the eighth day, Sunday symbolizes the age to come, the eternal life. History's closed and hopeless mill of boredom is given a radically new opening and meaning. Sunday is the initial point of creation and re-creation, as well as the transition point between history and eschatology.

The Christian Pentecost, the day of the coming of the Holy Spirit on the apostolic community, is related to the Jewish Pentecost only in name, both referring to the 50th day. The 50th day after the resurrection of Christ falls on a Sunday. The weekly Easter is strengthened sevenfold. So Pentecost is called the Great Sunday or the Sunday of Sundays. The coming of the Holy Spirit on Pentecost makes this day the symbol of the new age; it is liberation from the clutches of history. The new age of new creation, which has already begun in the resurrection of Christ, is consummated in Pentecost.

The material, socio-economic resonance of the jubilee idea is clearly audible in the life of this Pentecost community as described in Acts 2:42-45. They abolished private ownership of property "and had all things in common; they would sell their possessions and goods and distribute the proceeds to all, as any had need". So Pentecost was understood as the Christian parallel to jubilee, but in a radically different way. The abolition of private property and the sharing of resources after the Pentecost experience were not conceived as a model for continuing historical practice, but rather were proposed in view of the end of history, the imminent coming of the Lord. Since history was about to lose its meaning, the sharing of goods was an act of redeeming history, anticipating the paradise experience of the kingdom of God.

Turning now to the other set of number relations — the sequential connection between 40 and 50 — we see that early Christian liturgical tradition took special note of the significance of the number 40 in Jewish history on the basis of the fasting of Jesus for 40 days and 40 nights at the very beginning of his public ministry. The liturgical prayers, especially in the East, also regularly refer to the 40-day fasting of Moses and Elijah and the 40-year wandering of the people of Israel in the desert.

St Augustine tried, rather simplistically, to give a scriptural meaning to the number 40 by noting that it is the product of the number of gospels (4) and the number of commandments (10). But in the Christian tradition what counts is not the number itself but the content of 40 days or 40 years. More concretely, this content is translated into the practice of the Great Lent, leading to the memory of the death and resurrection of Christ. The Lenten prayers and rituals highlight three elements: repentance, both collective and individual; reconciliation/forgiveness; and liberation/restitution. Like the 7-day week, the 40 days of the Great Lent symbolize history and human life. It should be a time of return to God through genuine *repentance*. The prayers of the church are very self-critical during this period. In some of the Oriental Christian traditions, people practise complete prostration during the prayers — more than 100 every day! At the beginning and at the end of the Great Lent, there is a special ceremony for asking mutual *forgiveness*. People also go for private confessions. There are special instructions and exhortations to restore the lost harmony of the community in social and economic life, to practise justice in concrete human situations and to redress the grievances of the poor and the powerless. Thus the *liberation* from all kinds of captivity, spiritual and material, is emphasized. The readings on this liturgical occasion draw heavily from the Hebrew prophets like Isaiah.

This 40-day period, the symbol of the historical order, which is marked by repentance, reconciliation and restitution, leads to the Sunday of resurrection. (In actual practice today, the Eastern churches reckon 50 days for Lenten fasting, which includes the Holy Week commemorating the suffering, death and resurrection of Christ.) This period of 40 or 50 days before Easter is to be compared with the 50 days immediately following Easter, which leads to the Sunday of Pentecost. The latter 50 days between Easter and Pentecost symbolize the renewed creation at the transition point between this world and the kingdom of God.

The qualitative difference between these two periods is ritually shown in the Orthodox tradition. In contrast to the Lenten practice, prostrations are forbidden during the Easter-to-Pentecost period. The faithful are exhorted to stand up and pray. This standing position symbolizes resurrection and the transcendent dignity of the new creation. (In Syriac the word *kyomtho*, "resurrection", and *koumo*, "standing", are from the same root.) There are no food restrictions and no fasting on Wednesdays and Fridays in this period. Thus it is a period of joyful celebration, feasting, singing and praising God. In fact, the whole period is an extended Sunday, because there is no fasting or prostration permitted on any Sunday of the year. The spiritual thread running through these 50 days of celebration is the quiet working of the Holy Spirit. It is the Spirit who perfects the creation, and we are called upon to receive the gifts of the Spirit and commit ourselves to a cooperative action (*synergia*) with God in bringing creation up to its true vocation of deification (*theosis*).

The social teaching and societal concerns of the fathers of the church definitely drew inspiration from the Hebrew Bible, which was copiously quoted and interpreted in the patristic writings. However, the early Christian theologians who shaped the doctrinal-ethical worldview of the church appealed directly to God's love and compassion for humanity (*philanthrōpia*) as manifested in Jesus of Nazareth. The union of divinity and humanity in the incarnate Christ was the only model for them. They did not propose any blueprint for an ideal society.

In their criticisms of the Roman imperial state and in their intransigent attitude towards worldly governments and political structures, fathers like John Chrysostom, Basil of Caesarea, Gregory of Nazianzus, Ambrose and others simply held on to a daring vision of the kingdom of God, whatever we may call it: utopia or eschaton or eternity. The weekly Sunday with its joyful celebrations in gratitude (*eucharistia*) for the death, resurrection and second coming of Jesus Christ was the historical locus for this vision.

It would be naive to think that we can combine the Jewish sabbath with the Christian Sunday. These are two different faith traditions that are rooted not in some intellectual concepts but in certain foundational experiences. We cannot negotiate foundational experiences between different religious traditions. But we can certainly reflect together and also act together as people believing in one God and in one humanity. There is ample common ground — historically, theologically and spiritually — between Judaism and Christianity.

The Jubilee: Time Ceilings for the Growth of Money?

Geiko Müller-Fahrenholz

My thoughts in this article are both utopian and fragmentary. Fragmentary because of my limitations, for I am not an expert in the areas of economics and finance but a layperson who likes to believe that he has seen something of what money does to people and to the good and blessed earth herself. And what I am seeing makes my heart angry. Nor am I an expert in biblical exegesis but at best one who tries to keep himself accessible and vulnerable to the word of God. And what I am seeing there makes my soul grateful.

It is from this anger and this gratitude that my fragmentary observations come. They are utopian in the saddest sense of the word. They have no "topos", no place in our world — or more precisely, no place yet. The category of the "not yet" is, as Ernst Bloch has insisted, a constitutive dimension of the capacity of human beings to transcend their historical conditions and to imagine possible developments.

The topos of anger

I spent five years in Costa Rica. This country took pride in calling itself the Switzerland of Central America, for it seemed like an island of stability and social concern surrounded by an ocean of civil wars, ruthless exploitation of the poor and violent oppression of opposition groups. Within those five years, however, I saw begging children appearing in the streets of San José, Costa Rica's squalid capital. I saw the fences around the houses of the rich grow higher and higher while the country plunged into an economic crisis that went deeper and deeper every year. "Structural adjustment plans" imposed by the international monetary system continue to suffocate what little economic breath the country possesses. Costa Rica is but one example of all the nations that are caught in the downward spiral of debts that cannot be redeemed and interest payments that keep growing with every "renegotiation" that takes place.

Costa Rica has probably the highest biological diversity per square kilometre of any country on earth, blessed with the bounty and beauty of nature, yet squandering most of it, selling it away, contaminating it. Through my experience there, I began to see that there must be something basically wrong with the ways in which we administer the household of the earth. (I understand "economics" simply as the science of administering the earth's household.)

The topos of gratitude

What does the sabbath add to a creation that is "very good" already? The creation myth in Genesis 1 makes it very clear that each day is imbued with goodness, potent and fertile, bouncing with blessings, animated by the Ruah, the breath and soul of life. What is there in the sabbath that is not already there in the works of the six days of creation?

It will not be enough to say that what is added is the rest. The sabbath is more than mere relaxation, more than a break. The text (Gen. 2:3) suggests that what the sabbath adds to the goodness of the working days is holiness.

The sabbath is the day (and the night) to celebrate the goodness and contemplate the great mysteries inherent in nature's ways, the day to be trained in the art of gratitude. This can be deduced very clearly from the scathing critique of the prophet Amos: "Listen to this, you who grind the destitute and plunder the humble, you who say... When will the sabbath be past so that we may open our wheat again, giving short measure in the bushel and taking overweight in the silver, tilting the scales fraudulently, and selling the dust of the wheat; that we may buy the poor for silver and the destitute for a pair of shoes?'" (8:4-6 NEB).

The prophet sees that the sabbath day is being observed, but only in a formal and ritualistic manner, as a day that the powerful use in order to imagine yet more ways of cheating the poor. The sabbath is perverted when it is used as a day to design new tricks to steal the silver from the poor and the last pair of shoes from the destitute. Why is it perverted? Because it is not kept as a day of holiness but as a day of cunning; not as a day of contemplation but of trickery; not as a day of training to be grateful and gracious but as a day of training to be wicked. The perversion consists in robbing the seventh day of its holiness.

In other words, it is this dimension of holiness that upholds the supreme goodness of creation. The sabbath is there to ensure that creation can remain very good. *Holiness protects goodness.*

It is not the break in work as such that makes us receptive for the blessings of creation. It is the active contemplation of God's blessed ways that keeps us receptive to the blessings at work in our bodies, in the lilies of the field and the beasts of the night and the flowing of the rivers and the turning of the stars. The relaxation of the sabbath day may well help to renew our strength. But there is more to it than getting fit again: the conscious meditation and celebration of God's wondrous ways helps to restore the order of creation because it helps us to see our place in this order of things and to search for our place again and again; for in the hectic course of our working days we may well lose track of the place given to us in the realms of life and trespass the limits imposed by its integrity.

The rhythms in time

In my view the sabbath is the most remarkable "invention" of the Jewish faith. It does more than institute the principle that goodness needs to be protected and upheld by holiness. Rather, it gives this tension a place in the course of time. Every seventh day is to be celebrated as the holy day among the working days. Thus is instituted a rhythm of six working days and one holy day. And this is not an arbitrary ritualistic sequence but something close to an anthropological order. Humans need to work, and to deny work, as is the case today with widespread and systemic unemployment, is thus a denial of an innate necessity, a destruction of human dignity. And what is equally important, human beings need to rest, to distance themselves from their labours.

So there is something to this rhythm of six-to-one that reflects a basic disposition in the nature of human activity. Jürgen Moltmann speaks of the sabbath as the "ecological order of creation". I would suggest that this rhythm of six-to-one constitutes the order that needs to be followed in history in order to keep it good and sane.

The Jewish faith has developed this rhythm of six-to-one in the sequence of weeks and then in the sequence of years. The sabbatical rhythm of the years is the sabbath of the land (see Lev. 25:2), the "sacred rest" needed for the household of life to maintain its regenerative potential. As a further sequence, the jubilee is introduced (Lev. 25:8-55). After seven times seven years the "liberation in the land" shall be proclaimed.

What does the jubilee add to the sabbatical order of things? Whereas the sabbatical years refer to the ecological order of the land, the jubilee refers to the socio-economic order of societies. It establishes a time ceiling for the accumulation of wealth and, by implication, the aggravation of dependencies.

Why is the 50th year made to be the year of liberation and restitution? Is there any particular reason for introducing this interruption after seven times seven sequences? My personal impression is that 50 years encompasses the productive time of human beings. One has moved from childhood to the time when one approaches old age and leaves things to the following generations. So the sequence of generations comes into focus, and the jubilee marks an interruption.

The jubilee is introduced as a means by which the socio-economic life of Israel is ordered. Two criteria are given that interact with each other. The first concerns the notion of property and trusteeship, and the second, the understanding of the corrective quality of time.

Regarding the first, God as the Creator is the only one to own the land. "The land is mine, and you are coming into it as aliens and settlers", says Leviticus 25:23. This is the fundamental criterion for the land rights in Israel. There is a sacred character about the land because it is imbued with God's creative powers. Therefore, the land can never be considered as an entity to be owned in perpetuity. The simple fact is that the land is not free, it is not up for sale, as it were. There is already one who has established his ownership rights for perpetuity, the eternal God. In fact, the only one who can claim land in perpetuity is the one who is eternal. Human beings are mortal, finite creatures, so they can claim only the leasing rights of the land and its products and potentials.

It follows that this land is entrusted to families as the basic productive unit in Israel. They hold their "patrimony" (*nahala*) in trust, which means that they owe it to God and to their posterity. The historical stability of the people of God is directly related to the stability and equity of the *nahala* system.

The notion of the corrective quality of time for social and economic processes is equally important. Since it is unavoidable that some families should be more successful and fortunate than others, so it is also unavoidable that some should get richer while others get poorer. That is the way things are. The potentials among human beings are unevenly distributed; some seem to be blessed more than others. There is a deep inequality in the way people are blessed.

This must lead to social and economic distortions if there are no time ceilings to correct them. This is the function of the jubilee. It restores the original *nahala* system by ending the dependencies of those who were impoverished and curtailing the accumulated wealth of those who "made it". The miseries of some and the fortunes of others cannot be carried endlessly beyond intergenerational lines. This would by necessity lead to feudal and oligarchic structures in society. The time ceiling has a "democratizing" and "levelling" effect. What must be preserved and safeguarded is not the successes of individual families but the well-being of all constituent members for the sake of the land and the future of the people as a whole. It is the people of God that count, not a particular group among them.

Money must be allowed to die

It is too easy to dismiss this idea of the jubilee by saying it was probably never realized. Ideas are like seeds that lie in the earth waiting for their opportunity to take root and to grow. Nonetheless, as we probe the usefulness of the ancient concept of the jubilee, the question I find more difficult to deal with is that the sacred orientation of Israel's land and time concepts has gone. The very idea that there is a God who owns the land and the time, this sacred dimension of our being, is alien to most people, and certainly alien to the way we do business today. The history of secularization, which is the most pervasive mark of modernity, is intimately linked to the reception of Roman property laws during the Middle Ages, basically the conversion of *patrimonium* into *dominium*,[1] and the emergence of the monetary system. The history of practical godlessness began with this subtle destruction of the sacred character of land and time, which occurred long before the academic disputes about atheism.

The mediaeval church still knew that any practice of usury was sinful because it was in the last resort blasphemous. For this very reason the Reformers, foremost Martin Luther, were angrily fighting the usury business. Time was a quality that belonged to God, they insisted, for no created being can make time. We enjoy the time, we are carried along in the flow of time, everything is embedded in its time, so the very idea of exploiting the flow of time to take interest on money lent seemed preposterous.

It does so no more because the sacredness of time has disappeared, even before the sacredness of the land vanished from the memories of our modern societies. Instead, capitalist market economies have been elevated to global importance; they are enshrined with the qualities of omnipotence that border on idolatry.

So the question arises: does it make sense to attribute to money qualities that no created thing can ever have, namely, eternal growth? Every tree must die, every house must one day crumble, every human being must perish. Why should immaterial goods such as capital — and its counterpart, debts — not also have their time? The capital knows no natural barriers to its growth. There is no jubilee to put an end to its accumulative power. And so there is no jubilee to put an end to debts and slavery.

Even bankers begin to see that there must be something wrong with the unbroken and limitless accumulation of capital. There are huge amounts of money floating around the globe that are no longer tied to national economies and to real products. Money that feeds on money, with no productive or social obligation, represents a vast flood that threatens even large national economies and drowns small countries. The famous "deregulation" policies imposed by the international capitalist system are further weakening whatever regulative power was in the hands of national governments and regional markets. But at the heart of this deregulation is the undisputed concept of the eternal life of money.

Let me take an example from nature. Over the last decades many rivers have been engineered into straight waterways. The meanderings of the river have been dammed up, thereby opening up wetlands for whatever use was deemed urgent. The river was turned into something like a channel. What happened when there were heavy rains and/or thaws? The waters that flowed to the river began to rush down the water highway. The meanderings that used to slow down the flow were gone, the wetlands that used to be flooded no longer available. So the waters stream with increasing speed and finally cause disastrous floods further down where nobody expected them.

This is what happens with the flow of money that knows no time limits and rhythms. Some may argue that it is inappropriate to use a river as an example. I have done this on purpose, for I want to point out that within the conditions of this planet earth, every type of activity must be compatible to the limits imposed by the exceedingly intricate interplay of factors that constitute the functional integrity of each element of life. In a finite world everything must be finite.

It is the fascinating insight of the sabbatical concept that the flow of activity must be regularly intercepted in order to keep it from accelerating beyond proportions. The sabbatical ordinances serve to maintain the regenerative and wholesome meaning of work because they stand in the way of unlimited progress. The sabbatical rhythms control the exploitative and demeaning impact of endless activity. And it is the fascinating insight of the jubilee that even the accumulative potentials of human endeavour must be submitted to radical interruptions. Whether the 50th year is the right moment to have such a break may well be disputable, especially since we don't know whether it worked this way at all. Important is the idea that the accumulative power of wealth and the accumulative impact of dependency must be submitted to time ceilings. In other words, money must be allowed to die; that is, its gaining power must be limited by the imposition of time ceilings.

How this can be done, I don't know. Bankers would know how to design systems by which deposits would be written off after a certain period of time. We can write off buildings or vehicles, for instance, because it is assumed that they lose their original value in the course of time. In a like manner capital would have to be written off so that after, say, 10 or 20 years its generative potential is exhausted.

From domination to inhabitation

Globalization is the big word these days. There is no need to describe the distortions and perversions that mark this process: loss of cultural diversity; loss of biodiversity; depletion of earth, water and air, including the ozone layer; increased disparity among nations; increased tension among peoples over access to vital resources; weakening of the state and its ordering mechanisms, including the welfare systems, to name but a few factors. We human beings are approaching the limits of *dominating* the earth. It is time to reflect on how we can *inhabit* the earth, together with all the other myriad forms of life that are needed to sustain the functional integrity of this planet.

It is time to learn how to inhabit, rather than to dominate, this wonderful blue planet.

One vital aspect of this learning process on which will depend the capacity of the human race to survive is to learn from the Torah that time is not a commodity but some unspeakable reality that carries us along. Inhabitation implies understanding and honouring the rhythms of life and human activity.

My friend Robert Muller used to say: "The universe was not created to make money." To fight for the domestication of money is in the last resort not only a matter of political sanity and economic reason; it is a matter of faith.

NOTE

[1] See Ulrich Duchrow, *Alternativen zur kapitalistischen Weltwirtschaft, Biblische Erinnerung und politische Ansätze zur Überwindung der lebensbedrohenden Ökonomie*, Gütersloh, Matthias-Grünewald-Verlag, 1994, p.45. See also Manfred Brocker's work on the theory of occupation, in *Arbeit und Eigentum. Der Paradigmenwechsel in der neuzeitlichen Eigentumstheorie*, Darmstadt, Wissenschaftliche Buchgesellschaft, 1992, pp.30ff.

Evaluating the Triumph
of the Market

Ronald J. Sider

This essay represents a preliminary attempt to describe how Christians today should respond to the phenomenal success and expansion of market economies at the end of the 20th century. [1] For its normative framework, the essay assumes the preferential option for the poor and the basic view of property and possessions outlined in my book *Rich Christians in an Age of Hunger*, plus the understanding of economic justice developed in my "Toward a Biblical Perspective on Equality" (1989). [2] God measures societies by what they do to the poorest and demands, as a minimum, that they care for those who cannot care for themselves and make available to all others economic opportunity to the point that they have access to the resources needed so they can earn a decent living and be dignified, participating members of their community.

Assuming those norms, how should we assess the success of democratic capitalism? Do market economies help or hurt the poor?

Democratic capitalism has won the most dramatic economic/ political debate of the 20th century. Almost every country in the world praises the ideal of democracy. Virtually every nation is taking concrete steps to move closer to "a market economy". Anybody concerned about the poor must struggle with how this momentous global embrace of market economies impacts the poorest.

But what is a market economy? Definition is crucial. There are a wide variety of actual market economies today. The "ideal type" of a pure laissez-faire economy where the government never intervenes in economic life does not exist anywhere in today's world. Whether in North America, western Europe or the successful "Asian Tigers" (Taiwan, South Korea, Singapore and Hong Kong), the government plays a substantial role in what everyone nevertheless calls market economies.[3]

A market economy, then, is an economic arrangement where the bulk of the wealth and means of production are privately owned and where most wages and prices are set by supply and demand. That does not mean that government never intervenes in economic life. It does today in all existing market economies — although in the US, for example, the government intervenes in the economy less than it does in Germany.

Communist economies were fundamentally different. The state owned the means of production, and its central planners determined wages, prices and production. (There actually used to be a central office in Moscow that set 25 million prices every year!)[4]

At the end of the 20th century, the modern world has rejected centrally planned economies in favour of market economies. Is that good news for the poor?

Yes, on balance, it is, although there are serious problems with the way present market economies are working.

Communism's state ownership and central planning do not work. They are inefficient and totalitarian. Market economies, in contrast, have produced enormous wealth. And not only in western nations. Many Asian countries have adopted market economies. The result has been a dramatic drop in poverty in the world's most populous continent. In 1970 chronic undernourishment plagued 36 percent of the people in all developing countries. Only 20 years later and in spite of rapid population growth, only 20 percent were chronically undernourished.[5]

All around the globe, countries are seeking to copy the success of the Asian Tigers, which have successfully combined a basic market framework with substantial government activity. The result? Stunning success. A recent United Nations report indicated that "about 80 countries were in the process of economic liberalization and privatization."[6] Whether in former communist countries, in sub-Saharan Africa or in Latin America, countries are adopting economic policies that place far greater emphasis on markets. Countries are privatizing government-owned corporations, reducing barriers to international trade and welcoming foreign investments.[7]

The evidence is overwhelming. Market economies are more successful than centrally owned and planned economies at creating economic growth. China's phenomenal economic growth rate over the last decade is clearly the result of its substantial adoption of free-market measures in both agriculture and substantial parts of industrial production. Throughout most of East Asia — not just in the much-discussed Tigers, but also in Malaysia, Indonesia and Thailand — market economies are producing explosive economic growth.

Central to this growth is the expansion of exports and international trade. The rapid growth of the Asian Tigers was directly related to their decision to reduce trade barriers and emphasize exports, along with substantial government activity (see below). Scores of careful studies show that greater concentration on goods for export almost always produces economic growth. [8]

International trade also tends to increase real wages in developing countries. [9] Wages in export-oriented firms in developing countries are, of course, very low in comparison with wages in developed nations. (That, after all, is a major part of a poor nation's comparative advantage.) But those "low wages" are often substantially higher — especially when trade unions have basic freedom — than the average wages in the country. Thus when international trading patterns use the comparative advantage of low wages in poor nations, two beneficial things can result: poor people receive higher wages, and all of us pay lower prices for the products. [10]

International trade creates forces that tend to cause wages for labour with the same skills to equalize among trading partners. [11] Obviously, that hurts higher-paid workers in industrialized nations, who must compete with much lower-paid workers in Indonesia, Mexico or China. But surely those most concerned with the poorest should support measures to improve wages in developing countries and then seek other ways (e.g., generous unemployment insurance and job training) to help workers in rich nations who are hurt by global trade. In this way, developed nations focus more on areas where they have a comparative advantage.

Substantial evidence indicates that moving towards free markets often promotes economic growth. *World Development Report 1995* reports a study of 29 sub-Saharan African countries. Between 1981-86 and 1987-91, the six countries that adopted the most market reforms experienced the strongest economic growth. Their economies expanded by 2 percent per year. GDP in those countries that did not adopt market reforms fell by 2 percent per year. [12]

In just a moment, we must look carefully at a number of significant problems that seem to accompany this market-led economic growth. But surely the first conclusion to draw is that market economies are better at producing economic growth than present alternatives. Furthermore, since poor nations need economic growth in order to provide a modestly decent standard of living for the world's poorest people, those who care about the poorest should accept markets as an important, useful tool for empowering the poor.

Weaknesses of the market economy

Unfortunately, today's market economies also have fundamental weaknesses. When measured by biblical standards, glaring injustices exist. Precisely as we adopt a market framework as better than known alternatives, we must examine and correct problems.

The most glaring problem is that at least a quarter of the world's people lack the capital to participate in any major way in the global market economy. Land is still the basic capital in many agricultural societies. Money and education are far more crucial in modern capital-intensive, knowledge-intensive economies. About one out of four people in our world has almost no land, very little money and virtually no education.

The market's mechanism of supply and demand is totally blind to the distinction between basic necessities (even minimal food needed to avoid starvation) and luxuries desired by the wealthy. Today, 20 percent of the world's people receive 83 percent of the income.[13] In itself, the market will supply whatever the wealthy can pay for — even if millions of poor people starve.

If we start with the present division of wealth, then the outcome of the market will be gross injustice. Only if redistribution occurs — through both private and public measures — will the poorest obtain the capital to earn a decent living in the global market.

A second problem is that, at least in the short run, the poorest seem to suffer (or at least fail to gain in proportion to the rest of society) when countries move towards a market economy — unless government takes vigorous and wise corrective measures. The data are not totally conclusive, and economists still debate the issue. But there is increasing agreement that as economic growth lifts per capita income, the initial result is growing inequality between rich and poor. [14] Then as per capita income continues to rise, the inequality declines.

This basic analysis raises crucial questions. In the earlier stages of economic growth, do the poorest actually lose real income? Or do they gain, although not as fast as the middle and upper classes? There are no widely accepted answers to these questions. The outcome depends in part on whether government takes appropriate steps to provide capital and other things to the poorest at the same time that market reforms occur.

The actual situation in the past decade, however, is that market reforms have been accompanied by a short-term increase in poverty in many places. Many of the people in eastern Europe and the former Soviet Union are worse off than they were under communism. A number of studies indicate that the poor in Africa and Latin America have also become poorer as market reforms were introduced. [15] Was that outcome an inevitable part of market reforms? Or was it because of choices by governments to cut things like education and health care rather than military budgets? The answer is not yet clear.

What is indisputable is that over time, the poor usually benefit. The poor in South Korea, Taiwan, Singapore and Hong Kong are vastly better off economically than they were 25 years ago because of a combination of market reforms and government activities. The same is true of vast numbers of formerly extremely poor people in China, Indonesia, Malaysia and Thailand.

Very disturbing, however, is more recent data showing that the gap between rich and poor is increasing again in very wealthy countries, especially the US and the UK — the two wealthy market economies with the greatest reliance on the market. In the US, the gap between the rich and poor has grown enormously in the last 20-plus years. From 1973 to 1992, the richest 10 percent gained 18 percent while the real income of the poorest 10 percent fell by 11 percent. [16] In contrast, wealthy European countries with more active governments have not experienced the same growing gap between rich and poor. The right kind of government intervention to help the poorest seems to be a significant factor.

Without corrective action, it appears that today's global markets create unjust, dangerous extremes between rich and poor. Robert Frank, a Cornell University economist, argues in his book *Winner Take All* that complex developments (modern technology, the globalized economy, mass marketing, economies of scale etc.) enable increasingly smaller numbers of people to acquire an ever larger share of the wealth. So, for example, Bill Gates of Microsoft makes $15 billion before he's 40 and becomes the richest American. [17] "The $20 million Michael Jordan reportedly received in 1992 for promoting Nike shoes exceeded the entire annual payroll of the Indonesian factories that made them." [18] Today, Michael Jordan earns as much for promoting Nike shoes as approximately 18,000 Indonesian workers who make these shoes (even after a doubling of wages since 1993!). [19] In response, Nike claims their workers earn 50 cents an hour (twice the country's minimum wage) as well as free meals and health care. [20]

Centralized wealth equals concentrated power. And that — as the conservative critics of communism rightly used to point out — is dangerous. It is not surprising that the relatively small numbers of wealthy people who control the largest corporations, which in turn own the media, also have vast political power. In the US, most of the private money for political campaigns comes from the richest 1 percent of the people. Not surprisingly, most politicians care more about the self-interest of their wealthy donors than about justice for the poor. Democracy is threatened, and the poor suffer.

A third problem is that pervasive cultural decline seems to follow the expansion of the market. [21] The most obvious, perhaps, is the sweeping materialism and consumerism that floods across the world as country after country joins the global market. Material possessions and the money that buys them become all-important to more and more people. The size of one's house and salary becomes more important than God, neighbour and the creation. In fact, increasing numbers of people value making money more than they do marriage, parenting, or even honesty.

The power of advertising

It is easy to see how materialistic consumerism develops. The competitive drive to increase market share encourages ever more seductive advertising. American historian William Leach's book *Land of Desire: Merchants and the Rise of a New American Culture* tells how this happened. The Puritans and other Christian traditions had shaped early 19th-century American culture to value thrift, frugality and modest life-styles. But that did not sell enough products. So large corporations developed advertising techniques to persuade us that joy and happiness come through fancy new clothes, more expensive cars, the latest fashions and increasingly sophisticated gadgets.

The director of research of General Motors, Charles Kettering, decided that business needed to create a "dissatisfied consumer". Annual model changes — planned obsolescence — was his solution. Success, according to advertising historian Roland Marchard, came to depend on "the virtue of qualities like wastefulness, self-indulgence, and artificial obsolescence". [22]

Diabolically clever advertising agencies use the most sophisticated combinations of beautiful women, gorgeous colour and splendid soundtracks to guarantee that self-indulgence and instant gratification replace frugality and simplicity. The great economist John Maynard Keynes put it simply: "Consumption is the sole end and object of all economic activity." [23]

Television is the most powerful medium. The average five-year old watches 3½ hours of TV a day. The average adult, five hours — that means watching 21,000 commercials a year. And the message is the same: "Buy something — do it now." It is hardly surprising that the largest 100 US corporations pay for about 75 percent of all commercial television. And the producers and writers develop what the advertisers will support. [24]

What started in the US has spread around the world. Even the poorest kid in India knows that Coca-Cola refreshes. And Avon's slick advertising persuades desperately poor Brazilian women to buy expensive skin cream. TV ads showing sensuous light-skinned women suggest that older women can shed their aging skin, tanned and wrinkled by years of hard labour in the sun. The product "Renew", which costs $40 a jar, works by burning off the top layer of skin. But Avon Brazil's communications director says it works: "Women do everything to buy it. They stop buying other things like clothes, like shoes. If they feel good with their skin, they prefer to stop buying clothes and buy something that is on television." [25]

Global corporations own the global communications networks whose programmes and advertising create a global lust for ever more consumption. Growing materialism creates growing markets and expanding profits. Tragically, this same materialism destroys social relationships and the creation. Increasingly, some people think the heart of parenting is supplying one's children with more and more material pleasures. And the consumption overload pollutes the environment.

The market also corrupts culture by rewarding immoral actions. If there is a demand for pornography and dishonest advertisements, the market generously rewards the producers, even if the process corrupts the character of both the producers and the recipients.

Cultural decay also flows from the imperialistic tendency of the market to dominate all of life. The efficiency that follows from making some relationships mere interactions of economic exchange based on supply and demand is good. It is often fine to choose a TV salesperson based on market prices. But should the same concern determine the choice of a spouse? Or the decision whether or not to have one parent stay at home with young children? It may be economically advantageous to pay a full-time nanny rather than have skilled professionals "waste" precious time on parenting. But something terribly valuable has been lost. There should never be a market in body parts or sex or infants for adoption. "If sexuality is made a commodity of exchange, it becomes prostitution."[26] The market's imperialistic tendency to become the sole way to organize all of life corrupts and destroys character and culture.

The environmental crisis reveals a fourth problem with our global market economy. Our rivers and lakes are polluted, the ozone layer is depleted and global warming has already begun. Unfortunately, markets pay little attention to the needs of future generations.[27] The market fails to account for environmental costs — both because national accounting systems fail to notice the loss of natural capital and because companies seldom count pollution costs in their profit-and-loss statements. Costa Rica experienced significant economic growth between 1970 and 1990. But environmental decay in its soils and forests produced lost natural capital totalling 6 percent of the GDP of that period. In Indonesia, the loss was 9 percent from 1971 to 1984.[28]

The market rewards polluters who pass on their costs to neighbours — those who live downstream from where they dump polluted water into the river, those who live thousands of miles downwind from smokestacks that spew pollution into the air that quickly circles the globe; or all our grandchildren, who will have to suffer the consequences of today's arrogant neglect. Unless government compels all companies to pay the real costs of environmental destruction, the market rewards those who pollute, preferring quick profits to environmental sustainability.

It is idolatrous nonsense to equate justice with the outcome of a pure laissez-faire economy. It is simply false to think that a market economy, if freed from all government interference, would create what the Bible means by justice. Masses of poor people lacking capital are unable to afford even basic necessities. Concentrated wealth threatens democracy. Materialistic messages and practices corrode moral values, family life and God's creation.

To pay this price in the name of efficiency is idolatrous. Christians know that Keynes was wrong. Consumption is not the sole end of economic life. The economy is made for people, not people for an autonomous, efficient, ever-expanding economy. Wholesome family life and wise stewardship of God's garden matter more than economic efficiency. Yahweh is Lord even of economics.

What should Christians committed to a biblical vision of economic shalom do? Here I discuss four corrective measures: providing the poor with basic capital so they can participate in economic life, insisting on the right amount and right kind of government intervention, finding new measures for economic life, and redefining the good life.

Capital for the poor

We must end the outrage where Christians celebrate the market economy and then fail to provide the poorest with the capital they need to earn a decent living in the global market. Supply and demand pay no attention whatsoever to whether the purchaser wants basic food to keep her children from starving or luxury items to parade social status. The market rewards only purchasing power.

We do know what to do to strengthen the purchasing power of the poorest. They need capital so they can earn their own way. The poorest billion have hardly any capital, so they and their children waste away in malnutrition and starvation. To endorse market economies without redistributing resources so the poorest have the capital to earn a decent living is damnable defiance of the biblical God of justice.

Today's wealth is divided in a way that flatly contradicts the Bible. God wants every family to have the basic capital — land, money, knowledge — to earn their own way and be dignified, participating members of society. [29] If we want to implement this biblical teaching on economic justice — and enable market economies to operate justly — then we must fundamentally change the terrible injustice where many of the world's people have little or no capital. The poorest billion plus have virtually none. Another three billion have very little. The poorest 20 percent of the world's people (just over one billion people) own 1 percent of the world's wealth. In fact, the poorest 60 percent (around three and a half billion people) own only 6 percent of the world's wealth. The richest 20 percent own 81 percent. [30]

t insist on redistribution — both private voluntary efforts and effective government programmes. The word "redistribution" is a red flag for some. Redistribution does not mean state ownership. Not every redistribution scheme is wise. But the right kind are essential and successful.

What kind of capital do people need? That varies with the situation. In a largely agricultural society, land reform is essential. In an information society, equality of educational opportunity is the most basic way to empower the poor. Wise schemes to enable the poor to acquire the money needed to buy a house, start a small business or prepare for retirement are also important. [31] Providing capital so the poor have economic opportunity to earn their own way can happen through both private voluntary programmes and the activities of democratic governments.

In the last few decades, pioneers in micro-enterprise development (MED) have demonstrated the great success of tiny loans to poor people. Many Christian development agencies have experienced stunning results with MED. Many secular organizations, including the World Bank and the US government (USAID), now also promote MED.

Mohammed Yunus, a Bangladeshi economist, pioneered one of the earliest and most successful MED programmes. He founded the Grameen Bank to make tiny loans to the rural poor — $50, $75 or $120 to buy a cow, a plough or a small irrigation pump. He soon discovered that women were more likely than men to use the profits to care for their children's health and education and expand their business. So the Grameen Bank concentrated on women. Today, it has about two million borrowers in Bangladesh, most of them women.

That many women with new opportunities, new wealth and new power are threatening the Muslim religious leaders and the politicians.

A vigorous backlash is occurring. Muslim clerics have confined some women to their homes or declared them outcasts. Dozens of elementary schools for girls have been burned. [32] Women empowered by micro-loans are challenging traditional established centres of power.

I believe that Christians today should greatly expand Christian micro-loan programmes. The Agra Covenant on Christian Capital calls on Christians around the world to devote 1 percent of their income to micro-loans:

> The God of Israel gave every Israelite family enough land to earn their own way. The same God now summons Christians to struggle for justice and to offer similar opportunity to the one billion persons almost totally excluded from today's growing economies. For some, the necessary capital will be land; for others, education, a small loan or a decent job opportunity. The God who summons all those created in His image to responsible work demands that they have the opportunity. There are many ways to provide the basic capital. Governments, churches, businesses and voluntary organizations all have important responsibilities.
>
> We believe that small loans to poor people for micro-enterprise development is one of the very promising ways to empower the poor to help themselves. In the last decade private Christian organizations making such loans have enabled the poor to create hundreds of thousands of jobs.
>
> Now is the time to expand this successful model a hundredfold. The Christians of the world enjoy an income of at least 10 trillion dollars a year. It only takes about 500 dollars to create a new job among the poor and improve the living standard of a family of five by 50 percent within a year. At 500 dollars per job, one percent of Christian income for just one year could create new small loans producing 200 million new jobs. In one year, that many new jobs could improve the well-being of one billion people! [33]

By themselves, private (and public) micro-loans are inadequate. Gifted, tiny entrepreneurs cannot flourish if they lack fair legal systems, infrastructure such as roads and communication systems, wise macro-economic policies and appropriate public services. But certainly one thing Christians today should do is increase on a massive scale the resources devoted to providing the poorest with needed capital through voluntary organizations.

The right kinds of government programmes of redistribution are also essential. Every tax-based system of education, health care and social security involves taxing those with resources to guarantee the basic resources of knowledge and health to everyone, especially the poorest members of society. Of course some government programmes are disastrously ineffective. We should abolish them! We must avoid both libertarian views that reject almost all government intervention in the economy as well as statist approaches that seek to abandon a basic market framework.

Measures such as the Pell Grants and the Earned Income Tax Credit (EITC) in the US illustrate the kind of government redistributive programme that works well. Pell Grants, which are awarded to college students from poor families, do not encourage long-term welfare dependency. They end in a semester or two if the student fails to study and flunks out. And they create capital for a lifetime. The EITC subsidizes the income of low-income workers who faithfully carry out their responsibility to work but can find only low-paying jobs that do not provide a living wage. Republican President Ronald Reagan called the EITC "the best anti-poverty, the best pro-family, the best job creation measure to come out of Congress", precisely because it rewarded work and responsibility and worked within the market framework.

Both private and public programmes to provide capital so that the poor have genuine opportunity to earn their own way are absolutely indispensable if today's market economies are to work with even minimal justice. Failure to do that would be like freeing illiterate slaves and then providing them with no land, money or education. [34]

Government intervention: what works and what does not?

We need intensive study of how much and what kind of government intervention promotes both political freedom and economic justice. Clearly the history of communist societies demonstrates that consolidating economic and political power in the same hands brings totalitarianism. We must avoid that kind of centralized power. But it is also clear today that the largest corporations and the elites who control them also wield vast political power. This concentration represents an ever-growing threat to democratic life. Through painstaking analysis and careful experimentation, we must discover how government can work within a basic market framework to empower the poor and restrain those aspects of today's markets that are destructive.

Libertarian views that condemn all government intervention make nonsense of 20th-century economic history. In the US, most elderly people are no longer in poverty precisely because of government-sponsored social security and medicare. A number of anti-poverty measures have failed and need drastic reform. But others — such as Pell Grants — have been very successful.

The lesson of the Asian Tigers is *not* that the market will produce magic if governments will just get out of the way. Governments played a major role in the "economic miracles" of South Korea, Taiwan and many other Asian countries. Michael Todaro, author of one of the most widely used texts on economic development, insists that "public-private cooperation, and not the triumph of free market and laissez-faire economics, is the real lesson of the success stories of South Korea, Taiwan and Singapore."[35]

The South Korean miracle started with government-organized land reform. From 1952 to 1954 the percentage of farmers who owned their own land rather than working as tenants jumped from 50 percent to 94 percent.[36] Something similar happened in Taiwan. The governments of both countries invested heavily in health, education and job training. The result? Their people were ready to use the most recent technologies. The productivity of labour has been growing by 10 percent a year — and half of that growth results from the state's investment in education and technical skills.[37] An activist government was central to the economic growth of South Korea and Taiwan.

Equally important was the way these governments intervened in the economy. They worked with the market rather than against it. They encouraged private enterprise and the growth of exports and refused, over the long haul, to protect the nations' companies from international competition. The right kind of market-friendly government activity is essential.[38]

The contrast between South Korea and Brazil is striking. Both countries have experienced rapid economic growth since 1960. But the South Korean government invested heavily in health care and education for the poor, and the Brazilian government did not. The result? In Brazil, tens of millions of poor people remained stuck in poverty, benefiting very little from the country's growing economy. In South Korea, by contrast, the poorest gained ground significantly (and the economy also grew faster!). The richest fifth of the Korean population have about seven times as much income as the poorest fifth. In Brazil, the ratio is 30 to 1.[39] Harvard economist Amartya Sen describes Brazil's pattern as "unaimed opulence" and South Korea's as "participatory growth." The Korean government's far greater investment in public health and education is a key to this strikingly different outcome.

Even the World Bank insists that "markets in developing countries cannot generally be relied upon to provide people — especially the poorest — with adequate education (especially primary education), health care, nutrition and family planning services". [40]

Governments, the World Bank says, should do less where markets work and more where they don't:

> Above all this means [government] investing in education, health, nutrition, family planning, and poverty alleviation: building social, physical, administrative, regulatory, and legal infrastructure of better quality; mobilizing the resources to finance public expenditures; and providing a stable macroeconomic foundation, without which little can be achieved. Government intervention to protect the environment is necessary for sustainable development. [41]

Growing market economies do not automatically help the poor. The right kind and amount of government activity is also essential if the poor are to benefit from an expanding GNP. Recent history demonstrates that government is an essential partner along with private business if we want just, participatory growth that empowers the poorest.

New measures of social and economic well-being

The Gross Domestic Product (GDP) is a poor measure of economic or social well-being, even though our politicians often use it that way. Is society better off when a huge oil spill costs a billion dollars to clean up? Or when a wealthy person hires expensive lawyers to arrange a complicated divorce? Obviously not. And yet the common (mis)understanding of the GDP would tell us exactly the opposite! In the minds of many, the GDP is our basic measure of economic progress. They think that if the economy is growing, then, presumably, society is improving. This widespread notion is absurd.

To begin with, the GDP only measures economic transactions — that is, activity where money changes hands. It does not count unpaid work in the family or the community at all! If one parent leaves paid employment to stay home to parent children, the GDP actually goes down. If Mom and Dad get a divorce — and therefore pay lawyers, pay realtors to sell one house and buy two others, pay for "professional" child care etc. — GDP goes up! Volunteering to improve one's local community does not count at all.

The GDP also counts many negatives as positive growth. Crime adds to the GDP. More lawyers, police, judges, prisons, plus all kinds of crime-prevention devices all raise the GDP. When TV and home videos replace story-telling by parents and grandparents, the GDP goes up. When cigarette advertising creates addictive smoking, the GDP goes up. Gambling, alcoholism and pornography all have the same result.

Environmental pollution raises the GDP twice! Once when a factory creates products with byproducts that pollute, and again when the nation spends billions to clean up the toxic site.

Obviously we need a better measure of social and economic well-being. The Genuine Progress Indicator (GPI) produced by people in an organization called Redefining Progress offers a good start. [42] Their GPI measures more than 20 factors the GDP ignores.

Parents at home to care for children or grandparents get counted. So does volunteer work in the community. These things raise the GPI.

Destructive things lower the GPI, including expenses that result from crime and any environmental pollution that damages health, agriculture, beaches or our buildings. If people work longer hours for the same pay, that also lowers the GPI. When a private company uses up its nonrenewable resources, that counts as a cost. But when a nation does the same thing to its oil and other minerals, the GDP counts it as a gain. The GPI counts a nation's use of nonrenewable resources in the same way a private business does.

This new, more accurate measure of economic well-being tells an astonishingly different story from that based on the GDP. Using the GDP, one might suppose things have gotten better and better in the US since the early 1950s. But the GPI shows that after some growth through about 1970, things have gotten progressively worse — roughly by 45 percent! What we call progress is to a large extent just correcting past mistakes, borrowing from the future or shifting activity away from the world of the home and community to the realm of the marketplace.

The researchers at Redefining Progress may or may not have all the details right. [43] We need not accept their detailed findings to recognize that they have raised a very basic issue. Indeed, in recent years many people, including the United Nations (see its Human Development Index), the World Bank and most European nations have been working on better ways to measure social and economic growth.[44]

One potentially far-reaching result of this kind of new analysis is that it is beginning to bring environmentalists and social conservatives together. Environmentalists deplore the way an unrestricted market economy destroys the environment. Social conservatives denounce the way that a preoccupation with economic growth demanding ever more consumption destroys the family and communal life.

Both groups, for example, rightly see problems with currently popular "takings" legislation. ("Takings" bills would force taxpayers to reimburse property owners when laws reduce potential income from the unrestricted use of their property.) The conservative preacher and anti-smut crusader Donald Wildmon recently denounced "takings" legislation as the "porn owners' relief measure". Why? Because the taxpayers would, for example, have to compensate the owners of topless bars if government passed any restrictive laws.[45]

The Redefining Progress group has raised some fundamental issues about the nature of "economic growth". But the problem really lies deeper than they indicate. During the 18th century Enlightenment, a human-centred, pseudo-scientific view of reality replaced the historic God-centred view. The autonomous individual replaced God as the source of ethics. The scientific method became the only avenue to truth. Nature, as naturalistic scientist Carl Sagan tells it, is all that exists.

Tragically, this new view abandons the limits of economic growth imposed by historic Christian faith. In a God-centred, biblical worldview, persons, family, and God's good creation matter more than money and unlimited material consumption. The scientific method, however, cannot measure love or joy in the family. But it can measure a growing bank account, larger cars and increasingly sophisticated gadgets. Modern people cast aside the limits imposed on economic life by the biblical truth that Yahweh is Lord even of economics. The result has been a preoccupation with economic growth that is now devastating the family, community life and the environment.

Jesus' question is still relevant: Do we want to worship God and therefore accept God's perspective on everything, including the relative importance of "economic growth", more gadgets and family time? Or do we prefer to absolutize the material world and the things that scientific technology can produce?

Getting a more accurate measure of social and economic well-being via some new Genuine Progress Indicator will not answer that fundamental question. But it will make it easier for us to think about it more carefully if we really want to choose God rather than Mammon.

Redefining the good life

It is idolatrous nonsense to suggest that human fulfilment comes from an ever-increasing supply of material things. Genuine, lasting joy comes from a right relationship with God, neighbour, oneself and the earth. As body-soul beings created for community, we do need significant material resources. But looking for happiness in ever-expanding material wealth is both theologically heretical and environmentally destructive. It also hardens our hearts to the cry of the poor.

We must redefine the good life. We must develop a theology of enough. We must develop models of simpler life-styles, corporate policies that permit people to choose parenting, leisure and community service over maximizing income and profits, and macro-economic policies and advertising practices that discourage overconsumption. Unlimited economic growth is an economic Tower of Babel, not a biblical goal.

The developed world should consume less and pollute less. But there are complications. As MIT economist Lester Thurow points out, given today's economic structures, environmental crusades that reduce growth and advocate greater pollution control may well benefit the middle and upper classes at the expense of the poor. Under current structures, reducing growth may lead to a rise in unemployment, which hits the poor (both here and abroad) harder than the rich. Increased pollution-control equipment may raise the prices of goods needed by the poor. Furthermore, a cleaner environment may well raise the standard of living of the wealthier classes, who retain their jobs and have enough money to get out and enjoy the enhanced environment. [46]

Few economists doubt the validity of this analysis. But that does not mean that we should ignore environmental pollution as we seek to help the poor. Rather, Thurow's warning illuminates the size and complexity of the obstacles that we must overcome.

The pervasive notion that increased consumption leads to greater happiness is at the heart of our dilemma. In fact, even some economists understand that economic growth and rising affluence do not guarantee greater happiness. Economist Richard Easterlin argues that people tend to measure their happiness by how much they consume relative to their neighbours. As all try to get ahead, most tend to rise together, with the result that people are frustrated by their unsuccessful efforts to achieve happiness by getting ahead of the others! Easterlin concludes: "To the outside observer, economic growth appears to be producing an ever more affluent society, but to those involved in the process, affluence will always remain a distant, urgently sought, but never attained goal."[47] Growth occurs, the earth is used and abused — but happiness is still beyond one's grasp.

To Christians this should be no surprise. We should be the first to reject this rat race in which everyone is trying to surpass the other guy. Knowing that material goods are not what brings ultimate happiness, we should be the first to experiment with simpler life-styles. As we reduce our demand for dwindling resources that pollute the environment, we witness to others that happiness is not found primarily in material possessions.

As we move in this direction, however, we need to be alert to Thurow's warning. If, in our advanced state of technology, significant numbers of people consume less, there will be less need for production. Declining demand will signal a decline in the need for workers. Therefore we need long-term structural changes if displaced workers are to find other jobs. Because of the monumental proportions of the changes needed, they must be slow and gradual. Therefore I offer suggestions both for the immediate future and for the more distant future.

In the short run, a simpler life-style lived by Christians will mean more money not being spent on consumer goods. If large numbers of people save rather than spend this income, severe unemployment might ensue. If, however, we donate the income we have saved to Christian agencies promoting development in poor nations, a major reduction in employment is unlikely. Aid recipients will spend the money on goods they need to create wealth and attain an adequate level of material well-being. As they do, the dollars spent on these goods will eventually return to buy things from businesses in industrialized nations. As the developed nations consume less and share more, we will also spur indigenous development in the third world, thus fostering a more just distribution of goods and assets.

As we adopt this short-run approach, Christians all over the world ought to re-examine priorities at a still deeper level. Suppose that by a miracle of God's grace we succeeded in ending the scandal of a world where a billion plus live in grinding poverty while the affluent live like kings. Even if we reached the biblical norm of distributional justice, we would have to ask ourselves the next question: Should we once again pursue the same sort of economic growth we formerly did? The obvious answer is no. The earth's resources are limited, and we dare not destroy the environment.

Christians must seek to redirect the demand for goods and services away from heavy resource usage and environment-damaging goods towards goods and services that make less demand on the earth's carrying capacity. Christians could spend more of their time and money creating vibrant, active Christian churches. Everyone could spend more money on the arts (drama, music, and other creative arts), thus creating an incentive for more people to engage in these activities instead of in the production of more material goods. People could work fewer hours at their jobs, and in their new leisure they could do volunteer work in their community or spend more time with their families or in constructive hobbies.

In the long run, then, sweeping changes will come. Christians, we can hope, will lead the way in redefining the good life by returning to a biblical understanding of what produces joy and happiness.

I am not a pessimist. Continued, wise use of modern technology and market economies can offer new hope to those who are still poor. It is possible, within the framework of market economies, to empower most of the world's people to enjoy a generously adequate level of material well-being without creating environmental catastrophe. But to accomplish that we must make sure that the poor have new access to capital, that government plays its proper role, and that society rediscovers the ancient faith that persons do not live by bread alone.

NOTES

[1] Much of this material is taken (with permission) from chapters 8 and 11 of the 20th anniversary ed. of my *Rich Christians in an Age of Hunger*. First published in 1977 by InterVarsity Press and Paulist, it has appeared in numerous translations and been revised in 1984 (IVP) and 1990 and 1997 (Word).

[2] *Interpretation*, April 1989, pp.156-69. Chapter 4 of the 1997 edition of *Rich Christians* incorporates the key ideas of this essay.

[3] See the helpful distinction of different types of economies today in *Transformation*, July-Sept. 1995, p.18.

[4] Democratic socialism, of course, sought to offer an alternative where politically the democratic rather than the totalitarian political process operated, but the democratic socialist vision, nonetheless, was to be largely centrally planned and state-owned. A different definition of democratic socialism is of course possible: namely a situation where a comprehensive welfare system exists but the economy is largely privately owned and central planning is far less dominating.

[5] Bread for the World, *Hunger 1995: Causes of Hunger*, Washington, DC, Bread for the World Institute, 1995, p.10.

[6] United Nations Development Programme (hereafter UNDP), *Human Development Report 1993*, p.44.

[7] Of the 373 changes in investment rules in developing countries between 1991 and 1994, all but 5 encourage international investment (which comes largely from multinational corporations) (personal memo from Linwood T. Geiger).

[8] See an article by economist Linwood T. Geiger, "Market Activity and Poverty", *Transformation*, July 1995, p.20. This article was prepared for the Third Oxford Conference on Christian Faith and Economics (Agra, 1995).

[9] World Bank, *World Development Report 1995*, p.5. One study covering 1970-90 compared 37 countries where the relative importance of the country's exports was falling with 32 countries whose exports were rising. Real wages grew an average of 3 percent per year in the latter countries and fell in the former. In the first set of countries, the ratio of exports to GNP was falling; in the latter, this ratio was rising (*ibid.*).

[10] Other possible negative factors may also occur. Local elites that work with global corporations to prevent poor workers from developing unions reduces or prevents the benefit of increasing wages. And unnecessary shipping of materials around the world is environmentally foolish.

[11] Paul Samuelson's "factor price equalization theorem", articulated decades ago, has been confirmed repeatedly.

[12] World Bank, *World Development Report 1995*, p.104. The data, however, are not entirely conclusive (and are debated!). The United Nations' *Human Development Report 1993* says: "Three quarters of adjusting countries in Sub-Saharan Africa have suffered declining per capita incomes and in Latin America the declines were at least as bad" (p.45). We must remain open to

further, more extensive data. Obviously, not every kind of privatization is good. See the section entitled "Seven Sins of Privatization" in *ibid*, pp.49-51.

13 UNDP, *Human Development Report 1993*, p.37.

14 Simon Kuznets first proposed the hypothesis of the "Inverted U". See Geiger, "Market Activity and Poverty", p.26.

15 *Ibid.*, pp.27-28.

16 *Ibid.*, p.28. See also Juliet B. Schor, *The Overworked American*, New York, Basic Books, 1992.

17 Lester C. Thurow, *The Failure of Capitalism*, New York, William Morrow, 1996, p.73.

18 David C. Korten, *When Corporations Rule the World*, West Hartford, CN, Kumarian Press, 1995, p.111.

19 Personal communication with Jeff Ballinger of Press for Change, a corporate watchdog group, on 22 May 1996. It is also true that the wages these 18,000 workers earn (around $2.50 per day) are higher than prevailing Indonesian wages.

20 *Time*, 17 June 1996, p.30.

21 Not all cultural change is bad. A small, poor nation with 20 small tribes and 20 different languages and no modern sense of time will be unable to participate in the global economy. Certainly they are welcome to retain their traditional culture, but they should not then blame the rest of the world for their poverty.

22 Quoted in Schor, *The Overworked American*, p.120.

23 Quoted in George F. Will, "The Politics of Soulcraft", *Newsweek*, 13 May 1996, p.82.

24 Korten, *When Corporations Rule the World*, p.152.

25 *Ibid.*, p.158.

26 M. Douglas Meeks, *God the Economist*, Minneapolis, Fortress, 1989, p.39.

27 This is not to say that communist societies did any better. In fact, the environmental destruction in the former Soviet bloc is much worse than in the West.

28 UNDP, *Human Development Report 1993*, p.37.

29 I am using the word "capital" in a broader sense than do most economists, as a shorthand for productive resources.

30 UNDP, *Human Development Report 1992*, p.36. Wealth is defined as domestic savings. The actual figures are much worse than this. The reason? In making these calculations, the UNDP used only averages for each country. If we took the poorest people anywhere in the world, the figures would be worse. The United Nations estimates that the richest 20 percent of the world's persons are at least 150 times richer than the poorest 20 percent. UNDP, *Human Development Report 1992*, p.3.

31 One interesting example is the Central Provident Fund in Singapore (see the *Economist*, 13 January 1996, p.38).

32 "Mothers vs. Mullahs", *Newsweek*, 17 April 1995, p.56.

[33] Quoted from *Transformation*, July 1995, p.8. It should be noted that the statement assumes that this efficiency ratio would remain the same when 200 million micro-loans were made. In practice it would change — and probably fall.

[34] This is precisely what American society did in the 1860s at the time of the civil war.

[35] *Economic Development*, 1994, p.590.

[36] United Nations, *Human Development Report 1993*, p.30.

[37] *Ibid.*, p.38.

[38] The World Bank's *World Development Report 1991*, pp.5-11, has a helpful summary of criteria for market-friendly government activity.

[39] Bread for the World, *Hunger 1995*, p.49. See also Jean Dreze and Amartya Sen, *Hunger and Public Action*, New York, Oxford UP, 1989, p.13.

[40] World Bank, *World Development Report 1991*, p.6.

[41] *Ibid,* p.9. One of the committees from the Third Oxford Conference on Christian Faith and Economics offered an excellent summary of what the market does well and poorly; see sections 3-4 of "The Market Economy", *Transformation*, July 1995, p.12.

[42] See "If the GDP Is Up Why Is America Down?", *Atlantic Monthly*, Oct. 1995, pp.59-78; the organization's address is Redefining Progress, 116 New Montgomery, Suite 209, San Francisco, CA 94105.

[43] Professor Lin Geiger has shared with me some substantial reservations about some of their assumptions.

[44] For example, the UNDP Human Development Index uses statistics on health and education as well as income to measure human development. See *Human Development Report 1992*, pp.12-25.

[45] This section is a revised version of my column in *Prism*, Jan.-Feb. 1996, p.34.

[46] Thurow, *Zero-Sum Society*, New York, Basic Books, 1980, pp.103-7.

[47] Richard A. Easterlin, "Does Money Buy Happiness?", *Public Interest*, no. 3, Winter 1973, 10. See also Martin Bolt and David G. Myers, "Why Do the Rich Feel So Poor?" in *The Human Connection*, Downers Grove, IL, InterVarsity Press, 1984; and Paul L. Wachtel, *The Poverty of Affluence: A Psychological Portrait of the American Way of Life*, New York, Macmillan, 1983.

Five Areas for Jubilee Today

Paul Spray

Jubilee might seem irrelevant today because our economy is so different from the biblical — for example, in size, in complexity, in the importance of market relationships. The sabbath and jubilee provisions are specific to particular circumstances and people. It would be quite wrong to appeal to some kind of biblical authority for applying these rules in different circumstances.

Rather, the question is whether we can uncover an underlying principle that may be relevant to our society, one that has more to say than simply a call to social justice. This is a serious task that must treat the text respectfully, and I am very poorly placed to do so. This Bossey colloquium has demonstrated, for me at least, that the sabbath and jubilee are actually very fertile biblical passages for such reflection.

This article looks at two of the principles that I hope can be legitimately gathered: (1) The jubilee and the sabbath are regular moments that counteract injustices thrown up by the operation of the existing system, and (2) they do so by reference to fundamental values.

The sabbath will recur every seven years, the jubilee every seven times seven. The implication is that the economic system — *any* human economic system — is fallible. The jubilee is not the moment when a perfect system is inaugurated, a new age. In that sense, it is not a utopia. To be sure, the new start is to be as good as possible, not only are slaves to be freed, but also they are to be provided with the resources needed to make a new start. Nevertheless, we should expect it to go wrong. It will be necessary to bring the new system under judgment in seven years' time, to counteract injustices once again, by referring to fundamental values. The message is that we have to subject our economic system to ideas of justice.

Several fundamental values seem to underlie jubilee and the sabbath. One of them, which I focus on here, is the idea of equality — or at least equality of opportunity. There is a further theological question about *why* inequalities should be redressed. Peter Selby, for example, argues that "all the efforts of the ancient equivalent of social policy were directed at ensuring that debt was not a means to exploitation or to depriving others of their freedom for the future."[1] But I have not explored these here.

There is not space to explore the existing economic system, whose workings and effects are the subject of considerable controversy. Furthermore, it is not static — in particular, it is becoming more globally integrated. Nevertheless, it is possible to outline five areas that cry out for action because of failures in the existing system: debt, primary commodity trade, global political institutions, global tax and work. In all these, we can look for *jubilee actions* to redress inequalities of income, wealth or work. I use the term "jubilee actions" in a very loose way, not to imply actions that are the same as in the biblical jubilee, but to identify ones that fulfil the two principles outlined above.

Debt

The most obvious candidate is international debt. It has built up to be an obscenely heavy burden on the poorest countries. A good number cannot possibly hope to pay it back. Other countries (Jamaica is one Christian Aid has been campaigning with) could repay, but only at the cost of deep cuts in public services.[2]

There are three categories of debt: commercial owed to banks, bilateral owed to governments, and multilateral owed to institutions such as the International Monetary Fund (IMF) or the African Development Bank. They need different treatment, but the debt must be considered as a whole; much of the past debt relief effort has been of little value because reducing bilateral debt has freed resources not for the poor but merely to service multilateral debt. The main merit of the current plan for multilateral debt that the IMF and World Bank are considering is that it does contain the principle of looking at all debt and planning an "Exit strategy".[3]

A jubilee action would cancel some or all of the debt owed. The most important point is to get worldwide agreement. There are two practicalities: (1) how to ensure that the benefit flows to the poor, and not to a small ruling elite; and (2), assuming that we believe that some lending is desirable, how to have a the method of debt cancellation that does not put off lenders. [4]

Trade in primary commodities

The majority of Africa's exports are primary commodities — coffee, cocoa, copper and so on. Their prices have been declining dramatically. They will go on declining, both because technological changes are promoting artificial substitutes and making things smaller and also because as people get richer they do not tend to drink a lot more coffee. The World Bank predicts that by the year 2000, commodity prices will be little more than half their 1950 level.

A jubilee action would be to reset the price of primary commodities, raising them or at least stabilizing them. This was attempted in the 1970s, with various commodity agreements where producers agreed amongst themselves to restrict supply, and consumers agreed to fund "buffer stocks". But these arrangements failed, partly because of pressure from northern companies and consumers wanting lower prices, and partly because, in a market, it is in the interests of a cheap producer to break ranks and outsell its competitors. It is difficult to see what can now be done, but it is worth thinking hard about.

If, despite this hard thinking, prices cannot easily be raised, another and more promising jubilee action would be to provide compensation. [5] The economists' solution to falling primary commodity prices is that Africa should diversify into other products. Is there some "jubilee" way that Africa can be helped to diversify?

Political control of the new global economy

The problems of primary commodity trade, and in some ways even the present debt crisis, are the consequences of a familiar world economic system. But the last decade has thrown up new characteristics of the global economy, which demand different kinds of jubilee action. [6]

The world economy has become more integrated as trade and capital flows have grown rapidly. They have been driven first by political decisions to liberalize trade and investment and, secondly, by new telecommunications and computer technology that allows very rapid international financial transactions and flexible production.

One consequence is the increased power of transnational corporations (TNCs). Five hundred of them account for two-thirds of world trade; 40 percent of that two-thirds is within one or other of those companies. Another consequence is that national economies are more vulnerable to economic changes elsewhere in the world, and their governments cannot so readily control their own economic policy. A third consequence is that areas of the world that are unpromising to these corporations (especially Africa) are being left out of the growth — it is not truly a *global* economy.

Counteracting the injustices perpetrated by this new system can be attempted in many ways. My colleague Peter Madden, reviewing globalization, concludes that "there will not be a single, simple solution. We are looking at overlapping, interweaving systems of responsibility and control, just as we have at the national level."[7] Some of the measures needed will indeed be national, protecting local economies and cultures.

Nevertheless, if we agree that a global economic system is here to stay, many jubilee actions would require political decisions at a global level. An example might be the global equivalent of anti-monopoly policy, or enacting basic labour standards as the Organization for Economic Cooperation and Development is now proposing.[8] But no political authority has an overview of the world economy. Establishing such an authority therefore becomes an early first priority, if there are to be effective jubilee actions. The most realistic proposal at present is for a UN Economic Security Council, with powers akin to the existing Security Council.[9]

Global income distribution

Market systems tend to benefit the rich and not the poor. In the last 30 years, the gap between the richest 20 percent and the poorest 20 percent in the world has doubled, from 30 to 1 to over 60 to 1.[10] Most obviously, if the poor do not have assets, they are excluded from most profitable opportunities.

We accept this analysis at a national level and, indeed, do something to redress the problem, to counteract the untoward consequences of the existing system: we have tax systems that redistribute income to those for whom the market does not give a decent income. The European Union (even the British government) accept it, in the idea of regional funds that automatically are made available to poorer regions.

But at the world level, we do not accept this analysis. Instead we have aid, which is seen as charity. Aid should be replaced by a global taxation system, perhaps on global corporations. [11] Whether this could be categorized as a jubilee action is debatable — it is, after all, proposing something that is built-in to the present economic system, rather than a periodic moment of pause and restitution. But it is certainly a nonmarket intervention to correct the injustices of the market.

Work
Our standard picture of the economy will seem laughable to future historians, and explicable only in terms of gender politics. Somewhat less than half of all human work we call productive, measure in money terms, organize through markets, and remunerate with money income. The greater part of work, sometimes called reproductive, is largely performed by women, often in very long hours per day, outside markets, and largely ignored in economic analysis. Putting these two together, the distribution of work and income is grossly unfair.

At the same time, the old pattern of paid work is collapsing in the North. Business studies experts think people will no longer have permanent full-time jobs for a lifetime. [12] In the new global economy, we have become familiar with "jobless growth": increases in economic income without corresponding increases in paid jobs. Keynesian economists have pointed out that successful industrialized countries have created jobs by protecting sectors that are not "efficient" in market terms, such as the private service sector in Japan or the public services sector in Scandinavia. [13] Less successful countries, like the UK, maintain high unemployment together with increasing hours for those in work. The resulting strains are very bad for social cohesion.

Counteracting the set of injustices around work may not best be done by a periodic jubilee action, which would presumably involve redistributing work in some way. A different, more permanent contribution to easing the problem would be to break the link between income and work, and ensure everybody a basic salary, a proposal that has obvious problems. But there should be no doubt that this is a set of injustices thrown up by the way we organize life at present. The extraordinary feature is the way it is invisible to standard economic analysis and discussion. It would help if at least we changed our analysis so that we recognized the importance of all types of work and of their interaction with each other. Then it would be easier to see if an appropriate jubilee action is called for.

NOTES

[1] Peter Selby, "Love in the City", in *Essentials of Christian Community*, D. Ford and D. Stamps, eds, Edinburgh, Clark, 1996.

[2] John Jackson, *Sacrificing the Future*, London, Christian Aid, and Kingston, Jamaica, Social Action Centre, 1995.

[3] In other respects the plan is deeply flawed.

[4] The lenders would have to be compensated, or they would have to believe it is in their long-term interest, or they would have to believe that this jubilee action will not soon be repeated.

[5] A parallel occurred in the negotiations for the most recent round of trade liberalization, the so-called Uruguay Round of the General Agreement on Tariffs and Trade (GATT). It was agreed that if any country lost out by introduction of freer trade in food, that country should receive compensation. The compensation mechanism was not specified, however, and pressure is needed to ensure that it is addressed at the first meeting of the new World Trade Organization, in December 1996.

[6] This phenomenon of "globalization" is explored in Peter Madden, "Economic Globalization", discussion paper for the Church of England Working Party on Faith, Poverty and the Globalization of the Economy, 6 pp., mimeo, Christian Aid, 1995.

[7] *Ibid.*, p.6.

[8] The OECD study "concludes that labour standards must not be left to market forces, and the global community should step in to stop the worst abuses", *Guardian* (London), 21 May 1996.

[9] The proposal is argued in Professor Frances Stewart, *Global Challenges: The Case for a UN Economic and Security Council*, London, Christian Aid, 1995.

[10] United Nations Development Programme, *Human Development Report 1994*. See also World Bank, *World Development Report 1995*: "For the past century rising inequality of incomes has been a dominant trend in the world economy", p.118.

[11] The most-discussed option, the so-called Tobin tax, would be not on TNC profits but on global capital flows. It was originally proposed by a Nobel prizewinner in economics, James Tobin, and taken up by the UNDP *Human Development Report 1994*. It is worth considering, though there are practical difficulties. Christian Aid commissioned a report on it from the London-based Overseas Development Institute, which is summarized in their *ODI Briefing Paper 1996/1* "New Sources of Finance for Development".

[12] For example, Charles Handy, *The Empty Raincoat*, London, Arrow, 1995.

[13] Paul Ormerod, *The Death of Economics*, London, Faber, 1994.

The Year of Jubilee:
A Model for the Churches?

Lukas Vischer

In recent years proposals have repeatedly been made to apply the idea and institution of the biblical year of jubilee to our own time. The suggestion has actually been taken up in certain countries. Churches have sought to use the year of jubilee as a framework for their present-day witness. Recently, in Switzerland, for example, church circles proposed that the 700-year anniversary of the Swiss Confederation (1991) should be celebrated in the perspective of the biblical year of jubilee. [1] Another example was the suggestion of a number of Korean churches to declare 1995 a year of jubilee, and to prepare for it jointly by way of a new commitment to justice. In the background here was the hope that this year might bring about the reunion of the two Koreas. Recently it has been proposed that the World Council of Churches might take the basic principle of the year of jubilee as its model for the 50th anniversary of the WCC, and for the assembly to take place in the jubilee year 1998.

How useful are these suggestions? More precisely, how can we meaningfully apply the biblical injunctions about the year of jubilee, as well as the ideas behind them, to the present time? What problems would arise in the process?

In an attempt to find an answer to these questions, I shall first say something about the Swiss celebrations. The experience gained during those celebrations shows that the transposition of the biblical texts is anything but a simple affair. In order to avoid any misunderstanding, an agreement needs to be reached on the basic idea of the jubilee year and its possible application today.

The Swiss "jubilee year 1991"

The jubilee of the Swiss Confederation

In 1991, the Swiss Confederation celebrated its 700th anniversary. Of course the choice of 1291 as the year in which Switzerland came into being can be questioned. The event that took place in that year concerned only a small part of present-day Switzerland. On August 1, 1291, the inner Swiss territories concluded a protective pact against Austria. Initially, the majority of the cantons making up Switzerland today were not included in this pact. We might say, to be sure, that present-day Switzerland gradually grew out of this original alliance. But we should not forget in this respect that the other areas of Switzerland have centuries of their own history behind them. Fundamentally, therefore, they can identify with the year 1291 only indirectly. The common history of present-day Switzerland began only in later centuries, at the latest with the Napoleonic occupation of the country, and fully with the establishment of the federal confederation in 1848. Nevertheless, there were various reasons for choosing 1291. One reason for making the choice was the confessional division of the country. Events that have occurred in the centuries after the Reformation are all inevitably emotionally loaded. The legends gathered around 1291, especially the William Tell narrative (also immortalized by Friedrich Schiller), were harmless in this respect. On this basis, the young confederation could pass over the conflicts of the past and celebrate its unity.

If the establishment of the confederation had been taken as the occasion for a celebration, the problems of present-day Switzerland would have been much more directly tackled. The opportunity for this will come in 1998, when 150 years will have passed since the foundation of modern Switzerland. It would be an important task to use this occasion as an opportunity to trace once again the history of the confederation, together with its achievements and its failures, and to consider the future in common.

In 1991, however, 1291 was chosen as a jubilee year, and a celebration was held. The population, however, was not in a festive mood. An initial project for a really major festival met with resistance in the cantons in question and was rejected by a plebiscite. Why was this? The reason was certainly the general uncertainty of the Swiss about their own country. What does it mean to be Swiss in the modern world? What is there really to celebrate about the many aspects of present-day Swiss society that have been brought into question?

Church circles then suggested that the jubilee year should be celebrated "along the lines of the scriptural year of jubilee". The "conciliar process of reciprocal commitment (covenant) for justice, peace and integrity of creation" proposed by the World Alliance of Reformed Churches and the World Council of Churches met with a widespread response in Switzerland. This was obviously something to connect with. Perhaps the jubilee year could be the opportunity for renewal as called for by the conciliar process? Perhaps it was possible to make a number of adjustments to the course the country was taking, and to make a small contribution to justice, peace and the integrity of creation? These questions were behind the 1991 jubilee year project.

The conception of the jubilee year

Two biblical themes were to the fore: God's covenant and the year of jubilee as described in Leviticus 25. We in Switzerland thought it was important that we should not merely confine ourselves to a number of recommendations to the government and to parliament but should emphasize the need for an inner renewal of church and nation. The idea of the covenant, which was in constant use in conciliar process circles, seemed appropriate to this design. God has entered into covenant with his people and has maintained it throughout an eventful history. The people have abandoned God, and if they want to live under God's promise, they must return to it.

The meaning of the covenant concept, however, is not so un-equivocal as it seems at first. Whereas the biblical terms *berit* and *diathēkē* emphasize God's initiative and subordinate the human response to it, the terms used in Western languages have another implication. "Foedus", "Bund", "covenant", "alliance" and so on, refer rather to an agreement between equally entitled partners. In general usage, the terms "covenant" and "alliance", for instance, evoke the idea of a human initiative. We conclude an alliance in order to serve God. This notion was also dominant in the conciliar process. We thought it important to query this "activist" interpretation of the covenant. We believed that a real basis for church discourse and action could emerge only if the divine initiative was stressed. We were talking not so much about concluding an alliance but much more about recalling God's covenant anew and responding to God's commitment to us.

The second idea that played a major part in our deliberations was the jubilee year. We based a series of recommendations to contemporary Switzerland on the injunctions in Leviticus 25. They also corresponded to the three key terms "justice", "peace" and "integrity of creation". It is quite evident that the prescriptions of the year of jubilee are not very far removed from this threefold guideline. In the declaration we published for the Swiss jubilee year we said:

> In order to recall in common the covenant that God entered into with humanity, the churches in the ecumenical movement have allied themselves in the cause of justice, peace and preservation of creation. God wants to liberate us for life. We maintain this out of trust in Jesus Christ, who said at the beginning of his public ministry: "The Spirit of the Lord is upon me, because he has anointed me to preach good news to the poor. He has sent me to proclaim release to the captives and recovering of sight to the blind, to set at liberty those who are oppressed, to *proclaim the acceptable year of the Lord*." We propose that Switzerland should celebrate the year 1991 as a year of jubilee in the biblical sense.

The practical recommendations

Three recommendations were made. First, on the occasion of the jubilee, the government should write off the poorest countries' debts to Switzerland. A petition to this end was organized under the slogan "Development requires debt remission." By the jubilee year, 250,000 signatures had been collected in support. In the same year the request was made that the new poverty in Switzerland should be ranked more explicitly among topics requiring political decisions.

Second, government and parliament were urged to introduce an alternative to military service. At that time, conscientious objectors were still punishable and had to serve prison terms.

Finally, we recommended that the consumption of energy in Switzerland should be "subject to an annual reduction of 2 percent". In this connection, we stated that we were prepared to adopt a "simple life-style". A "self-commitment" campaign stressed our seriousness in this respect.

In addition to these practical recommendations, we urged that the jubilee year be a year of reflection, reconciliation and conversion.

The effects of "jubilee year 1991"

The effects of the jubilee year were twofold. The proposal was accepted favourably by many people. It led to a widely ramified discussion. Some of the recommendations met with general approval. Government and parliament accepted the idea of the petition and made available the sum of 700 million Swiss francs for debt clearance and related aims. Since 1991 a solution to the problem of conscientious objection has also emerged.

Otherwise, the effects of the church initiative remained limited. In all honesty, it must be admitted that the two above-mentioned steps forward (especially the introduction of an alternative to military service) on the part of the government and parliament would probably have been taken even without the voice of the churches. Our movement was no more than an intensification of developments that were in the air anyway.

One difficulty was in the twofold attitude of the churches themselves. The group responsible for launching the jubilee year did indeed have the express approval of the Swiss Protestant Church Federation. It soon became evident, however, that official church circles, especially the Swiss bishops' conference, offered only half-hearted support for the initiative. The spirit that had governed the European Ecumenical Assembly at Pentecost 1989 had disappeared relatively quickly. The Roman Catholic Church had distanced itself from the conciliar process for justice, peace and the integrity of creation proposed and conducted by the World Council of Churches. The church leaders in Switzerland began to realize that the concept of the jubilee year meant more than a number of individual recommendations, and that it basically committed them to consequences that went much further than their judgment of the present-day situation led them to think were feasible.

The official state committee for the organization of the jubilee year took hardly any notice of the proposal. Apart from the provision of the 700 million Swiss francs, therefore, the official celebrations as a whole remained extremely conventional. Although there were constant claims that the festivities were not to celebrate the status quo, the profound malaise of the Swiss population scarcely changed. Shortly afterwards the major debates on joining the European Economic Area began. The question of how our society might overcome the major challenges of industrial development — new technologies, competitiveness, unemployment — had the first call on people's attention. The major issues of social responsibility, both at home and internationally, faded increasingly into the background.

Open questions

What do the experiences gained allow us to say about the application of the year of jubilee to the present time? I suggest four considerations for discussion.

Tangible social-ethical solutions or symbolic actions?

The prescriptions of Leviticus 25 are a piece of Jewish legislation. Even if we do not know the extent to which they were ever applied in reality, their intention is clear. They were designed to ensure a just distribution and due cultivation of the land in Israel. The injunctions are contained in a "liturgical" framework. Both the Day of Atonement and especially the sabbath tradition were decisive in this respect. They gave additional weight to the prescriptions. Just distribution and due cultivation of the land were a part of Jewish spirituality.

Is it at all possible to transfer these regulations to our own time? Are the requisite preconditions available? The agricultural economy of Israel has been replaced by a complex industrial society. The liturgical context that gave additional authority to the ordinances has vanished, even in the churches. Today the prescriptions of Leviticus 25 are scarcely more than a text that we may recall in Bible studies but that actually no longer has any roots in the practice of the churches, still less in that of society.

In the publications on the Swiss jubilee year, therefore, we said that something "corresponding" to the scriptural year of jubilee ought to happen in Switzerland. But that would mean that the churches would have to propose solutions today whereby the land throughout the world could be justly distributed and cultivated, and at the same time would have to indicate how these solutions might possibly be put into practice.

In reality, however, something different occurred. A "year of jubilee" was proclaimed. The idea was that a particular effort at a specific time could make possible a new beginning in our world. The jubilee year was now no longer a solution but had become an appeal to people of good will to take at least one step in the right direction. The objectives of the year of jubilee were understood as a utopian social programme that would indeed point the way, but in all probability would not be implemented. The desiderata formulated as "corresponding" to those of the year of jubilee were symbolic steps in the direction of utopian goals but fundamentally so modest that society as a whole was not really affected by them.

Inherent in all attempts to apply the jubilee year to the present time is the danger of transforming a programme that was meant to be realistic legislation into a comprehensive utopian programme. Whatever value utopias may have, such a transformation does not do justice to the biblical text. To be in harmony with the text, we would have to attempt to offer concrete solutions and to practise them within the bounds of the church.

The celebrants of the year of jubilee

The prescriptions in Leviticus were addressed to the people as a whole. It was a matter of ensuring that the people returned to the sources and restored justice in their midst. If the churches proclaim a jubilee year today, its celebrants are a minority set over against society as a whole. Today, the churches are not capable of pointing society in a certain direction. They can remind political authorities of God's commandments. They can stand up for the restoration of justice. But everything depends on the kind of response they get from the public. Possibly their voice will be heard. But in many cases they will be no more than a protest movement with no real influence on the course of things. The difference is not unimportant. The society that is trying to rediscover its due order under God's promise has been replaced by a minority seeking to influence society.

What was legislation in ancient Israel can be no more than an appeal under these altered circumstances.

The acceptable year of the Lord (Luke 4:19)

Certainly, in trying to apply Leviticus 25 nowadays, sufficient thought has not been devoted to asking how the efforts and institution of the year of jubilee are to be understood after Christ. Christians, however, cannot avoid this question. Between the chapter in Leviticus and our present time stands the New Testament. What part did the year of jubilee play in Jesus' own proclamation? He alludes to it in the synagogue at Nazareth at the beginning of his public ministry. He quotes the prophet Isaiah (61:1-2) and thus gives the year of jubilee a messianic emphasis. The biblical law is extended to become a comprehensive vision. It is no longer a matter only of the just distribution and sensible use of land. A perpetual year of grace — "the acceptable year of the Lord" — opens up with the coming of Jesus. God's justice breaks into this world. The lame walk and the blind see. Signs declare emphatically that there are limits to suffering and to repression.

Accordingly, the year of jubilee is placed in a new context. Jesus' disciples wait for the dawning of the ultimate kingdom of God. Is it possible to speak in any way of sabbatical and jubilee years after Christ? Surely the community must first proclaim, "in season and out of season", the coming of the kingdom? Surely every moment must be used to reveal something of God's inspiring presence? To be sure, the coming of God's kingdom also finds expression in precise recommendations, and these certainly include the just distribution and due use of the earth. But now the motivation for advances in this direction is to be found in the coming of the kingdom. In respect to every transposition of the idea of the year of jubilee, we must enquire expressly how the proposed solutions relate to the coming of the kingdom of God.

The kingdom of God is not a utopia but the kingdom of love that manifests itself among us now, in the midst of persistent injustice and suffering.

Can things still be put right?

Finally, we are faced with an urgent question in the present situation. Can we still count on the restoration of justice? Behind the injunction in Leviticus 25 is the expectation that in sabbatical and jubilee years Israel can heal whatever went awry in the everyday life of the intermediate years and decades. The people's sin can be effaced; it is possible to restore the order appropriate to God's commandment. Is this expectation justifiable today? Or have injustice and destruction prevailed to such a degree that the way back to a wholesome world is already blocked? It could indeed be true that adjustments are possible but that there can be no full restoration of the order as God foresaw it for his people.

It is significant that in our pronouncement on the Swiss jubilee year we said the following: "We have no complete, indeed not even a coherent, programme to offer. We do not know how the future order of society will and must look in detail. But we believe that certain steps have to be taken *whatever the circumstances*." Many people felt that this "modesty" was unsatisfactory. What do you want, then? we were asked. What alternatives do you propose?

But there were good reasons for our reticence. It was based on the conviction that humanity is now steering a self-destructive course and that the future can open up only if the thrust of this development is stopped. The time for comprehensive social projects is past. Utopian visions of a just world are so far from the lived reality that they have, quite rightly, lost their capacity to inspire. Before all else, it is a matter of avoiding any further irreparable damage.

The big questions are: How can we really bring about any kind of reversal in this self-destructive world? And if it is no longer possible to bring about any such change, what witness should the churches bear? And is the concept of the jubilee year the appropriate way to find an answer to these questions?

What inspiration does the year of jubilee afford nowadays?

Does all this mean that reference to the year of jubilee necessarily leads us astray? Must we conclude that when preparing for its next assembly, the World Council of Churches would do better to avoid any such reference?

I think, in fact, that any too direct recourse to the idea would create more problems than it would solve. At first sight, the biblical prescriptions seem straightforwardly illuminating and appealing. Accordingly, there is a strong temptation to take them as a motto or, as is sometimes said nowadays, a "source of inspiration". Yet the experience of the Swiss jubilee year shows that the real meaning of the scriptural text vanishes when it is reduced to the level of a utopian programme.

The text, however, is still relevant. It shows us how the land was justly distributed and used at a particular time. It invites us to do something equivalent today. Is it possible, accordingly, for the World Council of Churches to concentrate its efforts on working out realistic solutions to the problem of how the debts of the poor nations can be controlled in the long term as well? The notion of a cancellation of debts was, relatively speaking, the most successful recommendation of the Swiss jubilee year. But in the end this too was no more than a symbolic gesture. We need an analysis that reviews the whole complex of problems and leads to tangible proposals for solutions.

An analysis of this kind must be as accommodating as possible and include the greatest possible number of partners in the discussion. It should neither disappear in a sea of generalizations nor try to address every aspect of present-day injustice but must focus on the single problem of indebtedness. In terms of this one question, it must try to show how to set limits to debt and to the impoverishment and destruction it produces.

NOTE

[1] Schweizerisches Ökumenisches Komitee für Gerechtigkeit, Frieden und die Bewahrung der Schöpfung, *Zum Leben befreien: Das Jubiläumsjahr als Chance* (Liberation for life: The possibilities of the jubilee year), Bern, 1990.

Economics of the Jubilee

Norman Solomon

As religious people, we do not identify progress with the increased provision of material goods and services. Moreover, quite apart from religion, it is evident that human happiness and contentment do not vary quantitatively in direct proportion to wealth. Nevertheless, our religions all teach us to look after the poor, to heal the sick, to provide food and shelter for those in need, to educate and to pursue justice. All of these demand material as well as personal resources, so that even from a religious point of view, we are justified in regarding the growth of wealth and material resources, with their equitable distribution, as a major element in human progress towards the kind of world we believe God wants us to partner with him in making.

Yet progress is marred by the inequitable distribution of wealth. For instance, recent estimates claim that the United States has a per capita income of $24,700, and Burkina Faso of $326. Even these figures conceal gross inequities within each of those countries; many individuals in the United States suffer greater economic privation than some individuals in Burkina Faso.

The result is social and economic injustice amongst and within nations, and the over-exploitation and destruction of natural resources. Third-world debt is one of the most worrisome symptoms of the disease; the disappearance of the rain forests and of large numbers of plant and animal species another.

What is the disease that leads to such deplorable results? What are the remedies to heal it?

The Bible, the jubilee, and third-world debt

If the scale of our problem is unprecedented, the root problem itself is not. A similar range of issues was addressed by the jubilee and sabbatical year regulations in Leviticus 25. These regulations, which are a summation and culmination of the Code of Holiness, ordain that land should return to its hereditary smallholders, who themselves hold it only on trust from God; wealth is not to be concentrated in the hands of a few. Further laws demand that slaves go free, that debts are remitted and that the land "rests" and recovers from its exploitation.

We do not know whether the Levitical regulations were ever fully implemented. Perhaps they represent an ideal programme that awaits fulfilment in the days of the Messiah. It would in any case be naive to apply to the contemporary global situation rules that were addressed to one particular society in the first millennium BCE. Yet with careful, contextual reading, it may prove possible to extract certain basic principles on which we can build an approach to modern problems.

Even within the rabbinic tradition, where biblical commandments are normally taken in a practical, though not necessarily literal, sense, the jubilee regulations are relegated to the allegedly glorious days of the Davidic kingdom that was and to the still more glorious days of the Messiah who is to come, while the sabbatical year regulations are applied only partially, one of the applicable parts significantly being the cancellation of debts. This reluctance to put the rules into practice is a recognition that they are fully relevant only within the idealized society of Israel as envisaged in Leviticus. In other lands and times, we may derive inspiration and learn lessons from them but must attend carefully to the specific needs of our own situation.

Several interesting assumptions underlie the legislation in Leviticus and must be borne in mind when we try to apply its lessons. One assumption is that population remains stable. If population increases, or even if population increases in some tribal areas and declines in others, the system of land distribution breaks down. On a grand scale, the decline of the Carolingian empire can be attributed to the simple fact that Charlemagne had too many descendants, each of whom claimed the inheritance. Leviticus's idealized picture of parcels of land allotted in the days of Joshua being enjoyed in perpetuity by the families to whom they had been granted depends on each of those families remaining very much the same size in perpetuity — not a likely situation.

Another assumption is that things will go wrong if left alone. This is probably the most important single lesson we can derive from Leviticus. We should always assume that even if we set up the best system of rules we can devise, things will go wrong. People will learn to "beat the system"; they will start to exploit one another, and some will seize the others' territory and amass wealth whilst others will get poor. So we must frame additional laws to put everything right every now and then, say every 7 years, with a major clean-up once in 50 years, like the sabbatical and jubilee years.

A third assumption is that slavery will continue to exist, both the enslavement of one Israelite by another and the enslavement of the heathen from the surrounding, or displaced, nations. Let us feel encouraged that in this respect at least we have made real progress. Pockets of slavery do persist in the world, and we must not close our eyes to them. When we refer to indebted third-world nations as "enslaved" to the rich nations, our rightful compassion should not be allowed to obscure the simple and blessed fact that bonded slavery, accepted as a universal norm in pre-modern times, has almost disappeared; we trivialize the evil of slavery if, like Marx, we refer to underpaid employees as wage slaves.

A fourth point is that Leviticus, in instituting the cancellation of debt at the end of each seven-year period, clearly has in mind accumulated private debt, in an agrarian, pre-industrial society. Is this concept equally applicable to commercial borrowing in a highly developed industrial society, or to the international financing of state economies? And if it is not equally applicable, is there perhaps some analogous debt remission that could be implemented in certain circumstances?

It is interesting that *yovel* (jubilee) and *shemittah* (sabbatical year) between them address the four major issues that confront us now in dealing with third-world debt, namely social injustice in the distribution of wealth, lack of work opportunities, environmental issues, and the stability of population as reflected in the sustained relationship between people and land.

Answers to the debt problem

From July 1 to 22, 1944, at Bretton Woods in New Hampshire, USA, 44 nations met at the United Nations Monetary and Financial Conference in order to plan currency stabilization and credit in the post-war economic order. They set up the International Monetary Fund (IMF) to provide short-term credit for the world economy, and also the International Bank for Reconstruction and Development, more familiarly known as the World Bank, to provide long-term credit. These organizations have remained, but the informal arrangement made at Bretton Woods to maintain more or less stable exchange rates between currencies was broken apart by speculative pressures in the aftermath of the oil price rises of 1973.

The IMF and the World Bank not unreasonably expect people who borrow money from them to pay it back, and with interest. If it has not been wisely invested by the borrower, the borrower may be unable to pay back or even to maintain interest payments. This is the situation of many third-world countries, with regard to both loans from the IMF and World Bank and loans from specific countries or banks.

It is in the borrower's interest, as well as the lender's, to repay debts, since if borrowers do not repay, their credit rating will suffer and they will find it difficult to borrow again. What can third-world countries do to fulfil their obligations? The sort of measures recommended by the IMF and economists include:

1. Devalue and export.
2. Raise local interest rates to depress consumption.
3. Lift trade barriers.
4. Take anti-inflationary measures (e.g., cut government spending).
5. Privatize national assets.
6. Make more effective use of aid (e.g., by encouraging internal enterprise within free markets rather than dependence on state activity.

Some of these measures might well help to reduce national debt. The problem is that the people who can least afford it are the ones who will suffer most in the short run if, for instance, their currency is devalued so that their wages and buying power are effectively reduced, and if their government cuts expenditure on education and welfare. Education cuts further weaken the country's longer-term prospects for economic prosperity, since people are unable to acquire the necessary skills for management, production and marketing.

Wouldn't it be better if the debts could be rescheduled or even cancelled? Rescheduling, now common practice, is sometimes successful, but it may also simply prolong the agony, especially as the IMF or other creditors will insist on stringent conditions such as those just listed.

Statistics

One of the most frustrating aspects of the third-world debt problem is that the world could indeed afford to cancel debts if it would serve a lasting, useful purpose. Take the following three cases:

— In 1995 the top ten Japanese banks wrote off Y6.2 trillion ($64 billion) of bad loans. The banks survived.

— Mexico was bailed out in 1995 by a "mere" $40 billion from the US and the IMF.

— Multilateral and bilateral banks lent $75-85 billion to African countries between 1985 and 1995.

Evidently, if the sum written off by Japanese banks alone in 1995 is almost as much as the total loaned to African governments in the whole of the previous decade, we are dealing with sums that the "rich" nations could relinquish without lasting harm.

If it is not because they cannot afford it, there must be other reasons why international banks and agencies are so reluctant to cancel outright the debts of third-world nations.

Cancel the debts?

Leviticus requires that debts be cancelled in the seventh year. Would a periodic cancellation of international debt work for the third world?

The problem is that in an economic system that depends heavily on the availability of credit, no one will want to lend if it is uncertain whether the debt will be repaid or interest payments will continue. Without credit, commerce is inhibited; barter is not an adequate substitute. The point was well understood by Hillel, two thousand years ago, when he circumvented the biblical cancellation of debt in the seventh year by the institution of the *prosbul*, explicitly in order "that the door be not shut before borrowers". Hillel moreover limited the *prosbul* to debts placed in the hands of the courts, thereby ensuring that this legal device could not be abused for extortion. (On the *prosbul*, see the essays by Klenicki and Jospe.)

An alternative to straight debt cancellation might be to devise some procedure of national bankruptcy, that is, to apply to insolvent nations the sort of laws that apply to insolvent businesses. The managers are sacked, and a receiver takes over the business, settling outstanding claims and seeking if possible to rescue the business in "rationalized" form. But the political implications of such a procedure for nations are unacceptable. The "managers" are the constitutionally established governments, in many cases democratically elected governments. No outside agency could be allowed to displace the legitimate government.

The question of the extent to which international bodies (governmental or nongovernmental agencies, or businesses) ought to interfere in national policies has led to some of the most difficult ethical dilemmas in international commerce. The present government of Nigeria, for instance, is widely perceived to be authoritarian and oppressive; its policies, it is safe to assume, would not meet with the approval of the board of Shell. Should Shell therefore renege on its existing contracts in Nigeria? Should it further undermine the country's economy and cause additional hardship to its poor by refusing to deal with Nigerian oil? Similar problems confronted businesses in pre-apartheid South Africa, and it is still unclear whether the moral high ground lay with those companies who pulled out or with those who remained in South Africa and used what leverage they could to work for greater racial justice.

Protectionist policies

One way to help third-world countries would be by international agreements for preferential trade. Such countries might be permitted individually or in groups to impose discriminatory tariffs or embargoes on goods imported from rich countries; at the same time, their own goods would be guaranteed tariff-free markets in rich countries.

To what extent openly protectionist policies of this nature would be acceptable to the international community is open to debate. But it does seem unjust that at the present time it is, on the whole, groups of rich countries, such as the European Union or the Association of Southeast Asian Nations, that engage in collective protectionism of this type by establishing so-called free trade areas. It is difficult to see how collective European or Southeast Asian practice can be reconciled with, for instance, the aims and policies of the Geneva-based World Trade Organization (WTO), founded in 1993 by the Final Act, which concluded the Uruguay Round of multilateral negotiations under the General Agreement on Tariffs and Trade (GATT), which it supersedes. One person's free trade is another person's tariff barrier.

It is also necessary to examine honestly, with due consideration for the interests of poorer countries, the distortions of free trade that are routinely practised in rich as well as poor countries, in so-called free-enterprise economies, in the attempt to secure national competitive advantages. These include "hidden" subsidies such as preferential tax regimes, export loans and exemption from social legislation, which confer economic advantages on selected national industries and thereby grossly distort the free operation of the international market.

Every subsidy is paid for by somebody. We have to make sure that it is the rich who subsidize the poor, not the poor who subsidize the rich.

Education

Appropriate education is a priority for any nation to create and sustain the economic base necessary to support what the United Nations' Universal Declaration of Human Rights acknowledges as the legitimate rights of all people to

> life, liberty, and security of person; to freedom from arbitrary arrest; to a fair trial; to be presumed innocent until proved guilty; to freedom from interference with the privacy of one's home and correspondence; to freedom of movement and residence; to asylum, nationality, and ownership of property; to freedom of thought, conscience, religion, opinion, and expression; to association, peaceful assembly, and participation in government; to social security, work, rest, and a standard of living adequate for health and well-being; to education; and to participation in the social life of one's community.

None of these rights comes cheap.

By saying that appropriate education is a priority, we imply that in the allocation of resources within a nation, education must rank high. How does any government decide how much of its budget to allocate to education, to welfare, or to defence? If such decisions are difficult for rich nations, they are deeply agonizing for poor ones. It is tempting to cut education, since the damage is not immediately apparent. No one is physically injured or hungry as a direct effect of lack of education. The damage is indirect, long-term, as the basis for future success is eroded.

Two sorts of education are vital for economic success, the technical and the moral/cultural. Technical education includes both skill training appropriate to the technological development and economic resources of the country, as well as management techniques to ensure that the skills are efficiently used in service or manufacture and that the end products are effectively marketed.

Moral and cultural education, in which religion has a part, must cultivate honesty and a work ethic based on a sense of responsibility to family, work associates (employer and employee), society and the environment.

Religions regard greed, envy and ambition as vices. However, some means must be found to harness these natural tendencies to productivity whilst moderating their less pleasant aspects. A wise story in the Talmud relates how the Men of the Great Synod prayed for the *yester hara* (evil tendency) to be removed from people. Their prayer was granted, but people then ceased cultivating crops and raising families; they had to pray again, this time that the *yester hara* be partially restored.

Corruption may well be the greatest single reason that international funds are locally diverted to ends other than those for which they were loaned, for instance to enrich and aggrandize governments, administrators and middlemen. Religion surely has an important part to play in moulding public culture to abhor corruption.

Structures of sin

Some liberation theologians have expressed a wish to "change the system" because it is "a structure of sin". But is "structure of sin" a helpful concept? Such a structure is not a particular type of socio-economic system, defined in socio-economic terms, but a socio-economic system in which people are motivated by greed, lust and sinful stimuli generally. This is a very confusing way to categorize socio-economic systems. People living under any known socio-economic system may individually and in specific instances act either through altruistic or through selfish motives, but these are characteristics of people, not of socio-economic systems per se.

What seems to underlie the concept is the Marxist idea that the nature of the capitalist system was such that capitalists were bound to exploit labour, hence greed was actually built into the system; in a classless, socialist society this would not happen. However, history offers no evidence that socialist societies are any more free from greed, envy, corruption and other human evils than are capitalist societies.

No one has designed a sin-proof system. The church itself (I speak here not of a specific church, but of the "establishments" of all religions), viewed as a social structure, is not claimed to be sin-proof.

There are three principal dangers in calling for radical revision of the system when one cannot say what is to be put in its place and how. First, such a call destabilizes society, thus providing opportunity for the strong-armed and the unscrupulous (of the Left or of the Right) to take charge. Second, it distracts people from constructive criticism of the existing system. Third, the absence of a clearly formulated alternative generates confusion and false hopes.

There may be some difference of opinion between Jews and Augustinian Christians as to whether humankind is inherently evil (carries a burden of sin from Adam), but there is no disagreement that humanity has a considerable propensity to evil. One need only turn to Freudian and subsequent depth psychology for confirmation.

Some "systems" lend themselves to particular types of evil. A system might depend on slavery (in the literal, old-fashioned though not yet obsolete sense rather than the metaphorical "wage-slave" sense of the Marxists). It is interesting that the Bible (and indeed the church, until recently) did not oppose the "system" of slavery, though it certainly modified it and sought to ameliorate its harshness; the actual abolition of slavery was the achievement of modern Western industrialized society, on the basis of an ideology that combined Enlightenment ideas with highly selective religious themes.

The way ahead lies not in the revolutionary substitution of novel socio-economic systems for the present ones but in the difficult and painstaking evolutionary process of curbing abuses that arise within the system. Moralists and preachers have a dual role in this process. They must persuade individuals to act in an upright and moral fashion, explaining how traditional values can be upheld in a modern society. They must also urge legislators to enshrine appropriate values in their laws. This point was well appreciated even by Adam Smith, the great apostle of the free market.

Can the classical debates of economics be settled on a genuinely theological basis? Amongst both Jews and Christians there have been thinkers who would maintain that socialism is the true expression of their faith, and also thinkers diametrically opposed to this view, to whom only a free-enterprise system harmonizes with the values taught by their faith. On the socialist side, compare the liberationist Mexican and former Jesuit José Porfirio Miranda [1] with the writings of the early religious socialist Zionists, who were equally convinced that socialism was the only just system and therefore what their religion was all about.

Julio de Santa Ana, in an impassioned essay on "How the Rich Nations Came to Be Rich" remarks how, "during the sixties, hardly anyone spoke about the situation of the poor. Poverty seemed simply something that was inevitably about to be eradicated." The rich nations were about to help the developing nations to become rich themselves. Such hopes, however, proved illusory. Santa Ana explains that the poor nations remained poor because the rich nations used mercantile means to extract surplus value from them. He seems to think that this is inevitable: "So we have to say that *development and underdevelopment are two faces of the same coin*" (his emphasis). [2]

Santa Ana has every right to be passionate, as he has before him the memory of the exploitation of the native Americans by the conquistadores, and the reality of present-day poverty. But one must be careful in suggesting comparisons. The conquistadores quite openly set out to plunder, conquer and take over the lands of the Americas for themselves, and with some honourable exceptions, they were unconcerned with the welfare and culture of the conquered. But the nations who assembled at Bretton Woods in 1944 to set up a new world economic order had already, by and large, rejected exploitative imperialism, even though paternalistic attitudes persisted. The World Bank and the IMF may have failed, as Santa Ana claims, to halt the growth of poverty in Brazil and other countries, but there is no doubt that whatever their profit motives and their errors of economic judgment, they have also had the consistent aim of stimulating the third-world economies in which they have invested.

Santa Ana insists that the cause of persistent poverty in third-world countries lies in the present "economic order". I disagree strongly with this assertion and believe that the causes of persistent poverty in Brazil and other countries lie elsewhere — after all, countries such as South Korea have successfully evolved from underdeveloped to developed under comparable external conditions, and there is some reason to believe that Brazil has begun to do likewise. J. K. Galbraith has exposed the lack of clear relationship between external conditions, including the availability of natural resources, and economic development. [3] The reasons why the rich nations failed in their intention of rescuing the underdeveloped nations from poverty can be ascertained only by careful economic argument and analysis.

False utopianism

Judgments in politics, economics and other technical subjects must be grounded in the special knowledge of those subjects. Theology may lay down broad aims — help the poor, seek peace, cease exploitation — but these aims must be implemented through awareness of the "facts on the ground" and the increasing knowledge available to us in the social and natural sciences.

We must be on our guard against any form of "utopian heresy". Ultimately, the success of any social or economic system depends not only on its draughtsmanship but on the efficiency and corruptibility of those who operate it. Unfortunately, no one knows how to draft the utopian economic system. If the new order cannot yet be described, what basis is there for the critique of present economic practice, other than that it results in deprivation for many? All "men and women of good will" agree that we ought to help the poor and that in economic (though not judicial) matters they should have some form of "preferential option". If theology gets us no further than that, it is superfluous. What we really need to know is how to combine effective wealth creation with just distribution, and this demands the specialized knowledge of economists, sociologists and politicians.

Other than in extreme circumstances, evolution is better than revolution, pragmatism superior to doctrinaire ideology.

Population

One major factor responsible for poverty is the inability to increase resources in step with population. As Malthus pointed out, resources tend to grow arithmetically, population exponentially. At the planetary level, moreover, there are limits to growth. One can no longer export excess population as the industrialized nations did from the 16th century onwards, building empires. With present technology, it would be far too expensive to create suitable habitats elsewhere in the solar system and to transport volunteers there in sufficient number to make a significant difference to earth's overcrowding.

Consider Brazil. The population of Brazil was 53.4 million in 1950 and 144.4 million in 1988, an average growth rate of 2.65 percent per annum. The estimated population for 1993 was 156.6

million, a fall in growth rate to 1.64 percent per annum. Based on the earlier figure, a population of around 157 million in 1993 would reach a billion by 2064, and five billion (close to the present world population) by 2126. Based on the later growth-rate figure, a population of around 157 million in 1993 would not reach a billion until 2107, and five billion until 2206.

Such statistics suggest that Malthus rather than Marx points the way forward. The church does not permit Catholics actively and openly to promote birth control in the barrios, but this does not alter the fact that population control is a prerequisite for economic improvement and long-term stability.

There is no way that any country can indefinitely support a population that grows by 1.64 percent per year, let alone by 2.65 percent. We are already witnessing precisely the type of social and environmental breakdowns that population experts have warned about for decades. It is surely no coincidence that the Rwanda conflict erupted in a country that has seen its population double every 16 years, one of the world's fastest growth rates.

Of course the population of Brazil will not actually reach five billion by 2206. Something will happen. War? Starvation? Disease? Shall we leave it to AIDS to decimate the population? Surely planned birth control is preferable to any of these.

Emigration on any useful scale is impossible. Movement within the country does not work either. Rondônia sounded like a good idea, but it rapidly exceeded its capacity in absorbing about a million people, a mere third of the annual population increase, and even this has been achieved only by widespread destruction of forest habitat and Indian tribal life.

Deforestation and desertification have driven people to the cities, destroying the city environment. In the neighbourhood of Rio, 400 shanty towns have come into being, and there is no way the city can cope. Millions of children are said to die every year from causes related to malnutrition.

Yet for the long term — not just for aesthetic or even moral reasons, but for the plain economics of survival — it is imperative that the environment be protected now, before it is too late. This can be accomplished only by government in cooperation with international agencies; it demands legislation, international cooperation and effective administration. And control of population growth.

Brazil is sometimes referred to as a middle-income country, for although its per capita income is far below that of Japan or the United States, it is higher than that of India or China. Brazilian Joelmir Beting calls his country Belindia — thirty million or so enjoy a Belgian standard of living, maybe the same number just get by, but the rest are as seriously deprived as the poor of India. The statistic does at least demonstrate that there is sufficient wealth in the country to raise the standard of living of the poorest significantly, even at the present population level. How can the redistribution of wealth be accomplished? More, how can it be accomplished in such a manner that the redistribution will not undermine the wealth-creation capabilities of the wealthier part of society? It is a fallacy to think that taking the wealth from those who have it and distributing it among those who do not, even if politically possible, would produce an economically viable solution. It would be more likely merely to destroy the wealth-producing ability of the country. Redistribution, presumably through public expenditure financed by taxation, has to be a more careful and finely tuned process, and once again we come up against the problem of a population exploding so rapidly that it is not administratively feasible to create the necessary infrastructures to channel wealth in these ways. For instance, with a workforce growing even faster than the general population, industry cannot be organized to create sufficient new jobs at a fast enough rate.

Mistakes have indeed been made in the past. With hindsight, perhaps Brasilia ought never to have been built, and various other prestige projects should not have been accorded priority over improving the infrastructure. Mistakes will be made in the future. We must learn from them, and not justify ourselves by imputing malevolence to those who took the risks and made the mistakes.

Santa Ana concludes his essay with the dramatic statement that "in reality, it is not the rich who are 'owed'. They have seized the value produced by the poor. It is really the poor to whom repayment is due."[4]

Not so. First, the rich have not "seized" anything. They have lent their wealth, and indeed there is a moral preference for lending with dignity over giving outright (see Lev. 25:35, but note that the next verse bans the taking of interest!). No one knew that interest rates would escalate, or that an OPEC cartel would quadruple the price of oil out of political spite in 1967. The general idea, which worked in other countries, for instance South Korea, was to enable under-developed countries to develop their own resources. If it didn't work, it was not on account of malevolence on the part of the IMF or even because of "the system". There was corruption, and honest mistakes were made as well, such as spending money on prestige rather than "seed" projects. The answer is not to drum up hatred against the helping hand but to eradicate corruption and invest wisely.

Santa Ana's words "this international usury is designed to consoli-date the security of the rich" are tendentious;[5] the payment of interest is designed to facilitate borrowing and hence commerce, and the nonpayment of debt simply leads to the non-availability of credit. Recently, where rescheduling has not enabled repayment, interna-tional banks have been writing off a large part of the debt. But this is a double-edged sword, as we saw earlier. The poor suffer, as well as the rich, if credit is withheld.

Conclusion

No permanent remedy, this side of eschatology, is available to heal the sickness of poverty and the maldistribution of wealth — "for the poor shall never cease out of the land" (Deut. 15:11 KJV). To believe in such a remedy is a utopian fallacy.

However, much can be and should be done to alleviate hardship both internationally and locally, even if the solutions are partial and impermanent. On this limited basis, "there shall be no poor amongst you" (Deut. 15:4 KJV).

There should be ongoing dialectic with scripture, not least with the sabbatical and jubilee passages. This is of value, not because it provides us with valid rules to organize the present world economy, but because when we enter into the dialogue of Israel with God about the people and land, wealth and poverty, we discover the universal values for which the Torah of ancient Israel is a paradigm.

We must engage in dialogue with economists, sociologists, educa-tors, and experts in natural sciences, including environmental studies. This will help to reveal the particular ways in which the universal values can be most effectively pursued in our time. Our approach must never be doctrinaire, but pragmatic, heuristic, with constant feedback and monitoring of the system, and a readiness to start again if things go wrong, as they certainly will from time to time. The Levitical laws

on economic matters can be summed up in a way that shows their relevance to contemporary society:
— Aim at the fair distribution of wealth, work and credit (numerous biblical laws on the care of those in need and the "marginalized"). *Global extension: let the rich nations assist the poor ones. Provide credit for finance with favourable terms.*
— Provide opportunity for remission of excessive debt (sabbatical release). *Global extension: reschedule and remit debt.*
— Do not over-exploit the land (let it "rest" every seven years). *Global extension: conserve the environment.*
— Preserve the bond between people and land (land reverts to original owner in 50 years). *Global extension: traditional land rights should be respected as far as compatible with economic realities; as fewer people work on the land, our ultimate dependence on its resources and our love for it must find fresh ways of expression.*
— The land is held as a trust from God ("for the land is mine; for ye are strangers and sojourners with me", Lev. 25:23 KJV). *Global extension: the planet is held as a trust from God.*
— Periodically when things go wrong, as they inevitably will in the course of time, joyfully "overhaul" the system (jubilee "year of freedom"). *Global extension: some will enrich themselves at the expense of others, some will be placed under the domination of others. Be ready from time to time to make the necessary adjustments to bring freedom to all, in joy, peace and common humanity.*

• The author wishes to record his debt to Prof. Leonard Minkes for a number of valuable suggestions.

NOTES

[1] For example, see J. P. Miranda, *Marx and the Bible: A Critique of the Philosophy of Oppression*, Maryknoll, NY, Orbis, 1974.
[2] Julio de Santa Ana, "How the Rich Nations Came to be Rich", in *Option for the Poor: Challenge to the Rich Countries*, L. Boff and V. Elizondo, eds, *Concilium*, no. 187, Edinburgh, T. & T. Clark, 1986, pp.3,5.
[3] John Kenneth Galbraith, *The Nature of Mass Poverty*, Cambridge, Harvard UP, 1979.
[4] Santa Ana, "Rich Nations", p.15.
[5] *Ibid.*

Jewish Farmers
and the Sabbatical Year

Yehuda Feliks

The Bible, in Leviticus 25, tells us that the seventh year, known in Hebrew as *sheviit*, which is also referred to as the year of *shemittah*, meaning "abandonment", is to be treated as a sabbatical year for the land. My researches into the subject have led me to two basic conclusions. First, agriculture in the land of Israel produced crops sufficient to feed the large population thanks to the industrious efforts of the farmer working small plots of land intensively on his own, or occasionally with hired labour (but not slaves). The link connecting the farmer with the inheritance of his forefathers was very strong indeed, as instanced by Naboth of Jezreel, who refused to sell his land to Ahab or even exchange it for another plot. The Jewish farmer was interested in farming. He was culturally at a much higher level than the farmers of other countries, who were in general primitive and conservative (farm work was generally done by slaves) and afraid of any innovation. The Jewish farmer was always willing to accept agro-technical innovations and to introduce new species. He would hand down the great expertise that he acquired to his descendants, from generation to generation.

Second, the *shemittah*, (the sabbatical, or seventh, year) was in practice observed during the period of the second temple, the Mishnah and the Talmud. Our literature bears evidence that it was not observed during the period of the first temple. The Torah issues a warning that non-observance would lead to exile: "Then the land will be recompensed for its sabbaths, all the years of desolation while you are in the country of your enemies... all (the time) that it did not rest on your sabbaticals when you were living on it" (Lev. 26:34-35). It was pointed out by Jeremiah (29:10 and quoted in 2 Chron. 36:21) that this was the 70 years of exile in Babylon.

Some researchers consider that in Mishnaic and Talmudic times there was a decline in the observance of the laws of the seventh year, but my research has proved that the basic laws were observed during this period and technical solutions were found to enable the observance to continue. The development of the economy at the time did not allow them to observe the law of remission of debts associated with the seventh year (Deut. 15:1-3), and Hillel the Elder (first century BCE) instituted the *prosbul*, a document that the creditor hands to the court before the seventh year begins, in which he details the debts that he intends to claim after the end of the seventh year. The court then claims these debts on his behalf; he himself does not actually claim them (Mishnah, Sheviit 10). This institution was created following a general refusal to lend money out of fear that the debt would be cancelled by the seventh year.

In order to strengthen observance of the seventh year, the rabbis added "defences" — stricter laws, including a ban on eating aftergrowths (crops that grow of their own accord) and a ban on ploughing in the summer preceding the seventh year. These bans did not withstand the test of practical implementation. The second ban was removed completely by Rabban Gamaliel the son of Rabbi Judah the President (editor of the Mishnah). The ban on eating aftergrowths was reduced so that the practical effect of this ban was almost nil.

The seventh year presented the Jewish farmer with professional and ecological challenges, which forced him to develop special means of keeping his farm going while abstaining from forbidden work in the seventh year. We can illustrate this with two basic agricultural activities: ploughing and manuring.

The Torah bans absolutely only two types of activity: sowing and pruning. "But on the seventh year the land is to have a year of resting — you are not to sow your land, and you are not to prune your vineyard" (Lev. 25:4). It then continues: "You are not to reap the aftergrowth of your harvest, and you are not to pick the unpruned of your vineyard, the land is to have a year of resting. But you can have the 'sabbath' of the land for yourselves to eat, for you, your male and female slave, and for your employee... who lives with you; and your domestic animals, and the wild animals on your land, will have all its produce to eat" (vv. 5-7).

The rabbis interpreted this passage to mean that reaping in the usual manner is forbidden, and the owner of the land must declare the produce ownerless, so that anyone who wishes may take it. Presumably not everyone did this, and at the time of Rabbi Gamaliel of Yavneh a severe decree was imposed, forbidding anyone from eating that which grew of itself. This decree was found in practice to be too difficult to implement, so Rabbi Simon bar Yohai permitted all aftergrowths except cabbage. Furthermore, other methods of renouncing ownership of aftergrowths were introduced such that even the owner of the land was able to benefit from them.

While the Torah did not specify any ban on ploughing on the seventh year, the rabbis included the ban on ploughing in the words "and the land will rest a sabbath to G-d" (Lev. 25:4).

This decree, intended primarily to prevent the farmer from preparing his land for sowing on the seventh year, lost its meaning because the Jews were very particular about not sowing on the seventh year, so that the ban on ploughing was not enforced. In particular, when the Roman authorities increased the burden of taxation during the third century CE and were not prepared to waive the tax on seventh-year produce, according to the Jerusalem Talmud the rabbis permitted "fallow ploughing" to prevent the land from being overgrown with weeds and to ensure good produce the following year. According to the Babylonian Talmud, Rabbi Jannai permitted even sowing ("Go out and sow on the seventh year on account of the tax"). The former version appears to reflect the authentic tradition.

Fallow ploughing (i.e., ploughing without sowing) proved itself on the seventh year as on other years, such that the farmer used to sow only half of his land each year, leaving the rest fallow but ploughing it up to seven times. This prevented the land being spoilt by weeds and at the same time improved the structure of the soil. Ploughing reduced evaporation of the moisture in the soil, so that rainwater would be stored there in the fallow year ready for the following year. Then, even if the rainfall was low, it would be augmented by the water already in the soil, ensuring a good crop. In practice, in most years drought was prevented, and a field that had been left fallow the previous year would produce double the crop produced by those that had not. The Jewish farmer thus obtained crops many times larger than farmers in other countries, and the size of their crops received praise even from the Roman agricultural writers, such as Pliny and Columella.

As I explained, ploughing was allowed in the seventh year because the Torah explicitly forbade only sowing and pruning. Initially the rabbis banned ploughing through their interpretation of the resting of the land but gradually permitted ploughing that was not for the purpose of sowing on the seventh year. Here I must stress that in the second-temple, Mishnaic and Talmudic periods the ban on sowing in the seventh year was rigorously observed. The Torah had already pointed out that in the event of an exile "the land would be required for its sabbaths" (Lev. 26:43, see 2 Chron. 36:21), and after the return from the first exile the Jews observed the laws of the seventh year; they did not sow and permitted the aftergrowth to be reaped provided that this was "not in the normal way".

So far we have talked about the achievements of the Jewish farmer. We need to point out that the rabbis were not chauvinistic and knew how to praise the expertise of the previous inhabitants of Canaan. They connected the name "Horite" with the Hebrew word *hor*, "a hole", and the name "Hivvite" with the Aramaic word *hevia*, "a snake", adding "they used to taste the ground like a snake, and say 'plant a vine here and plant an olive here'" (Babylonian Talmud, Shabbat 85a). This is the way the rabbis considered Israel's predecessors in the land. In their legends they even praised those who remained in their time, telling of a certain non-Jew who had a very small field from which he received a very high crop yield (Babylonian Talmud, Ketuvot 112a).

In this connection we must consider the traditional Arab farming methods that we encountered in the land of Israel at the beginning of the present century, in which scientists all observed a reflection of earlier Jewish agriculture. I will not denigrate this type of farming, which has preserved for us the country's scenery, and in particular has guarded the soil against erosion, by building stone terraces on the hills. At least they treated and preserved the land. Even today I still enjoy the beauty of the terraces of olive trees in the Nablus (Shechem)-Jenin-Tulkarm "Triangle" in Samaria. And how well nurtured and tasty are the vines of the Hebron Valley! The standard of traditional Arab arboriculture is high.

The same cannot be said of their ground crops, especially wheat and barley, whose yield during the period of traditional Arab agriculture declined drastically, reaching about one-fifth of the amount that the earlier Jewish farmers had produced. (Arab agriculture today has utilized the methods used by their Jewish neighbours and made great progress.) There was a tremendous gap between traditional Arab farming and that of the earlier Jews in two spheres in particular: (1) *ploughing*, which the Arab peasants did minimally and superficially, whereas the Jewish farmer, as we have already pointed out, did this intensively and in depth; and (2) *fertilizing*, which the Arab farmer scarcely bothered with, throwing his manure onto a dunghill at the edge of the village, where it remained uncollected.

Let us now deal with fertilizing. Here we encounter an important ecological topic. In Mishnaic and Talmudic times the farmer valued manure very highly and put it on a par with "jewels and precious stones". The Jewish farmer knew how to return to the land whatever was taken from it in the form of manure and compost, although for reasons of purity, human excrement was not used. A householder would keep all the organic waste that was in his yard and use it for compost with which to fertilize his field. On the seventh year, when manuring "in the normal way" was forbidden and the farmer wanted to get rid of all the organic waste products in his yard, the rabbis allowed baskets of manure to be piled in heaps ready for use after the seventh year. Such methods prevented the manure from being spread so as to lose all its valuable chemicals through evaporation. This system, which seems to have been first used in the seventh year, was later developed for use in other years.

Droppings from sheep that fall during pasture do to some extent fertilize the pasture field, but most of the fertilizing components evaporate, are burnt in the heat of the sun, and go to waste during the long time they are left in the field. To prevent this, a special procedure was adopted (mentioned in the Mishnah) whereby the sheep were penned during pasture in special mobile enclosures, or sheepfolds, to fertilize the soil. As soon as a portion of land was fertilized, the farmer would quickly plough it so as to cover the manure. This procedure was forbidden in the seventh year, as it resembled fertilizing, a forbidden activity, but the use of mobile folds was permitted on condition that soon after use, the owner of the flock or of the land would collect the manure in a heap, from which the manure could be taken and spread on the field after the end of the seventh year. In such a heap the dung lost only a small amount of its value as fertilizer. This is in fact the most efficient way of utilizing sheep droppings.

The Jewish farmer did not bother much about rotation of crops. It is worth mentioning that in modern agriculture less importance is paid to this than in the past, and many crops have been found that grow very successfully year after year. The system of fallow ploughing that the Jewish farmer used gave the land rest, so that nothing grew on it for a full year, although it was ploughed frequently. The Jewish farmer introduced a large variety of crops and even sowed five types of cereals, while in neighbouring countries they grew only wheat and barley, and occasionally spelt.

The farmer was receptive to the idea of introducing new species from other countries both near and distant. This is testified by the list of crops mentioned in rabbinic literature, which includes various species imported from east and west. We will mention just one of them — rice. It is generally accepted that this was introduced into the region after the travels of Alexander the Great. At the time of the Mishnah the rabbis were already in disagreement over which blessing to say before eating rice. A few generations later rice was already mentioned as an exported produce of the land of Israel, recognizable by its high quality, and the rabbis insisted that it should be tithed even outside Israel (Jerusalem Talmud, Demai 2:1).

It is worth noting the technical innovations introduced into agriculture by the Jewish farmer. At the end of Isaiah 28, the prophet describes the correct approach of the farmer, "which comes from G-d, wonderful is his counsel and great is his wisdom" (v. 29), before which he enumerates five methods of threshing used in his day, some of which began to be used in neighbouring countries only hundreds of years later.

All these produced crops of blessing, which we have achieved again only in the present generation. Some of these achievements are the result of observing the laws of the seventh year, the sabbatical, the year in which the Jewish farmer relaxed partially from working the land. One may assume that during that year he occupied himself also with religious and spiritual matters. It was the Jewish farmer of old who confirmed and publicized the name of the land of Israel as "the land of milk and honey".

Down to Earth Religious Education

Vivienne Cato

Out of the morass of detail that is Leviticus 25, two major themes emerge: social equality and liberation for the land. Every 50th year, the Israelites were to let go of their accumulated possessions in human and earthly property. The jubilee reminds us that, like our ancestors Adam and Eve, we are put on the earth to till and tend it but not to own it. We are simply stewards who have the usufruct of land (and people), whose ultimate owner is God. It was not Adam and Eve's choice to give up their garden. Fulfilling the requirements of the jubilee is our choice. When we do so, we are symbolically letting go of inappropriate control.

The environmental crisis of which we have daily evidence, in the heavens above, the earth below and the waters under the earth, has come about precisely because we have assumed we do have control over our surroundings. We have sought to "tame" and "subdue" the wild. Our very use of such language implies that we see ourselves naturally positioned in competition with nature.

The history of Western philosophy represents a struggle between religious and materialist worldviews. The mediaeval world managed to embrace both Genesis 1:28 ("subdue it and have dominion") and the inherent humility of the Great Chain of Being. Likewise, the rationalists of the Enlightenment were simultaneously deeply religious. Kepler, for example, who is famous for describing the "celestial machine" as akin to clockwork, reads geometry in religious terms: "Why waste words? Geometry existed before the Creation, is co-eternal with the mind of God, is God himself (what exists in God that is not God himself?)."[1]

The exploitative view of a nature manipulated by humanity was, intentionally or not, the inevitable consequence of this mechanistic materialism. Descartes' scientific rationalism reduced all life forms to predictable permutations of physics, chemistry and ultimately mathematics. As the late 20th-century Information Age knows so well, knowledge equals power. For the materialist, it is the *product* of reasoning; it is derived from the supposedly objective analysis of empirical phenomena. For the religious, knowledge *precedes* reasoning; it is the fruit of revelation that bypasses the mind. For Bacon, turning Descartes' arguments from pure form to applied, holding such scientific knowledge was the key to power over nature.

The split between head and heart initiated in Europe three hundred years ago did not take a straight and uninterrupted route until the present day. Blocking the path in the early 19th century was the Romantic movement. In granting nature an independent right to existence, Romanticism's bioethic and its animism were direct descendants of the mediaeval mind-set, and indeed can be seen in retrospect to form a stepping stone to today's environmental movement. Even if not always by name, Romanticism focused on the immanent spirit of God lodged within nature.

I have learned
To look on nature, not as in the hour
Of thoughtless youth; but hearing oftentimes
The still, sad music of humanity,
Nor harsh nor grating, though of ample power
To chasten and subdue. And I have felt
A presence that disturbs me with the joy
Of elevated thoughts; a sense sublime
Of something far more deeply interfused,
Whose dwelling is the light of setting suns,
And the round ocean and the living air,
And the blue sky, and in the mind of man.[2]

Like Romanticism, Judaism (and the Jewish influence on Christianity) sees God as being as much immanent in nature as transcendent. The Hebrew Bible is sown with evidence of a natural world infused and driven by the divine.

The Lord replied to Job out of the tempest and said...
"Who provides food for the raven
When its young cry out to God
And wander about in search of food?

Do you know the season when the mountain goats give birth?
Can you mark the time when the hinds calve?...
Do you give the horse his strength?
Do you clothe his neck with thunder?"

(Job 38:1, 41; 39:1, 19)[3]

Wordsworth would have found a fellow-traveller in the 11th-century Jewish poet Abraham ibn Ezra, who wrote:

Wherever I turn my eyes, around on Earth or to the heavens
I see You in the field of stars
I see You in the yield of the land
In every breath and sound, a blade of grass, a simple flower,
An echo of Your holy Name. [4]

All religions see the world as created in a state of perfection. All share a mythic understanding of a primordial world of unity and simplicity within which humans live in harmony and, fundamentally, in relationship. Since the materialist sees humanity as complete in itself, nature inevitably becomes the enemy. Bacon's vision was of humanity endeavouring "to establish the dominion of the human race itself over the universe", an ambition quite opposite to the religious messianic view of the time to come when

...you shall go out with joy And be led forth with peace.
The mountains and hills
Shall break forth in song before you,
And the trees of the fields shall clap their hands.

(Isa. 55:12)

The religious and materialist views are therefore in direct conflict. Except that any interpretation of the world gives rise to a specific set of behavioural outcomes, each might have carried on its separate path of development indefinitely. As it is, however, ascendant materialism has made a victim of the environment. Climate change, pollution, loss of biodiversity, of farmland and forests: all are evidence of utilitarian readings of the place of nature for humans. Thus at its heart the environmental crisis is a crisis of values. To borrow for a moment the language of materialism, choices have to be made in the supermarket of moral values. And no more so than when planning the education of the young, for it is in the curriculum of the school — both overt and hidden — that values are transmitted. Since the democratization of schooling approximately one hundred years ago, and especially since the second world war, educational philosophy in Britain has been inspired by a vision of equal opportunities for all, razing inborn differences of wealth and privilege. This almost biblically prophetic mission, of a time when the factory worker shall lie down with the aristocrat, stands fundamentally in antithesis to the materialist credo now taken as the norm by almost the entire world. A market-driven, competition-based economy has no time for empowering the under-privileged; it is quite happy for dog-eat-dog competition in the interest of a better life-style for a few.

Sadly, as regards the British education system at least, the egalitarian vision that once lay at its centre has become somewhat tarnished during the last 15 or so years of High Conservatism. The national curriculum and especially its associated system of assessment have brought in their train a focus on producing results that are perceivable and quantifiable. Accumulated knowledge can be made visible, categorized and ticked off on a check-list; inner moral development, compassion or spirituality cannot. Education for its own sake is giving way to training for business and industry. We are reverting to an equivalent of the 19th-century objective of educating young people just enough (and not more) to make them useful factory fodder. Seeing education as a follower of trends rather than a shaper of them, and watchful of "the bottom line", educational policy-makers seem to have bought into the prevailing materialist ethos. They have allied themselves with the empiricism of scientific rationalism ("all that is real can be observed and counted") and its related utilitarianism ("the purpose of knowledge is to manipulate the world").

Yet there remains one corner of education that has escaped the attention of the materialists. Whilst in the UK the content of every main subject is prescribed by law, religious education has somehow escaped this fiat. Schools must teach religion (Christianity plus at least two of the other five major religions) and must meet daily for worship "wholly or mainly of a Christian character". Beyond this, however, the choice of additional religions and the specific content to be transmitted through each is decided on a local basis by an Agreed Syllabus Conference comprising representatives of interested parties. Furthermore, the conference can choose to make its entire agreed syllabus prescriptive or to give schools the freedom to choose from some sections of it. Religious education in Britain is officially acknowledged to play a part in pupils' spiritual, moral, cultural and social development. In terms of its potential for subversion of the dominant materialist ethic, therefore, this subject with Cinderella status in law may actually be the princess.

Religious education as currently conceived inverts the pedagogic model of filling empty bottles that is implied by a knowledge-based curriculum. It follows, rather, the literal meaning of education, that of "leading out" what is already known. Rather than seeing a lack within the child, it values children's lack of ignorance and delusion. That we all possess understandings that teachers draw out from us is reflected in this Talmudic commentary: "Before a child is born, a light is held behind its head with which it can see from one end of the world to the other, and they teach it the whole of the Torah. But at the moment of birth an angel touches it on the lips, and it forgets all. So all of life is spent remembering what we once knew."[5]

The Alister Hardy Research Centre based at Westminster College, Oxford, has found that religious and transcendental experiences are most common in children, whose experience of being taught by the angel was perhaps more recent. As we grow older, it becomes an uphill struggle to regain that primal innocence and connection. It is the role of religious education to throw off the embarrassment that usually attends any mention of an awareness of the divine and instead to embrace it.

One way of doing so is to connect metaphysical understandings of the divine with human rapport with nature. Significantly, children's mystical experiences most commonly seem to occur in outdoor settings. Children often have an intrinsic affinity with nature, such as that described by Thomas Traherne: "Certainly Adam in Paradise had not more Sweet and Curious Apprehension of the World than I when I was a Child. Is it not strange that an Infant should be Heir to the Whole World and see those Mysteries which the books of the Learned never unfold?"[6]

Indeed, amongst all age groups in society, awareness of nature and concern over environmental problems is highest among the young. Their sense of shock and outrage is at its strongest. Young people make up the bulk of membership of many environmental organizations, and an estimated 25 percent of teenagers have become vegetarians.

Religion explores our connections with and responsibilities for the created world, and environmental studies should (not that they always do) look beyond the numbering and counting ways of geography and science to ethics, values and spiritual respect. For teachers, there are many ways of bringing the two together:

1. Allow opportunities for direct, contemplative experience of nature. Avoid the constant pressure to rush from one time-tabled lesson to the next and instead create space for "stilling", meditative, silent periods of relaxation.

    The awareness of grandeur and the sublime is all but gone from the modern mind. Our systems of education stress the importance of enabling the student to exploit the power aspect of reality. To some degree, they try to develop [the] ability to appreciate beauty. But there is no education for the sublime. We teach the children how to measure, how to weigh. We fail to teach them how to revere, how to sense wonder and awe. [7]

    Although one should hardly dare mention Heschel in the same breath as a government quango, even the UK Office of Standards in Education recognizes the need to nurture a sense of innate amazement at the world we so take for granted. Difficult as it might be to find, its handbook asks inspectors to find evidence of "the extent to which pupils display... a sense of awe and wonder as they become more conscious of deeper meanings in the apparently familiar features of the natural world or in their experience".

2. Create opportunities to explore the beliefs of societies that have succeeded in living in harmony with nature. Assess critically the beliefs of our own in this regard and compare the two in a manner that does not "anthropologize" the former as obsolete thought-systems irrelevant to us today. Teachers should make connections between personal and social issues experienced by their pupils and the solutions offered by religious belief.

3. Once they have been explored, allow time to reflect on the teachings of various religious traditions in order to extract those in which students personally believe. How does what they have learned of other societies impact on their understanding of their own?

4. Finally, all these stages must culminate in action. Without this, understandings remain marooned at the academic level, and the model of passivity in the face of problems remains unchallenged. Participants at a Jewish Tu B'Shvat (New year of the trees) Seder often round off the ritual by planting some trees, in person. It is

the hands-on connection with action in the world, and here specifically with the restoration of our damaged earth, that makes real both understanding and commitment. School projects are potentially diverse, from setting up recycling schemes for paper and cans to creating a wildlife garden (a Garden of Eden?).

In suggesting that pupils need to look at a range of religious belief-systems that respect the natural world, it's easy to assume that this must mean Hinduism, Buddhism or Native American animism. Yet, despite the record of the public voices of Judaism and Christianity, which have largely kept silent on environmental abuse, each of these traditions has an authentic history of respect for nature. To be sure, neither gives animals and plants equal status to humans, and their arguments for conservation tend to err towards the utilitarian. But even within this framework, voices asserting the intrinsic right to exist of nonhuman creation can be heard: "Do not believe that all things exist for the sake of humanity. On the contrary, one must believe that... everything exists for its own sake and not for anything or anyone else. [8]

It is now up to the established churches and synagogues to reclaim this part of their heritage in the interest of a planet whose support is needed from committed Christians and Jews. In this supermarket of choices they must select with deliberation which moral values to place in their baskets. It is time for them to pull out the cans and jars of environmentalism that have got pushed to the back of the shelf.

This article has outlined the contradictions between the materialist and religious outlook, accused education of forgetting its visionary purpose and suggested that by infusing religious education with pro-environmental values, it can reclaim that purpose. By subverting the dominant exploitative ethic, religious education can help to heal the world. The jubilee represents a cameo of this aim, bringing together as it does the needs of humans and the needs of the land. Humans need the land: without rest and respect, the land will cease to provide for humanity (and if we do not give these freely, the land will take them for itself anyway through desolation). The land needs humans to till and tend it, to serve and preserve. Our livelihoods and our fate are intrinsically tied up with nature's. The biblical tradition has an intuitive understanding of the interdependence we have only recently come to call ecology. Judaism, simultaneously mystical and practical, has always been about bringing religion down to earth.

NOTES

[1] Kepler, *Harmonici Mundi* (1619).
[2] William Wordsworth, "Lines composed a few miles above Tintern Abbey", in *William Wordsworth: The Poems*, 2 vols, ed. John O. Hayden, New Haven, CN, Yale UP, 1977, 1.360, lines 88-99.
[3] Transl. by David E. Stein, in *A Garden of Choice Fruit: 200 Classic Jewish Quotes on Human Beings and the Environment*, Shomrei Adamah, 1991.
[4] In Daniel Swartz, "Jews, Jewish Texts and Nature: A Brief History", in *To Till and To Tend*, Coalition on the Environment and Jewish Life, n.d.
[5] Based on Babylonian Talmud, Niddah 30b.
[6] Thomas Traherne, *Centuries of Meditations* 3.1-2.
[7] Abraham Joshua Heschel, *God in Search of Man: A Philosophy of Judaism*, New York, Farrar, Strauss & Cudahy, 1955, p.36.
[8] Maimonides, *Guide of the Perplexed*, 3:14.

Partnership to Eliminate the Debt: A Historical Perspective

Josef P. Widyatmadja

Henry Kissinger, former US secretary of state, has stated that history is often comprehended as "the memory of states". As a consequence, history often neglects the role of the oppressed and views truth only from the perspective of the conqueror. It is typically never viewed from the oppressed's perspective.

History writing often tends to a bias for the strong. The king's needs and his role are considered more important than a soldier's or than the lives of the common people. Eusebius, the early church historian, wrote the history of the church from the point of view of Emperor Constantine. For him, the Christians' enemies were the Montanists and Donatists, which were considered as false sects, but not Constantine's government or the rich who oppressed the poor. History becomes a report or formal statement of the rulers. Historical truths that threaten rulers will be omitted or told in another way.

In contrast, history can be defined as "the memory of people". Such history is a form of rebellion against tyrannical and corrupt rulers. It is usually transmitted orally from generation to generation through folklore and cultural resistance.

History as the memory of people is not only a blueprint made by rulers for the people, but also tells about the fight and struggle of the weak, who try hard to survive against the blueprint and the ruler's manipulation. This struggle is not easy because it is often banned and not given space in a state history. For this reason, the historian's task is not only to receive observations and formal statements from rulers but to transform the memory of people into objective report.

This article is dedicated to the celebration of the jubilee of Indonesia's freedom, first declared in 1945. It concerns more the people's perspective than that of the rulers and reflects primarily the voices of the underside. The jubilee of Indonesian freedom cannot be separated from the perspective of colonial history, the effect of which can be seen in all aspects of life.

Five hundred years ago

Globalization (in economy, politics and religion) began, not in the 1990s, but five hundred years ago, when Christopher Columbus reached America (1492) and Vasco da Gama arrived at the Cape of Good Hope, Africa (1497). With the permission of the Catholic Church, Portugal and Spain divided the colonies to be explored and colonized, which became the source of gold, spices and slaves. The imperialists engaged in conquest, slavery and genocide, with many people perishing in the 15th and 16th centuries through war, starvation and disease. In *A People's History of the United States* Howard Zinn reports that the population of Arawak Indians in Haiti, estimated to number 500,000 in 1495, had been reduced to 50,000 by 1515. By 1550 there were only 500. In 1650 there was no native Arawak left in Haiti. Furthermore, he states that from 1494 to 1508 altogether more than three million persons died because of slavery, war, and mining. [1] As the Indians decreased, the number of European immigrants increased.

To colonize and explore America required cheap human resources. To solve this problem, the Europeans brought slaves from Africa. By 1800 some 15 million African slaves had been brought to America. Millions more began the journey but never arrived: hunger and disease claimed the lives of between 15 and 75 percent of each shipload. The slaves were badly treated, even, when they had run out of food, being killed and their flesh given to feed living slaves. Altogether, about 50 million Africans died as slaves.

How much was the price of a slave? Around 1800 James Madison reported that it was about US$257 per slave. When the English and Dutch governments abolished slavery in 1863, the Dutch government compensated former slave-owners at a rate of 300 guilders per slave. As the effect of abolishment, in 1819 the Dutch began to send Javanese as contracted workers to Suriname.

In the process of colonization, highly valued objects were taken by the colonialists. M. P. Josef, an Indian theologian, stated that when England colonized India, the English annually plundered Indian valuables to the extent of £500-1000 million.

The church and colonization

History notes that religious teaching supported the colonization of America, Africa and Asia. Mediaeval churches were controlled by noblemen and royalty. These noblemen influenced church officials to support colonization and slavery. As a consequence, church interests were parallel to economic interests (i.e., establishing a monopoly) and colonization. Church doctrines approved the shipping of slaves from Africa to America. Only a few preachers opposed this slavery. From his pulpit in Vlissingen, Pastor Smitjtegeld spoke out against slavery. [2] J. G. Kals in his book *Nederland Hoofs — En Wortelsonde* (Courtly Netherlands — a probe of its roots, 1759), criticized the relation between trade, colonialism, and the gospel. [3] In the Catholic Church, Van Lith, who came to Java as missionary from 1846 to 1926, was well known as a radical opponent of colonialism. He thought that "the period of the white man is over. Not forever will one white man stand firm against 100,000 Asians." Furthermore, he argued that the effort to dominate the Javanese was useless and too risky. He wanted the Javanese to be treated like the Dutch in the church, because in Christ there was no difference between Javanese and Dutch. The Dutch, Indian and Javanese were able to live peacefully because Christ had united his believers.

Not all missionaries sent by the Dutch missionary association supported the government policy. They did not do so because most of them came from the middle or lower class, which witnessed the people's suffering. Affected by humanism and socialism, they opposed all kinds of colonialism and discrimination. In the colonized countries they worked as teachers to develop education, and eventually it improved the political awareness of the colonized people. It should be noted that missionaries also took part in the struggle to apply ethical politics, although exclusively neither conservative nor liberal. They include Abraham Kuyper, Hendrik Kraemer, C.L. Van Doorn and his wife, Willy. Johannes Verkuyl has ably discussed this ethical political movement in his book *The Tension between Western Imperialism and Colonialism and Mission in the Era of Ethical Colonial Politics.* [4] The following subsections develop several of Verkuyl's points.

The motives of imperialism and colonialism

Verkuyl states that there were four motives of Western imperialism and colonialism: economy, religion, culture and imperialism.

These four motives led to great suffering for people living in the third world. When it is examined, the root of these motives is greed and arrogance. The economic and imperial motives were embodied in a lust for riches and power, and the religious and cultural motives showed themselves in an arrogant attitude towards the religion and culture of conquered nations. It needs to be noted that the conquered nations already had a developed culture before the Westerners invaded their countries. For example, the American Indians, who came from Asia 25,000 years before Columbus's arrival, had built cities around the Ohio River Valley, in the time of Jesus Christ and Julius Caesar.[5] When Europeans first arrived in Benin, Africa, in 1602, they reported finding big cities with wide roads and houses as nice as theirs in Holland. In his book *The Cities of Africa*, Basil Davidson writes that the Congolese system of law in the 16th century was better than those in Portugal and England.[6] In England, someone could be hung for stealing a piece of cotton cloth. In Congo, persons caught stealing were sentenced to hard labour or were fined because Congolese law did not have private ownership rules. A Congolese once sarcastically asked a Portuguese, "What is the punishment for a person trespassing on someone's land in Portugal?"[7]

A presumption that the colonized nations had uncivilized cultures was wrong. It happened because there was misunderstanding and arrogance about the meaning of civilized and uncivilized culture. Can a nation having nuclear weapons be considered as having a more civilized culture than one that fights with daggers or scythes?

The impact of colonialism

Verkuyl writes that the socio-psychological impact on colonized countries included prejudice, a sense of incompetence, and ignorance.[8] Such a list is not wrong but is woefully incomplete. Besides the socio-psychological impact, we could list the economic, social, political, cultural and environmental. In the area of economy, the colonizers explored and expropriated the riches of the colonized countries, including coffee, spices, tobacco, and mining products. Dr Soemitro, the chief of the economic committee delegation, made clear the Dutch debt to Indonesia during the colonial era. Ironically at the Round Table Conference, it was not the Dutch who were charged with war reparations but Indonesia, which was ordered to pay the Dutch DFl.871 million plus DFl.420 million to the third world. Indonesia ultimately cancelled the conference and did not pay DFl.871 million to the Dutch, but it did have to pay the World Bank DFl.420 million. As a newly independent country, Indonesia was forced to pay the colonizer's debt. In this case, the colonizers were unwilling to admit that they had exploited the riches of the colonized countries and, after the declaration of independence, the unwarranted yoke on them of having to pay war reparations.

Colonialism has influenced many socio-politic aspects of the former colonies, as it has in effect left behind a time bomb for the new independent countries. Race conflicts have emerged in many areas of Asia and Africa because of the impact of colonialism. It also damaged the environment and local culture through the exploitation of natural resources, the destruction of religion and the ethnic languages, and changing the traditional law of land ownership.

Positive aspects of colonialism?

Verkuyl cites K.M. Panikar's opinion that colonialism had six positive aspects:

1. Principles of law were implanted in the colonies.
2. The colonial government overturned laws supporting local despots.
3. People's councils became operational in big cities.
4. The races became integrated.
5. A cultural exchange occurred between West and East.
6. Asia was delivered from its isolation.

I disagree with this assessment because it wrongly tends to mitigate the cruelty of the colonizer. Was the Congolese or any Asian system of law worse than the European? Were Europeans more civilized and cultured than Asian-Africans before the birth of Christ? Was there no relationship between Asia or Africa before the arrival of Europeans? Historical study notes that before Vasco da Gama arrived in Africa, Majapahit Indonesians had already landed there. Chinese landed in California before Columbus reached the Caribbean. Cultural and trading relations existed between China and Persia before Western imperialism began. Through the historical crime of colonialism, the world came to be dominated economically and politically by the West.

Partnership in church service

Partnership between churches planted by the mission bodies and the colonizers' churches was not a real partnership, simply because the West dominated the church. Local Christians were well aware of the Western domination of their local churches and of their being only an object of mission and religious propaganda. Social works in the form of schools, theological schools, hospitals and orphanages were founded by the mission bodies with government support, which sometimes had double functions. On the one hand, it supported the colonized people; on the other hand, it gave definite advantages to the mission bodies and colonizer.

Such partnership was first criticized in 1910 by Indian bishop V. S. Azariah at the World Missionary Conference in Edinburgh. Azariah said, "Through all the ages to come the Indian Church will rise up in gratitude to attest the heroism and self-denying labours of the missionary body... You have given your bodies to be burned. We also ask for *love*. Give us *friends!*"[9]

C.Y. Cheng from China confirmed Azariah's criticism and declared that the frictions between the missionary bodies and Christian sects only confused Chinese Christians. The Edinburgh Conference was attended by 400 delegates, but only 17 came from the colonized countries, and these 17 were the fruit of the missionary bodies. Since the Edinburgh Conference, the criticism about the paternalism of Western missionaries was heard. Later conferences (e.g., Madras 1938, Whitby 1947) discussed more fruitfully the partnership between European churches and third-world missions.

In the decades of development through the 1960s, the partnership between Western churches and those in the third world was not limited strictly to religion but included also cooperation in development issues. The Commission on the Churches' Participation in Development (CCPD) was formed in the wake of 1968 WCC Uppsala assembly. Through the CCPD, churches engaged in a partnership to keep peace and justice and to preserve the environment. Other church development organizations also arose, including the Interchurch Organization for Development Cooperation and Bilance, both in the Netherlands, and the Protestant Association for Cooperation in Development in Germany. The missionary bodies were also involved in supporting development.

For four decades, such partnerships in church development worked to reduce poverty in the third world. In fact, however, third-world countries were not getting richer but poorer, and the gap between the rich and the poor countries widened and increased 60-fold. This happened because wealth was not transferred from rich countries to poor ones but vice versa. In this period third-world debt reached $1 billion.

Partnerships in the era of development ultimately accomplished no more than did those of the colonial era. They had different names and forms but the content remained the same. This can be summarized in the accompanying chart:

Colonial era	*Development era*
• Created colonial regions	• Created market and debt
• Transferred the wealth to the West	• Transferred the wealth to the West
• Formed the Far East Corporation	• Formed the World Bank, etc.
• Colonial troops were present	• Transnational and multinational corporations were present
• Involved bilateral and international agreements	• Involved bilateral and international agreements
• Power rested in the missionary bodies	• Power rested in the development bodies
• Trained missionaries	• Trained people for development
• Considered the "natives" as uncultured and needing development	• Considered the "natives" as undemocratic and backward in technology
• Sought legitimation of religion in colonialism	• Sought legitimation of religion in development plans
• Formed puppet governments	• Formed puppet governments

Some missionary and development bodies were less practical and sensitive in the new form of colonialism, but some persons from church or secular organizations continued an ethical, political approach, as in the colonial era. In the third world and in Western countries movements emerged to restore the ancient lands of Indians, Aborigines and the Maori; to wipe out debts; and to resist the World

Bank/IMF and GATT/WTO. Such movements are mostly minor and do not command real power in either government or church structures.

Debts, 50 and 500 years old

Now, 500 years after Columbus and Vasco da Gama's navigation and 50 years after the end of the second world war, colonialism and economic exploitation continue. In modern times, colonialism has changed its form to what is called globalization in economy and the free market.

Charity and support for development have been given by the former colonizers to the former colonized countries through multilateral or bilateral agreements. What is wrong with such cooperation? "You lack one thing; go, sell what you have, and give the money to the poor," said Jesus in Mark 10:21. The former colonizers have given their bodies to be burned, but they have not given love, justice and true friendship as their partners hoped. Through private organizations or churches, development and humane support has been given via unfair economic policy. The formerly colonized countries demanded love and justice, not economic support and pity. Past mistakes and debts cannot be continued indefinitely. In order to obtain salvation, Zacchaeus had to give back whatever he took. The debts and mistakes in the colonial era must be repaid. [10]

"Debt is the debt having to be paid," according to creditors from developed countries and the World Bank. Eugene Rotberg, the former treasurer of the World Bank, has said that debt is an economic issue, not a theological concept. [11] Jesus' prayer "forgive us our debt", as well as the jubilee year, when the debt is erased and the slaves are freed (Lev. 25), is viewed only theologically.

Not paying one's debts, however, is considered a crime. Then how is the 500 year-old crime of the colonial era to be atoned for? How are the exploitation of natural wealth, the shipment of the slaves and the slaughter of the innocent people of the colonized countries to be paid for? These state crimes have not been paid for by all the colonizers. These questions were asked by former Nigerian president, Ibrahim Babangida, by the Nobel prizewinner for literature Wole Soyinka, and also in the document "Kairos 1998", drafted by participants in the Forum on African and Asian Spirituality, which was held in July 1994, in Sri Lanka.

The principle that debts must be paid applies to all kinds of debts. Financial debts can be paid with cash. But how are debts of blood to be repaid, or the debt of environmental destruction that happened in colonial history? The WCC jubilee of 1998 could take seriously such issues.

NOTES

[1] Howard Zinn, *A People's History of the United States*, New York, Harper & Row, 1980, pp.4-5,7.
[2] L. Schellekens, "Nederlands belang oversee: Vier gouden eewen", in F. Wijsen, *The Dutch and the Making of the Third World*, Occasional Paper, Nijmegen, Catholic University Third World Centre, 1978.
[3] Quoted in J. Van Engelen and J. Van Lin, *Church in the Netherlands and the Third World*, Occasional Paper 5, Nijmegen, Catholic University Third World Centre, 1978.
[4] Johannes Verkuyl, *Ketegangan antara imperialisme dan kolonialisme barat dan zending pada masa politik kolonial Etis*, Jakarta, Badan Penadit Kristen, 1990.
[5] Zinn, *People's History*, p.19.
[6] Basil Davidson, *The Cities of Africa*, Boston, Little Brown, 1939, p.191.
[7] C.I.R. James, *The Black Jacobins*, New York, Random House, 1963, pp.7-9.
[8] Verkuyl, p.22.
[9] V.S. Azariah, "The Problem of Co-operation between Foreign and Native Workers", in *The Ecumenical Movement: An Anthology of Key Texts and Voices*, eds Michael Kinnamon and Brian E. Cope, Geneva WCC Publications; Grand Rapids, MI, Eerdmans, 1997, p.330.
[10] See Verkuyl, p.80.
[11] Quoted in Christen A. Bogdanowecz-Bindert, *Solving the Global Debt Crisis*, Jakarta, Institut Bisness, Ekonomi dan Keuangan, 1993, p.23.

Sound the Trumpet
for Justice, Liberty and Freedom

Carmelita M. Usog

Writing here as a Filipina who does theology, I begin with an untitled poem that speaks of how people survive in my native country. [1]

I have been stripped of my basic necessities;
my stomach craved for food to appease the pangs of hunger;
my back longed for a decent bed or even bamboo slats
to ease out the tired muscles from the day's labour.
I have been searching — but nothing is in sight.
Cries of starving children chorused,
prompting me to listen,
Shouts of humiliation were the lot
of the mothers who continued to scout for food.
Insults hurled numbed the senses,
but one could not help but strive to survive.

Misery, poverty become an institution,
made heavier and stronger by
wealth and power-starved individuals,
reinforced by the values caught from the foreign masters,
sapping every minute possession of the poor and the exploited ones.

Out of the "inhuman" situation the exploited rose:
I am not destined to be poor, you made me into one;
I am not destined to be dumb, but you snatched the opportunity from me.
I am not destined to be "half-human", yet you formed me into one.

Curse be to you blood-thirsty
and power-starved elite.
You feasted on the peasants' produce
and the profit from the workers' labour
and have no plan of putting an end

to your evil deeds.
And so the exploited must act.

Enough of the oppression;
I don't deserve it.
Enough of the exploitation;
I need to get my share.
Enough of senseless killing;
I will rise up to protect my people.
There has to be an end to plunder and dominion.

Armed with our quest for JUSTICE and PEACE
I, we will chart our own destiny.
We will continue to struggle for our LIBERATION.
And after the bondage, our nation
will be free from tyranny.

Sr Maria Luisa David

This poem describes how it is with us, as people keep on forgetting our right to survive and simply take from us what they want and need. The poem also echoes the polyphonic cries of the people from the South, especially the women. What have we to do with this haunting cry? What makes it a sustained one? Is the situation in consonance with the intent of Yahweh that we should keep the sabbath, till the land and allow whoever tills it to partake of the produce? I quote here the text from Leviticus 25:

> You shall count off seven weeks of years, seven times seven years, so that the period of seven weeks of years gives forty-nine years. Then you shall have the trumpet sounded loud; on the tenth day of the seventh month — on the day of atonement — you shall have the trumpet sounded throughout all your land. And you shall hallow the fiftieth year and you shall proclaim liberty throughout the land to all its inhabitants. It shall be a jubilee for you: you shall return, every one of you, to your property, and every one of you to your family. That fiftieth year shall be a jubilee for you: you shall not sow, or reap the aftergrowth, or harvest the unpruned vines. For it is a jubilee; it shall be holy to you: you shall eat only what the field itself produces. In this year of jubilee you shall return, every one of you, to your property. (vv. 8-13)

Our Judaeo-Christian tradition has a very rich heritage, but did we ever take time to reflect and ask where we have failed in our expression and interpretation of it? Are we really observing the three key concepts of Leviticus according to the Jewish tradition: the day of rest, the sabbath of the land, and the jubilee year? If the sabbath is an embodiment of the belief that all are equal and that equality means nobility of each person, why the growing disparity between those who have and the exploited?

Since my focus here is women, and in order to achieve a clearer picture of the context, I would like to use Elisabeth Schüssler Fiorenza's framework. She speaks of kyriarchy instead of patriarchy. Fiorenza defines kyriarchy as the rule of an emperor/master/lord/father/husband over his subordinates. This involves a more complex social pyramid of graduated domination and subordination than patriarchy implies, which is defined simply as the rule of men over women. [2]

The context

The evil of kyriarchy let loose in the third world or in the South breeds poverty, violence, migration and exploitation — and the hardest hit are the women. I use the term "South" here to refer to the impoverished peoples of Latin America, Africa and Asia. This symbolic term likewise embraces all the poor and the outcast of the rich countries throughout the world. In contrast, "North" signifies the power centres, which are basically in the richest and the most industrialized countries. [3] But likewise it stands for all the rich and powerful who maintain, enjoy or manage those power centres.

In numerical terms the North represents 20 percent of the world population (about one billion people), and the South represents the remaining 80 percent (about four billion people). According to statistics published by the United Nations Development Programme, the North, the richest 20 percent of humankind, receives 82.7 percent of the world's income; the South, the poorest 80 percent, receives 17.3 percent. [4] The worse off are certainly the women and children.

The global picture is characterized by economic and political inequality, with built-in structures (such as the International Monetary Fund and the World Bank, plus the General Agreement on Tariffs and Trade and the World Trade Organization) designed to perpetuate the control of the North over the South. The IMF and World Bank, for example, collaborate with government leaders of first-world countries in pressuring governments of the third-world countries along the lines of what could be called development aggression. In general, the common denominators for third-world countries, or those in the

South, are UNEMPLOYMENT, UNDEREMPLOYMENT and NON-AVAILA-
BILITY OF WORK.

Let me focus now on my own country. Like other developing
countries, the Philippines has fallen prey to this international conspi-
racy particularly because of the United States' hold on us as a former
US colony. Our government's development thrusts have always been
heavily influenced by United States foreign and economic policies.
The Western kyriarchal model of progress called development continues to work havoc on us. The Ramos government's effort to
transform the Philippines into a "tiger" economy under the Medium
Term Philippine Development Plan (MTPDP or "Philippines 2000")
has caused more harm than good to our country's natural resources.
Our forests and agricultural lands are being destroyed and depleted.
Steel bars and iron poles for factories are replacing the trees; golf
courses and plush residential areas are taking the place of the rice
fields and other forms of technologies employed in newly built
industries have proved to be destructive to all life forms. Development
— understood as capital accumulation and commercialization of the
economy to produce high profits [5] — has created wealth for 10 percent
of the population, but extreme poverty and dispossession for the
remaining 90 percent. It seems clear that the "Philippines 2000"
project of President Ramos has already failed to meet the needs of the
people.

The 40 so-called growth centres that are part of the whole MTPDP
package have been created mainly for multinationals and large foreign
firms, including the provision of residential, commercial, service and
recreation facilities for expatriate executives and consultants. This
peripheralizes the surrounding backward rural areas. It deprives peasants of land and induces massive urban migration. The urban migration in turn spawns more social problems, such as criminality and
prostitution, because state resources cannot cope with the demand for
basic services. If government leaders really are serious about developing the nation, should they allow prime agricultural lands to be
converted into golf courses? Should indigenous communities be
displaced in favour of developing the infrastructures?

I could mention here the plight of the lahar survivors in Pampanga
who sought refuge in the former US Clark Air Base but who now are
under threat of eviction because of plans to construct another international airport on the site. This former American base nestles in a total

land area of 55,000 hectares (22,227 acres). This sprawling former American territory now houses five-star hotels, duty-free shops and recreation centres not for our own use but for foreigners. It is also a magnet to attract tourists to exploit us further. Where is development in this venture? Is this for a just cause?

The situation of women

A few years ago I had a chance to listen to the country reports of women who participated in the three-month-long Inter-cultural Course on Women and Society at the Institute of Women Studies of St Scholastica's College, Manila. These women from various Asian countries spoke of the struggles of women coupled with women's attempts to help themselves. They had the same refrain: women are being marginalized, exploited and subordinated. If human beings are created according to God's image and likeness, and if God created them as equals, then why the disparity?

Poverty all too often pushes women into odd jobs or into joining the work force full-time, where they are prey to exploitative employers. The slogan "first to be fired but last to be hired" applies particularly to women. Most big business firms use labour-only contracting (LOC) to avoid giving benefits to workers. One example is Shoemart, a department store chain owned by a Chinese national that has only 1,731 regular employees out of a total of 20,000 workers. This situation is typical of most transnational corporations (TNCs) or industrial enclaves. Since women are treated as a secondary labour force, they lack the benefits and privileges due them, such as maternity leave, health and safety equipment or just and humane working conditions, especially for those involved in assembly plants and export processing zones. The daily wage for a worker in the Philippines is $4.72, or P145.00, and with an average of five or six mouths to feed, hunger, malnutrition and sickness regularly stalk families and communities.

Prostitution

A more serious effect of poverty is prostitution, even child prostitution. In the Philippines alone around 500,000 women are engaged in prostitution. According to UNICEF, 100,000 of this number are child prostitutes, second only to Thailand in number. In Thailand 80 percent of the prostitutes come from peasant families.

The tourism business in third-world countries, which aims at adding dollars to the national treasury, also means selling women to tourists.

In Angeles, Pampanga, for example, site of the infamous US airbase, the sex tour is a "promising business." From the Ninoy Aquino international airport, the tourist goes directly to the sex hotel, where he pays about P500 ($15-20), and yet only 60 percent of that is given to the prostitute by the owner. According to research by the Centre for Women's Resources, in the red-light district in Angeles, the (40-70) bars and the 18 hotels are owned by foreign nationals.

The majority of the prostitutes come from agricultural families who have no financial guarantee of their annual production. Most of them are illiterate or have finished only grade school. The majority of their families work on land owned by others.

Migration
The lack of satisfactory employment opportunities in the Philippines is partially due to the increasing number of migrant workers. Also, many Filipinos have opted to seek employment in other countries, mostly as domestic workers or entertainers, although a few have white-collar jobs. This is encouraged by the government because the remittance of these "Overseas Contract Workers" (OCWs) provides a buffer to the economy. Of the 6.21 million Filipino OCWs scattered all over the seven continents, 60 percent are women.

From the macro- to the micro-situation of the third world there appears to be a vicious cycle, which must be broken. We can see the interconnection of the earth, human labour and social behaviour. If one of these elements is not respected, there is a chain reaction. In this framework I would like to spell out what jubilee means for the people in the South, especially the women. How will social justice, liberty and freedom be operative in this situation?

When will we be free? When shall we experience jubilee?
The basic issue is the land, the seed-bed of all forms of domination. If the third world is going to live in abundance, there is a need for a rethinking or reform in the use of the land. Because we have distanced ourselves from the land and adopted the capitalist mode of using the land for profit, we have forgotten its sanctity. A complete remoulding of values and outlook is needed so we view the land as our temple. A symbiotic relationship is needed instead of one of domina-

tion and exploitation. Only when we break the structures that support kyriarchy will women really be free.

It is important that the North respect the refusal of the South to be controlled by the North. The South refuses to surrender the sovereignty of its peoples or to forgo democracy. The South needs to live and to share its abundance. The South envisions the whole world (including the North) having life and dignity and the cosmos being re-created and saved from further destruction.

What is the cry of the South? Liberation of the body, liberation of women, liberation of youth, liberation of indigenous and black people in order to build a world in which all may have life.[6]

We need to go back to the basic tenets of our faith to truly live the jubilee — to reclaim the promise of the God of life, of justice and of caring, and thus to respect the sacredness of all life forms. Only then shall we be changed and no longer be numbed to women and children who are prostituted, to workers who are exploited and to families who are broken because one member has to seek employment in another country.

Is it so difficult to let go of our superfluous items and needs so others will survive? Is it so difficult to feel the pain and connect with other women whose bodies are corrupted and desecrated? Is it so difficult to make a stand for genuine land reform where land should be given to the tillers? Where is the passivity coming from? Surely, your God and my God are the same, your breath of life and mine are one. And God calls us today to be in solidarity for life and with life.

The power and strength for our future should emerge from the accumulated experience of survival and resistance of oppressed and vulnerable peoples, as well as the subjugated and marginalized. The emerging people's movement in the third world can only endeavour to influence different social systems and challenge life-styles in the direction of actualizing the values we uphold and questioning death-dealing trends and forces.

In closing, let me reiterate the moaning of the land and peoples of the South — we need a respite, we need to claim the space due us, we need those people scattered all over the world seeking employment one day to be united with their loved ones so that we can sound the trumpet and proclaim the jubilee year. Certainly for us in the third world, the road to liberation is tied to the attainment of a truly nationalist and democratic system of government. To respond to the cries and lamentations of the women for liberty is to give women equal access to employment. The peasant women should be able to enjoy the produce of the land, and prostituted women should be provided with the necessary support systems when they decide to leave the sex trade. We need to claim our special space. When you and I together with other women join hands and hearts, the conditions to sound the trumpet and celebrate can finally be made visible. And the time is now!

NOTES

[1] Untitled, unpublished poem, personal collection.
[2] Elisabeth Schüssler Fiorenza, *Jesus: Miriam's Child, Sophia's Prophet: Critical Issues in Feminist Christology*, New York, Continuum, 1995, p.14.
[3] Pablo Richard, "A Theology of Life: Rebuilding Hope", in *Spirituality of the Third World*, eds K. C. Abraham and Bernadette Mbuy-Beya, Maryknoll, NY, Orbis, 1994, p.102.
[4] *Ibid.*
[5] J. Badapadyay and V. Shiva, "Political Economy of Ecology Movements", *Economic and Political Weekly*, 18, 1982.
[6] *Ibid.*, p.106.

Contributors

Vivienne Cato is director of education at a London synagogue, and a teacher trainer in Jewish environmental education.

Yehuda Feliks is professor of biblical and Talmudic botany at Bar Ilan University, Israel.

K.M. George is principal of the Orthodox Theological Seminary, Kottayam, India.

Norman Gottwald is professor emeritus of biblical studies at New York Theological Seminary, USA.

Raphael Jospe is senior lecturer in Jewish philosophy at the Open University of Israel, Jerusalem.

Leon Klenicki, a rabbi, serves as director of the department of interfaith affairs of the Anti-Defamation League of B'nai B'rith, New York.

Jacob Milgrom is emeritus professor of biblical studies, University of California at Berkeley, presently living in Jerusalem.

Geiko Müller-Fahrenholz is a Lutheran theologian and writer who lives in Bremen, Germany.

Jacques Nicole, who was director of the Ecumenical Institute, Bossey, near Geneva, from 1989 to 1996, is now a pastor in Martigny, Switzerland.

Konrad Raiser is general secretary of the World Council of Churches, Geneva.

Ronald Sider is professor of theology and culture at Eastern Baptist Theological Seminary, Wynnewood, Pennsylvania, USA.

Geraldine Smyth is an Irish Dominican theologian and director of the Irish School of Ecumenics, Dublin and Belfast.

Norman Solomon, of Wolfson College, Oxford, is fellow in modern Jewish thought at the Oxford Centre for Hebrew and Jewish Studies, and lecturer in the faculty of theology, University of Oxford.

Paul Spray is the policy director of Christian Aid, London, the development agency of the British and Irish churches.

Carmelita Usog is principal of St Scholastica's Night Secondary School, Manila, Philippines. She also teaches gender sensitive catechetics at the Institute of Formation and Religious Studies, and women and religion at the Institute of Women's Studies of St Scholastica.

Lukas Vischer is professor emeritus of ecumenical theology at the University of Bern, Switzerland.

Josef P. Widyatmadja is a pastor at the Indonesian Christian Church for Social Ministry in Surakarta, Indonesia. He has also been the general secretary of the Social Welfare Guidance Foundation since 1974.